P9-CFA-050

DARE TO MAKE
HISTORY

Chasing a Dream
and Fighting for Equity

★ ★ ★

U.S. OLYMPIC WOMEN'S ICE HOCKEY TEAM

GOLD-MEDAL WINNERS

**Jocelyne
Lamoureux-
Davidson**

**Monique
Lamoureux-
Morando**

RADIUS BOOK GROUP
NEW YORK

Radius Book Group
A Division of Diversion Publishing Corp.
New York, NY 10016
www.RadiusBookGroup.com

Copyright © 2021 by Monique Lamoureux-Morando and Jocelyne Lamoureux-Davidson

All rights reserved, including the right to reproduce this book or portions
thereof in any form whatsoever. No part of this publication may be repro-
duced or transmitted in any form or by any means, electronic or mechan-
ical, including photocopying, recording, or any other information storage
and retrieval, without the written permission of the author.

For more information, email info@radiusbookgroup.com.

First edition: February 2021
Hardcover ISBN: 978-1-63576-727-8
eBook ISBN: 978-1-63576-728-5

Library of Congress Control Number: 2020913230

Manufactured in the United States of America

10 9 8 7 6 5 4 3 2 1

Cover design by Tom Lau
Interior design by Neuwirth & Associates

Radius Book Group and the Radius Book Group colophon are registered
trademarks of Radius Book Group, a Division of Diversion Publishing Corp.

This book is dedicated to our parents, who always encouraged us to dream big. To our brothers, who never pulled any punches and taught us we could compete with anyone. To Anthony and Brent, whose consistent love in tough and exhilarating times is our rock. And of course, to Mickey and Nelson; may you set ambitious goals and dreams and chase them with endless passion.

CONTENTS

★ ★ ★

CONTENTS

FOREWORD

★

I have interviewed many female athletes and gender equity trailblazers and advocates throughout my career, but none as tenacious and dedicated to the advancement of women in sports, in the workplace, and in life as Jocelyne Lamoureux-Davidson and Monique Lamoureux-Morando. Their athletic accomplishments speak for themselves. They have won twenty international medals between the two of them, including six world championships, two Olympic silver medals, and one Olympic gold—all before turning thirty years old.

But it's their sense of justice and willingness to risk it all that created real change.

I was on my own personal odyssey of trying to understand and appreciate my worth when I met Jocelyne and Monique. I was a successful national television anchor and on a mission. I was tired of seeing young girls and women shut down, self-deprecate, and apologize their way through a conversation or challenge. This had played out in all aspects of my life, so I knew there were legions of women out there struggling the same way.

I became a fierce advocate for women and girls once I forced myself to dig deep and evaluate my own sense of value and confidence. It took me twenty-five years to understand that I played a role in quantifying my success.

I've learned women are ferocious when it comes to protecting, defending, and augmenting the success of others—their spouses, their children, their bosses, anyone who isn't themselves! I came to realize that women everywhere could find their own value and appreciate it.

I decided to travel the country and interview as many women as I could about their own value. It was part of my own self-discovery expedition, and during that journey, I witnessed other women's lost dreams and buried ambitions, which is something that can be fixed. Those conversations were published in my first book, *Knowing Your Value,* in 2011.

Shortly thereafter, I launched my own women's empowerment platform called Know Your Value. I held events around the country, highlighting women's stories of failure and success, and celebrating how they dug themselves out of their insecurities and stopped using the same old patterns and techniques that were not working. I clearly struck a nerve with women and a community was born.

It was during this process that I met and got to know Jocelyne and Monique. I was in awe of them: twin sisters from a small town in North Dakota who had dreamed of winning an Olympic gold medal together, who played on three Olympic ice hockey teams, and who finally brought home the 2018 Olympic gold medal from Pyeongchang, South Korea, one scoring the goal that tied the game, the other netting the dramatic final shootout goal to win it all.

What truly captivated me was their determination to fight for gender equity in hockey and sports, but also in the broader context to show the world what was going on behind the scenes. USA Hockey was so disconnected from women's ice hockey, generating limited sponsorship dollars, zero marketing initiatives, meager support for girls' hockey programs, unequal travel and living arrangements, unequal benefits, and the list went on and on. Jocelyne and Monique and their teammates were determined to change the culture. And they did.

This book takes you on Jocelyne and Monique's wild ride to success and what it took to get there. It's more than a story about hockey or sports. It's more than a story of hard work, determination, and embracing adversity. This is a story of clear and serious purpose. It's a close look at how two female athletes empowered their teammates, and female athletes all over the world, to stand united for change. This is a story of leadership and the role that personal values play in developing the strength and the conviction to see a mission through to the end. It's a story of incredible courage as Jocelyne and Monique and their teammates put their Olympic dreams on the line to fight for lasting change that would largely benefit future generations of female ice hockey players.

Jocelyne and Monique are both married mothers now and juggling the complexities that come with being working moms. In fact, they are the first two women in USA Hockey history to take advantage of the maternity benefits that they negotiated for with USA Hockey. They have traveled the country and amplified the conversations and perceptions surrounding athletes, women, and motherhood. Their fight for gender equity in sports and in the working world continues, but their mission goes beyond women's ice hockey. They are now agents of change for social justice.

We all have to make a life for ourselves. How we do it and who we do it with is the single most critical question we can ask ourselves. We are all incredibly lucky to have Jocelyne and Monique as role models.

Jocelyne and Monique chose ice hockey, but in reality, no matter what their vehicle, I believe they would have ended up on this same impactful road. The rearview mirror may show them as young girls playing on boys' hockey teams, but as they matured into elite athletes who competed at the highest level, there was more to their journey. They were beginning to unlock doors for young girls and advocate for those less fortunate in a way that I feel blessed to have witnessed firsthand. There is no greater gift in life than creating an opportunity for the next generation, and Jocelyne and Monique are doing just that.

It's said that we journalists are eyewitnesses to history. Watching the evolution of Jocelyne and Monique's careers is a significant milestone in the history of athletics and in the modern fight for gender equity. Their story will be an important one to tell for generations to come.

Mika Brzezinski
Cohost, Morning Joe
MSNBC

Making the Team

★

MONIQUE

I t was August 4, 2019, and our predawn flights from Grand Forks, North Dakota, to Minneapolis to Albany were delayed. After fifteen years of repetitive road trips, we were used to travel challenges. But this trip presented a new set of experiences. My identical twin sister, Jocelyne, and I were on our way to the USA Hockey Women's National Festival in Lake Placid, New York, less than a year after we'd given birth to boys, Mickey and Nelson. We'd gotten up at 3:30 a.m., only to find out we had to completely rearrange our carefully made plans to travel with our sons for the first time.

Our little boys, now nine months and seven-and-a-half months, were resting peacefully—for now—beside us at the airline check-in counter in a double stroller. We were traveling with a nanny who was keeping an eye on them as we discussed our flight schedules with the airline rep, who sighed along with us. We all knew that we had our work cut out for us. Mickey, in the midst of teething, was gnawing on a toy and momentarily quiet; Jocelyne was going to need to nurse Nelson soon.

Next to us on the ground, ready to be checked, our bags were packed with the usual sticks, skates, pads, and other gear we'd lugged around for years as elite athletes who'd played in three Olympic Games, seven World Championships, and countless tournaments and hockey festivals and camps. Thanks to our new traveling companions, the bags also contained diapers, toys, formula, baby clothes, wipes, extra sheets, and even a Pack 'n Play. Even though we were Olympic athletes, our travel was not glamorous. We served as our own drivers, valets, trip planners, and baggage handlers. Our goals have always been about pursuing the next gold medal, but this trip was about chasing a new and different kind of mettle, our ability to adjust and adapt.

We were only five hours late when we finally arrived at the Olympic

Training Center. The boys' usual feeding and nap schedules? They had long since been blown up. After three flights, a hotel overnight, and a two-hour drive, we had made it. Jocelyne and I were tired and eager to get settled in our rooms with Mickey and Nelson. We were also excited to be returning to our day jobs. Neither of us had played in a competitive hockey game for eighteen months, the longest we'd gone since signing up for hockey at age five, but that didn't mean we were lounging on the sofa, watching television.

Since helping the U.S. Women's National Team capture a gold medal against our archrivals, Team Canada, in the finals at the 2018 Pyeongchang Olympics, we got pregnant, had our babies, and cheered from the sidelines as Team USA won the 2019 World Championship while we were on maternity leave. Throughout our pregnancies, we maintained a full schedule—working virtually every day—traveling to dozens of cities, representing our sponsor, Comcast Corporation, as brand ambassadors, and serving as national spokes-people for the company's internet program for low-income Americans. We also continued to promote equity within our sport, an effort that began with a near boycott of the 2017 World Championships before we came to an agreement with USA Hockey. That focus grew into a passionate public advo-cacy program for gender equity beyond our sport.

Now we were the first two players to benefit from the maternity-leave benefits we'd negotiated, which included full pay, a childcare stipend, and a guaranteed invitation to two national team tryouts.

Our battle for gender equity in hockey had always been focused on the next generation of girls. We wanted to make sure that they would not face the same barriers that we had—that they knew the times were changing in edu-cation, sports, and the workplace.

2019 seemed to represent a certain maturation of the gender equity battle. The #MeToo movement in Hollywood and the very public sexual harassment/ assault allegations in women's gymnastics put a glaring spotlight on issues of sexual harassment in the workplace and in sports. Our battle for gender equity in women's hockey was followed by an amazing stand by the U.S. Women's National Soccer team, which fearlessly and courageously won a World Cup while in a pitched battle, including litigation, with their governing body for equal pay.

There was also increased attention on pregnancy and maternity leave, some-thing that we were living quite personally. Pregnancy and maternity leave have long created conflicts and tension in the workplace, but women in sports put a spotlight on these issues in 2019. It's hard enough to be elite in your profes-sion—whether as an athlete or in the traditional workplace. But layering in motherhood—the physical challenges and the guilt of juggling your job as a mother and your job as an athlete or professional—can be daunting.

We were not alone in confronting these issues. Serena Williams, Allyson Felix, Nia Ali, Skylar Diggins-Smith, and other elite athletes who'd added motherhood to their résumé were all dealing with pregnancy and motherhood in the midst of elite athletic careers. There was a well-publicized spat between Allyson Felix, Kara Goucher, and Alysia Montano and Nike relating to the lack of maternity protection in Nike's sponsorship agreements and the penalties that all three of these premier track athletes experienced during their pregnancies. Fortunately for us, our main sponsor and partner, Comcast Corporation, fully supported us through our pregnancies (and after birth as well), and frankly, we were surprised that this was not the norm.

For all of us, our return was proof that the dreams of women athletes like us didn't have to end with marriage and babies, as they did in the past, unless we wanted them to. We'd competed in three Olympics and accomplished everything we had dreamed of in hockey. But we wanted to see if we could make it back to a national team post-childbirth—and maybe even play in one more Olympics in 2022 in Beijing.

But first things first. We had to make the team again. This week's camp was part of a long process leading up to the 2022 Olympics, including camps like this one every six to eight weeks and numerous international competitions. Jocelyne and I resumed training two weeks postpartum, not that we ever stopped since we worked out through our whole pregnancies with guidance from my husband, Anthony, who's managed our fitness program since 2014. Once the boys started day care in early summer 2019, we were able to commit more of our days to training full time and getting back into elite shape.

We were doing the thing that made us happiest, with the understanding that spots on the team weren't guaranteed. That's right. None of our contributions since we first made the U.S. Women's National Team in 2009 counted. Not the World Championships. Not our silver medals in the 2010 and 2014 Olympic games. Not the fact that we were responsible for the tying and game-winning goals in the 2018 Olympic finals against Canada, called by some the greatest game in the history of women's hockey. It all had a shelf life. There was new team leadership—new coaches. We hoped we would get a fair shot even though the head coach had never seen us play—that we would be given a fair opportunity to prove ourselves in terms of time on the ice and even getting a timely decision on whether I would be playing defense or forward. We had to prove ourselves all over again.

But that's life, especially in sports.

JOCELYNE

Our first full day in camp was spent greeting teammates, many of whom we hadn't seen in person for almost a year. Hilary Knight slowed her car down and waved as she drove into the facility and headed toward the parking lot. Soon we were introducing our boys to Kendall Coyne, Lee Stecklein, Emily

Matheson (Pfalzer), Annie Pankowski, Dani Camernessi, Kelly Pannek, and other teammates who were eager to meet them for the first time. Throughout all of the competitions—through the long battle for gender equity with USA Hockey—our team and teammates meant everything.

Then we got down to business. We breezed through off-ice fitness testing and initial team meetings before getting on the ice at the Herb Brooks Arena, the site of the 1980 Olympics where the men's hockey team triumphed over the Soviet Union in the historic "miracle" game (on the same date as we won our gold medal thirty-eight years later) on their way to a gold medal. But more history was being made right in front of us. A record number of women were on the ice, competing for spots on the U18, U22, and national teams, all with the dream of playing in the 2022 Olympics.

The turnout was powerful evidence of the growth of girls' and women's hockey across the country. We knew that negotiating better working conditions, pay, benefits, and most importantly, support for future generations of girl hockey players in the US would grow the sport. And it did—girls' hockey was now one of the fastest-growing sports for girls in America. An increasing number of veteran players were also receiving the support they needed to extend their playing careers after college. This was what we had believed in and fought for, and why we were returning to the sport we loved: a shared sense that all of us—veterans and up-and-comers—had the power to advocate for a playing environment that worked for us and let us determine our own fate.

Monique and I reminded ourselves not to stress or get frustrated at our play. Having turned thirty in July, we were among the oldest players in camp—and after taking a year and a half off from playing competitive hockey, it would have been unrealistic for us to think we could step back in where we left off, no matter how hard we had trained and prepared since giving birth. But once we were back on the ice, it didn't feel like it had been eighteen months away from the game.

Except for my first entrance onto the ice. Right in front of our new coach, as I was stepping onto the ice, I tripped and fell flat on my face. I looked up and said to the coach, "I swear, I've been practicing!"

When it came to my first real game-like situation against other players, I made a couple moves that felt good—a toe drag, a nice backhand-pass back-door for a tap-in goal. During my last five minutes on the ice, Monique popped into the rink before her team started warming up and stood along the glass in time to see me wind up for a slap shot below the top of the circle. The puck hit the crossbar with a piercing crack. Monique nodded approvingly, a smile brightening her face. I could literally hear her think, Jocelyne's still got it. She's just fine.

Afterward, I caught a bit of Monique in action. During her shift, she enjoyed a couple moments that showed why she'd been considered one of the best defenders in the world. Overall, the first day went well for both of us. We were on our way, but certainly not there yet. The ups and downs of a camp and a season were ahead of us, but the first full day of scrimmages made us feel like we were where we belonged—and on the right path.

MONIQUE

Our biggest challenges came at night. In my case, Mickey refused to sleep. He got four new teeth during the week of camp. He was a crabby, teething, tired baby, gnawing on anything he could put in his mouth and trying to pull himself up on whatever he could reach. At home, my husband and I had guided Mickey into good sleeping habits early on. He typically slept twelve hours a night and might wake up once. Not at camp. There, he woke up two to three times a night. And these weren't your typical quick change, feed, and back-to-sleep interruptions.

The night before our second game, I walked around in circles for an hour, gently bouncing him, trying to coax him back to sleep, while also asking myself how I was going to have enough energy for the game the next day.

After the game, I was getting an old injury looked at in the training room, and our dietician walked in. She asked how I was feeling. I am normally so stoic—so focused on my training and the game. But that simple question triggered an unexpected outpouring of exasperation from lack of sleep, exhaustion, and just everything. "I'm just so tired," I said, and then I started to cry. I couldn't even blame it on hormones. Like many mothers, I just felt overwhelmed.

That was a turning point. When Mickey was ready for sleep later that night, I put him down in the nanny's room, and I got a much-needed ten hours of uninterrupted sleep. I woke up refreshed and clearheaded. Like many moms trying to do all things all the time, I initially felt that asking for help had meant I'd failed. Fortunately, I quickly figured out—with a lot of pride—that I hadn't failed at all. I realized it simply meant that I had my limits, that I could only do so many things in a day, and sometimes needed an extra set of hands. Not a big deal, totally normal—and necessary. But like so many other new mothers juggling parenthood with a career, the mom guilt got to me. It took time for me to "be where my feet are," as our sports psychologist, Colleen Hacker, would put it.

My responsibilities as a mom made camp more complicated, but also more worthwhile. As the scrimmages wrapped up two days later, Courtney Kennedy, an Olympian in '02 and '06 and one of our coaches, pulled me aside and said she was happy to see Jocelyne and me back in camp. "I think it's really great you guys brought the boys with you," she said. "It's good for the younger players to see you return and play and compete and do it all as moms. It shows them they don't have to give up hockey. So just keep it going."

We planned to.

JOCELYNE

Quiet confidence—but not arrogance or overconfidence—has always been one of our competitive strengths. If we didn't make the team this time, we felt like we would get there in the long run. We were just starting our comeback. There were multiple teams to compete for. And whether we made it all the way to our fourth Olympics was almost beside the point. We really wanted to prove that, as mothers, we could make it back to the national team.

At the end of camp, we felt we had played well enough to make the team— we were not where we wanted to be, but we had competed well. One of the coaches left us with some encouraging words. But we didn't know. It had been a long time since we had faced this uncertainty—and it was unnerving. Three weeks later, we received the email. We had made the team. While we had never wanted to consider not making the team, that message was an important first step and a tremendous relief—and we could both take a big sigh.

But we had many more camps and teams to go before 2022, and we knew progress isn't always linear. We expected that there would be dramatic ups and downs for us to face. Time away from Mickey and Nelson was inevitable—and no one can prepare you for what it will feel like saying goodbye for weeks at a time. Even though winning another gold medal was a goal of ours, it wasn't the only one, not like it had been when we were younger. Ever since we first put on the USA jersey, we knew our efforts weren't solely for ourselves. But with winning came a greater sense of responsibility to others. Our careers were no longer just about us. We competed to celebrate potential and defy limits—to set an example. By returning as moms, we wanted to show that women didn't have to choose between a career and motherhood, between being athletes or anything else and being moms. Or if a choice was necessary, it was their decision to make. We wanted to continue improving the future for the next generation of female hockey players and level the playing field for all girls as they pursued their dreams in school, in sports, or in the workplace. And even just making this team had proved our point.

Coming out of the disappointment of the 2014 Olympics in Sochi, Monique and I realized we had the opportunity to have a greater impact than just being Olympic medalists. That softened the blow of losing the gold, and opened our eyes. We could be agents of change and role models, which was what we had always been taught. Our dad told us to be difference makers— and our mom taught us to cheer and fight for the one behind. This book, which we began to write in the weeks before we went to our first camp as moms, is about how our pursuit of a childhood dream to play together in the Olympics and win a gold medal gradually turned into a mission to change the opportunities and rewards within our sport, to inspire dreams and unlock doors for women and girls beyond women's hockey, and as an even broader matter of social justice, to advocate for those in our society who were being left behind.

We are two identical twin sisters from a small town in the middle of America who, not without our share of bumps, landed on a big stage where we came to understand we're part of an ongoing dialogue and movement, with women like Wilma Rudolph, Billie Jean King, Pat Summit, Michelle Akers, Jackie Joyner-Kersee, Julie Foudy, Cammi Granato, Abby Wambach, and others who pushed the limits and fought to get rid of them altogether.

Our parents nurtured a passion in us to make a difference as we grew up playing against our four older brothers and competing into our teens against boys. After a certain point, we knew we'd never be as big or as strong as the boys, but we were never told that we couldn't be as good as them or better. At boarding school, we helped our team win three national championships. As college freshmen, we made our first United States national team, and a year later, at age twenty, we played in our first Olympics.

All told, we have won twenty international medals between us, including seven World Championships (six of them being gold), two Olympic silver medals, and one Olympic gold. But we were taught that statistics and medal counts aren't as important as whether we're remembered as good teammates, leaders who empower, and friends who are there to help. To that end, we're going to take you inside all the bumps and successes of our career, including the hard-fought negotiations between the U.S. Women's National Team and the sport's governing body, USA Hockey, and our reluctant threat to boycott the 2017 World Championships.

MONIQUE

People have asked why our team was willing to risk the many years of hard work and sacrifice we'd invested in getting to the World Championships and ultimately, the Olympics. The answer is easy. We did it to get what was fair and right not only for our team, but mostly for new generations of girl hockey players.

As you'll discover, we've never been afraid to take off our gloves. But this book isn't just about our path to the Olympics or the fight to bring more equity to women's hockey. It's not just about reliving the risks we took to succeed and encouraging others to do the same in their own pursuits. It's also about the role values play in developing the strength, character, and conviction needed not only to win championships, but also to cheer for the ones behind, those who need a level playing field, those who might not have had all of the advantages and support that we had, and those who are next. It's our job to leave our sport and the world in a better place for those coming up after us.

Our parents ingrained this notion in us so deeply, that we wouldn't be ourselves or think of ourselves as winners if we didn't promote the importance of equity and inclusion and making sure those who need a break in the bigger game of life get it.

As we write this book, we are like so many other working moms balancing the competing demands on our lives: our hockey careers; running the Monique and Jocelyne Lamoureux Foundation; continuing the fight for equity in ice hockey, in sports, and in life; reflecting on the devastating impacts of the coronavirus pandemic and the social unrest following the murder of George Floyd by Minneapolis police; and most importantly, taking care of our children. Some days, the balance is completely off, and you feel like you have failed, and other days you feel like Superwoman and can do it all. As we move closer to achieving our personal goals and check off accomplished ones on the list, we always remember the most important benefit of our medals—that they create a platform to make a difference for others.

We naturally gravitated to the fight for gender equity and diversity in and out of sports. We learned that winning a sports competition—even winning an Olympic gold medal—has its limits. But what it means to be a winner has no limits and is up to us to define. Knowing that girls have traditionally been told they are less than, we want to be examples for girls everywhere that they can be more than—more than ever before. This might be you. If it is, you don't ever have to think in terms of limitations. You can think of dreaming big and having it all. Like those who paved the way for us, we're here so you can dare yourself to make history.

We did.

Part 1

THE DREAM

★ ★ ★

1

IT BEGINS WITH A DREAM

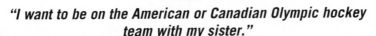

"I want to be on the American or Canadian Olympic hockey team with my sister."

JOCELYNE

It begins with a dream. We can trace our dream back to third grade. It was the start of the new school year, and we each were assigned to write about ourselves. Our teachers wanted to get to know us better. Not that they didn't have an idea. With four older brothers, the name Lamoureux was familiar to most of the school's teachers. But we were girls, and identical twins. That had to make them curious.

We were in different classes, something our parents preferred to give us some time to develop as individuals. Monique's assignment was slightly different than mine, but the work we turned in shows a glimpse into our determination even at that young age. Monique used our family computer to print out a five-pointed star and then drew a stick-figure self-portrait in the middle and filled the rest in with descriptions of herself. "I like sports," she wrote. "I like to play street hockey. I am really good at hockey. I like to run the mile. I get my work done right away. I try to figure things out for myself. I am not afraid to try."

For my assignment, I sat in the new computer lab at school with my computer screen in front of the window, peering into the library. I was eager to use the new computer skills I'd learned in tech class. I put a picture of myself in the middle and surrounded it with four boxes. They were labeled Favorites, Activities, Family, and Dreams. In Favorites, I listed the color green, Chinese food, and Harry Potter books. For Activities, I wrote hockey, gymnastics, track, throwing, violin, flute, piano, baseball, soccer, dance, basketball, skiing, tubing, and swimming. Under Family, I wrote, "All of my brothers and sister play hockey. My mom runs marathons, and my dad played hockey in college. I play on the same team as my sister, and my oldest brother is a goalie." Finally, in the top left, in the box labeled Dreams, I wrote, "When I am seventeen years old, I want to be on the American or Canadian Olympic hockey team with my sister Monique."

That project is still in my mother's scrapbook. The beginning of our dream.

For the first time in the 1998 Winter Games in Nagano, Japan, women's hockey was an Olympic sport. As ten-year-olds, we were caught up in the excitement of watching women's hockey on the ultimate world stage. These women weren't just paving the road. They were building it. Our four older brothers were all serious players who dared to dream big. They aspired to play in the NHL. So we dreamed big too.

When I am seventeen years old...

With dual citizenship, Monique and I would have our choice of playing for either the US or Canada if our ability allowed us. But we grew up in the US. We considered ourselves Americans. Proud Americans. We grew up saying the Pledge of Allegiance in school. We dreamed of playing for the red, white, and blue. We saw ourselves standing with gold medals around our necks and hands over our hearts while the "Star-Spangled Banner" played like we watched the '98 team do.

Our mom was into the Olympics. *Really* into the Olympics. She was an Olympics trivia queen. Summer and winter. For as far back as we can remember, she made watching them a family event. The trials and qualifying events leading up to them introduced her to the athletes and got her emotionally engaged in their lives. By the time the athletes walked in the opening ceremonies, she was emotionally invested, and eventually we were too.

She was enthralled with the human side of the competition: the people, the drama, the dedication and years of training, the tears, the joy, and how sometimes it was just one little slip or a hundredth of a second that was the difference between gold and silver. A year after I scored the final shootout goal to win the 2018 Olympic gold medal, I saw a picture of Scott Hamilton in the stands, fists in the air, cheering for Team USA, and the goal I had just scored. I stared at the screen and thought, "Wow! Scott Hamilton, an Olympic legend, cheering us on during our greatest Olympic moment." I know it might sound silly, as I was a three-time Olympian myself, but it was a bit surreal.

One of Mom's absolute favorites was Jackie Joyner-Kersee. Long and lean, with a big, inviting smile, Jackie won two gold medals at the Seoul games in '88, in the long jump and heptathlon. Four years later, she took another gold in the heptathlon in Barcelona. Altogether, her career spanned four Olympics, including six medals in those games. Away from track and field, she focused on philanthropy and advocated for children's education, health issues, and women's rights. By third grade, we knew all about Jackie Joyner-Kersee, even though we had never watched her compete.

Mom read Jackie's autobiography as if it was a blueprint for success. *Sports Illustrated* named Jackie the greatest female athlete of all time. Amazingly, her world-record performance in the heptathlon still stands today. Mom would marvel at her accomplishments and ask herself how Jackie and so many athletes who had come from very little became the world's best. That was her favorite part of the Olympics—how people from all over the world, many from the tiniest, most faraway places on the planet, and from every background imaginable, were able to accomplish so much.

In a true small-world story, Jackie preceded us as spokesperson for Comcast's Internet Essentials program. We got to meet her—and brought our mother to Washington to meet Jackie as well. And that autobiography—we got to present our mother with another copy, personally autographed by Jackie!

Jackie and the other Olympic athletes we followed were proof that success was available to anyone who worked for it.

MONIQUE

Mom kept Jackie's book in the kitchen, where she filled nearly every flat surface other than the counters with inspiring articles and motivational quotes she found in the newspaper. If you didn't live in our house, you wouldn't know what color our refrigerator was because it was plastered with quotes and photos. If it was one she really, *really* liked, she would laminate the piece of paper, which meant she "Linda-laminated" it by using clear packing tape on both sides and trimmed the edges that stuck out.

There was a picture of Oregon long-distance runner Steve Prefontaine and his famous quote, "To give anything less than your best is to sacrifice the gift." And there was a copy of the letter the city's fabled athlete Clifton Cushman, a silver medalist in the 1960 Rome Olympics, sent to the local newspaper after falling on a hurdle in the '64 trials and failing to make the US team. Addressed "to the youth of Grand Forks," he wrote, "Don't feel sorry for me...I would much rather fail knowing I had put forth an honest effort than never have tried at all." As we got older, I always wondered what our mother's motivation was in putting these snippets in front of us, and when I asked her, her response was, "I just did."

Our mom was low-key but quietly determined. Soft and pretty on the outside, with her blonde hair always perfectly coiffed and nails painted, she was tough as steel inside. She grew up in Grand Forks, one of six children, with parents of Scandinavian descent. Her mom, our grandma Edith, used to tell us, "To whom much is given, much is expected." She also taught us the importance of a firm handshake and to look people directly in the eye when we spoke to them. "Those little things help make a good first impression." I suspect my mom heard that many times when she was growing up, as did we.

Mom swam competitively, starting in junior high school. She was one of the few girls who went out for the team. "Maybe I was a little bit of an oddball," she once said to us, "but I didn't care." She liked getting in the pool and getting her laps in. She was hardwired for the mental discipline of setting her mind to a task and achieving it. She won high school state championships in freestyle, butterfly, and backstroke.

Interestingly, most people assume that we get our grit, tenacity, and work ethic from our dad. We've heard that our entire lives: "You must get that from your dad." And yes, we credit him for a lot of things, but our mom has always flown under the radar with respect to our genes for athletic ability and competitiveness. Dad has the outward appearance of seriousness and intensity, but a big part of our intense focus, competitiveness, and drive certainly comes from our mom. If you put her in a competition, it's as if a switch flips inside her, and she goes into an all-or-nothing gear.

The desire to do her best came naturally to her. As a young competitive swimmer, she dreamed of going to the Olympics, and although she was realistic about her ability, she always pushed herself to see how good she could be. She didn't get to the Olympics, but she did swim on the team at the University of North Dakota (UND), which was where she met our dad, Pierre Lamoureux.

JOCELYNE

It was 1979, and they were both freshmen and had a class together, Introduction to Physical Education. They never spoke. Dad remembers her frequently coming in late. To this day, Mom has trouble showing up on time for anything, and Dad is ready to go at least five minutes early. Mom laughingly acknowledges the interruptions she caused. She wore wood-soled clogs, which she loved, but they made a clip-clop sound that distracted everyone from the professor's lesson as she made her way to her preferred chair in the back corner of the room. So, of course, Dad noticed her; a beautiful, athletic, stylish blonde coed, trying to sneak in unnoticed and capturing everyone's attention in the process.

Their paths wouldn't cross again for another two years when they ran into each other at a local bar, and they soon started dating. Born and raised just outside of Edmonton, Alberta, in a little town called Fort Saskatchewan, Dad was an exceptional athlete. In college, he was a goalie on UND hockey teams that won two NCAA National Championships in 1980 and 1982.

They got married on Saturday, May 14, 1983, and the next day, Dad attended his graduation. Since they were already engaged and Dad's family made the long drive into town, they decided to make it easy and convenient for everybody and double up on the celebrations. That's typical of the way our dad thinks: strategic, analytic, and efficient—even for his own wedding.

Soon after marrying, our mom became pregnant with our oldest brother, Jean-Philippe, who was born in 1984. Two miscarriages followed before she gave birth to Jacques in 1986. The rest of us arrived each summer after that: Pierre-Paul, Mario, and finally, Monique and me. That's six kids in five years!

Mom says that when Mario was born, people said, "Oh, another boy?" and tried to console her, as if she might be disappointed. She wasn't. She was used to having boys and was grateful that her babies were healthy.

Then she got pregnant with us. Back then, she worked part-time in the radiology department at the local hospital. With four kids at home ranging in age from four to not quite one, she says going to work was like taking a break. When her pregnancy reached the three-month mark, one of her coworkers scanned her belly and, as Mom recalls, "It got quiet, and she left the room." She came back five minutes later with one of the doctors. They explained the scan showed something unexpected: two heads.

Mom was confused and nervous. "There are two babies," the doctor said. Mom relaxed. She already had four at home. As long as the babies were healthy, two more was good with her. She called Dad, who was with one of his business partners in Fargo. "Oh my God, she's having twins," he said. "I have to get a second job."

Dad's parents were stunned when they heard the news. One of our cousins, watching them during that phone call with our dad, saw their reaction and thought someone had passed away. Nope, our grandparents said afterward. Pierre and Linda were expecting again. Their fifth child—and their sixth. Twins!

For the last two months of Mom's pregnancy, Philippe and Jacques stayed with our grandparents in Canada. It was too hard for Mom to take care of the two more active boys and the little ones while being pregnant with twins. Mom was hoping for Fourth of July babies and a celebration with fireworks. She came up short by a day. We arrived via C-section, with Monique, weighing seven pounds, seven ounces, arriving two minutes before me. I was a little over seven pounds, and both of us were healthy, alert, and, given the way one of us came out just before the other, competitive right from the beginning.

MONIQUE

Despite the sonogram pictures, Mom refused to believe she was having girls until she saw us with her own eyes. Once we were in her arms, she called us a miracle. When the news of our arrival reached Dad's parents at their lake cabin in Canada, where they were taking care of Philippe and Jacques, Grandma went outside and rang the bell on their porch, determined everyone should know that the Lamoureux family had two new additions—and they were girls! As Mom says, we were celebrated in two countries.

As babies, Mom painted my fingernails to make it easier to tell Jocelyne and me apart, but Philippe never got the hang of it and simply referred to us as "the missies," as did most of our brothers and their friends until we were teenagers. Before we were even one year old, Mom started taking us to swimming classes, as she did with our brothers. She took a different kid—or kids, in our case—every day.

She needed to get out of the house for her own sanity, she says. She also believed in starting everyone in activities at an early age. One day, our dad came home with a van that had belonged to one of the UND athletic teams. It was one of those extended models—big, institutional, and very uncool in the eyes of our mom. "There's no way I'm driving that thing," she said to our babysitter, Nikki.

It had room for four car seats, two rambunctious older boys, and everything Mom needed for our daily outings, and it became her home away from home. As we shuttled between practices and games, it was more of a locker room on wheels, filled with skates, hockey sticks, uniforms, balls, schoolbooks, food, and even a TV that we watched on long road trips. I have vivid memories of Mom pulling up in front of the rink when Jocelyne and I were about three or four years old and all of us piling out of the van with our skates on, a hive of clamoring kids hurrying across the parking lot to get on the ice. I imagine those already inside the rink running for cover. There was no mistaking the storm that was about to hit.

The Lamoureuxs had arrived.

2

YOU HAVE TO SWIM THE LAPS

"You can't buy the things that help you succeed."

JOCELYNE

In our family, everyone skated.

Mom took us to preschool skating classes when we were two-and-a-half years old, the same year the International Olympic Committee voted to add women's hockey to the games starting in 1998. While the timing may have been prophetic, she was simply being practical in putting us on the ice at that age. She was a mom with six kids, with the oldest two, Philippe and Jacques, already whirling-dervish fireballs who streaked across the ice, and so all of us went to the rink and skated.

I baby-stepped my way around the rink right away, a natural if I do say so myself; Monique clung to Mom's leg and cried the whole time. She didn't want to be left alone. It was an early glimpse into our personalities: me jumping right into something and not always thinking it through, while Monique surveyed her options before making any rash decision. A year later, Monique took off on her own. The difference was night and day. The lady who ran the candy concession, Clara, marveled, "Is that the same little girl?"

Now, both of us, with our bouncing ponytails, chased our brothers around the rink. They were wild men. They took turns sitting atop walkers—skating's version of training wheels—and crashed them into the boards like they were bumper cars. I'm pretty sure Monique and I were calmer skaters. Mom says the two of us skated nonstop, waving as we passed her sitting in the stands while she did paperwork. We would've skated for hours if she let us—and sometimes she did. Why not? Afterward, everyone took good naps.

Monique and I shared a room. Mom decorated it with rose-colored wallpaper and tried to introduce lots of girly things, but we gravitated to our brothers' toys and games. How could a doll be as interesting as the way Philippe flipped our old playpen on its side as if it were a hockey goal and tried to block whatever the rest of us attempted to throw past him? No one ever kept score. The game usually ended when someone cried. But Mom saw the writing on the wall. Barbie was never going to get the same response from us as Gretzky. And in our house, Super Mario referred to Lemieux, not the video game.

I was right-handed and Monique was left-handed (known as "mirror twins"). The differences ended there. We behaved like we were a unit. When Mom took me to the doctor to get a wart burned off my thumb, I sat in her lap while the doctor cauterized the ugly little bump. Monique hid under the chair and screamed, begging the doctor to stop, as if she were the one in pain. "It's okay," I told my sister, trying to calm her. "It's okay."

We wanted to try anything and everything athletic—and Mom and Dad encouraged that. We started dance lessons at three. The next year we added gymnastics. Around five or six, we were on soccer and swim teams. Enthusiastic and fearless, we watched our brothers and mimicked their moves. We also took piano lessons. In fourth grade, we begged and pleaded to take violin. Mom said we were maxed out, but Monique and I cried, and eventually Mom gave in. She didn't know how we were going to fit it in our already-full schedule, but she said she'd try—and somehow she fit violin in too.

Mom kept a detailed schedule that she constantly updated. Dad kept a master monthly calendar with everyone's practices and games, so they knew which one of them was going where to watch which kids. They had a hard-and-fast rule. You had to finish what you started. You might not sign up for the sport or the lessons the next time, but you couldn't quit midway through. Take swimming, for example.

Swim practice began at 6 p.m., and we normally headed to the pool from a different practice or lesson. We liked swim meets, but didn't love practice. We pretended to fall asleep as Mom drove to the pool and made her shake us awake after she parked. We wanted her to think we were too tired to swim laps. If that didn't work, we told her that we didn't feel well. Anything to get out of swim practice, but it never worked, not even once. Swimming was important to Mom in a way we didn't understand at the time. What she knew from her own background as a competitive swimmer was that you couldn't fake it. You had to swim the laps. There is no hiding in the pool. So when she dropped us off at practice, it wasn't about conditioning as much as it was about character and values.

She had a plan. Our parents didn't have a lot of spare money growing up, and she wanted us to learn that just because we saw a kid get new skates or some other piece of equipment, that wasn't how you got to be good—not in sports, and not in life. The point they wanted to get across to all of us was that you can't buy the things that help you succeed. You can't buy desire. You can't buy drive. You can't buy discipline. You can't buy confidence. You can't buy a commitment to a team. You have to build those things within yourself.

You have to swim the laps.

MONIQUE

Not only did Mom tell us, but she also showed us. Before having kids, she started running and worked up to competing in a half marathon. She picked it up again about a year after we were born and carved out quiet, alone time for herself and fought to get back into shape. In the beginning, she trained with a girlfriend, but then, as she recalls, she got more serious and started getting up at 5:30 in the morning to run longer distances. In the winter, she ran around the inside of the UND arena, often with the ROTC guys, who were also training in the predawn hours.

Her discipline was world class. If one of us had practice at the UND arena, Mom ran around the concourse during practice. Sometimes she got her run in on the treadmill we had in the basement before we awoke for school. In the summers, Jocelyne and I sometimes rode our bikes alongside her while she was on a run. Even on bikes, her runs were too long for us, and we typically turned around and rode home while she kept going.

By the time we turned seven, Mom's goal was to qualify for the Boston Marathon. In 1997, she ran the first of what would ultimately be five Boston Marathons. The race was in mid-April, which coincided with the worst flood in Grand Forks' history. We'd had nine blizzards that winter and a late spring storm that pushed the Red River to record high levels and beyond. For weeks, everyone in town filled sandbags like crazy. Then the air force took over the effort. We helped distribute bags. It was a race of human will versus the rising river.

As the last in a series of intense blizzards hit, a storm the local paper called "hard-hearted Hannah," city officials closed schools in the middle of the day and called parents to pick up their kids. Our dad was on his way to get us, but his truck got stuck in the snow just outside the driveway. He walked back into the house and called the school office and left a message for us to walk home. All six of us were still in the same school. We got together and marched home, single file, one line of little Lamoureuxs with Philippe leading, and the rest of us tucked behind whoever was in front of us.

In the spring, the river rose past record levels with no end in sight. We were given warnings to evacuate the town ahead of the unstoppable floodwaters. Mom and Dad packed our clothes into garbage bags, and Dad drove all of us kids to our aunt and uncle's house in Hillsboro, about thirty-five miles away. The next day, our grandfather picked us up and took us to Canada, where we spent the next two months. We enrolled in school and resumed something of a normal life. We were too young to realize the direness of the situation back home or when we might return.

With evacuation sirens blaring throughout town, Mom packed her running gear and flew to Boston on Sunday morning. Dad cut short a business meeting out of town and returned to Grand Forks to keep an eye on the house and help those in need. On Monday, Mom ran the Boston Marathon in three hours, twenty-six minutes. That night, she turned on the TV in her hotel room and saw news reports of downtown Grand Forks on fire amid widespread flooding and evacuation of many of its fifty-two thousand residents.

On the day we finally returned from Canada, Dad drove us around town before we went home. Shocked, our mouths agape and faces pressed against the windows of the van, we saw the widespread damage. I spotted a car halfway inside someone's living-room window. In many cases, the waterline had been above the roofs of the one-story homes. Trash was strewn all over the berms from people having come back and emptied their homes from the water damage. Dad wanted us to see how lucky we were to be able to sleep in our beds that night, while others had lost everything or were cleaning up and figuring out what to do next.

Over the next few weeks and months, we saw our hometown move forward. We heard people recount extraordinary acts of kindness and caring for each other during the crisis and then talk about how they were reopening their businesses, rebuilding their homes, and getting back into life's normal routines. This was an early lesson about the importance of being resilient—of not letting blows that you receive in life keep you down. The effort to recover left you exhausted. But you did it anyway. You cleaned up, rebuilt, reopened, and banded together with your neighbors and community for what it built inside you.

Twenty years after the fact, I read a story online in the *Grand Forks Herald* in which Grand Forks mayor Michael Brown made the same point. "There's a Chinese proverb: adversity builds character," he said. "You could sense the pride in the community that comes from facing adversity...You could see a character you could be proud of." It brought back memories. At the time, Jocelyne and I understood as much as we could as eight-year-olds, but that's why our dad had driven us around town before going home.

The things we saw stayed with us. They became part of us and defined the way we lived our lives and pursued our goals later on. The way we worked hard, bounced back after losses, and continued fighting for a gold medal after "winning" two silvers. Life wasn't guaranteed to be easy. But human beings were resilient if they worked at it.

3

THE PATH TO WINNING

★

"If you have the will, you can find the way."

JOCELYNE

At age four, Monique and I were finally old enough to tag along with our brothers when they ran across the street to play hockey on the pond. Fed by a nearby drainage ditch known as an English coulee, the "pond" was a depression two hundred feet long and seventy feet wide that froze every winter and turned into our private rink. As soon as the temperature dropped, our neighbor Mr. Howe, who had three boys, flooded it with water. The day it froze was the best day of the year, even better than Christmas. Christmas was just one day. The pond was our practice rink for months.

We laced up our skates, put our skate guards on, bundled up, and hurried across the street with our sticks over our shoulders and pucks in every pocket and pouch. No one was concerned about thin ice or falling through. "If by some chance you do, you'll be able to stand," our dad once said. "It's not a big deal."

We were the only girls among the pack of neighborhood boys who played on the pond. They just added us to their game after we began running after our brothers. Philippe, Jacques, Pierre-Paul, and Mario were used to me and Monique wanting to do everything they did, whether it was baseball in the backyard, street hockey in the summer, or ice hockey on the pond. Their friends were fine with it too. We were two more bodies. We could skate. We didn't cry or complain. And we helped carry more practice pucks from the garage.

The Howes installed a floodlight that extended playtime past dinner and sometimes past bedtime. At one of our brothers' behest, we would call: "Can you turn the lights on?" But only after Monique and I battled about which one of us would actually pick up the phone. "I don't want to call." "I called last time. You call." "No, I don't want to." "Fine, then no one's calling." "Okay, I'll call. But you have to next time."

Monique and I were always on opposite teams. The boys, as we referred to our brothers collectively, showed us no mercy, which may be a kind understatement considering all the times we were sent flying into the snowbanks. "There's no way to cookie-cut it," Pierre-Paul later told a journalist from *Time* magazine. "We were assholes to our sisters." Our mom would check on us every once in a while to make sure they weren't getting too physical, but she let us play. She didn't want to break up the action every ten minutes. Like a good ref, she let us figure things out on our own.

Once, while we were playing street hockey in front of the house, Jacques and I were racing for a ball. It didn't matter that I was in third grade, and he was obviously older and bigger. We were both fierce competitors. He accidentally slashed my fingers pretty hard, so I whacked him back on the leg, then he swung his stick and instead of getting the ball, his blade sliced into the back of my leg, just above my ankle, and sent me to the ground. Bleeding, I tossed my stick on the front lawn and ran inside, crying. When my mom asked what happened, I simply said, "Jacques."

Years later, as I recalled this story to my parents, my dad shrugged and acknowledged that Jacques could be a bit of a hack in that he had no qualms about chopping someone to get the puck, including his little sister. Mom said as much at the time. "That's what you're going to get if you play out there with the boys," she said matter-of-factly. I nodded, let her bandage the cut, and then hurried outside and back into the game.

MONIQUE

At six years old, we signed up for Termites, the level of hockey for the youngest kids. You started there and graduated to Mites, Squirts, PeeWees, and Bantams. Kids spent two years in each, moving up according to age.

When asked about our start in organized hockey, we have always said that we were following our brothers. But the truth is, we were all following our dad. He started playing goalie as a kid on a house team when he was eight or nine years old. He used a baseball mitt and wore cricket pads over his shin guards. Even without the proper equipment, he was better at goalie than the other kids, so his coach kept him there.

In his early teens, he was asked to try out for one of the traveling teams as a goalie. With typical understatement, he says he must have been decent (his word) because his teams always had a winning record. Whatever he had, it was the right stuff.

Dad was pursued by the University of North Dakota as a recruited walk-on, meaning the hockey coach encouraged him to try out and said if he made the team, they would help him with tuition. Nothing was guaranteed up front, but he made the team as a backup goalie, got half his tuition paid for over four years, and played on two NCAA Division I National Championship teams in 1980 and 1982, sometimes as a starter. He loved the challenge of earning a spot in the starting lineup, especially coming in as a walk-on, where nothing would be guaranteed.

He also liked doing things the right way. After Philippe and Jacques started in Mites, he watched a few of their practices and went home disgusted (his word again). "It was pretty brutal," he remembers telling our mom. "I could at least teach those kids some basics."

He did—for about the next ten years. Once one of us aged out of Mites, he was back down with the next child in line. He coached all six of us and got satisfaction from knowing that we were learning the game correctly. He was an excellent coach, too. By the time Jocelyne and I followed Mario into Mites, Dad had honed the practice routines to a place where eight-year-olds were learning how to pass, defend, break the puck out, and move it up the ice without everyone going for the puck all at once, which still happened with players that age, no matter the coaching.

As long as they knew what they were supposed to do, he says. It was a start.

JOCELYNE

Mites looked and felt more like hockey. Games were on Saturdays. In the morning, we all dressed in our gear in the piano room, which was off the front door. We wore our red long johns and long-sleeved horizontal-striped turtlenecks; mine was blue, and Monique's was purple. Mom drove us to the rink a couple minutes down the road in our full gear. We climbed out of the van, put on our helmets, and ran straight onto the ice ready and eager to play.

I remember one game at Purpur Arena where I was in a free-for-all for the puck. I had my head down and was skating at full speed when I ran into a boy. He went down and immediately started to cry. I got stung, too, but I said to myself, "I can't cry," and stifled the urge to let the tears fall. I'm not sure if Dad had given us the speech yet about not showing if something hurt, but this foreshadowed the hundreds of moments we would hide the pain with a grimace, swallow the tears, and skate away, appearing unfazed by any collision.

He also reminded us that if we got hurt and lay on the ice waiting for a coach to come check on us, it better be because we couldn't physically stand because our leg was broken. In other words, there was no crying in hockey.

We were playing on two teams at this point—a traveling team and an in-house team of all local players, which Dad coached with a friend of his, Mike McNamara. At the end of the season, we played in a tournament against the East Grand Forks team, our rivals from just across the river. For whatever reason, we were missing some players. Maybe kids were sick or traveling with their families. East Grand Forks had three full lines of forwards and defense, which is fifteen skaters, and we only had eight kids—one line, a goalie, and two extra players on the bench. Their bench was packed.

I played goalie, as I did every now and then, and Monique and Mike's son, Patrick, played defense the entire game. The two of them did not come off the ice unless they got a penalty. Even though we were outnumbered and completely exhausted by the end of the game, we won by one goal. Our opponents were mad and frustrated, and making matters even worse, as many of them said, was the fact that two of the players on the team that beat them were girls. It was like, *Girls...gawd...unbelievable.*

It was the first time we heard players and parents make comments along those lines, as if we were less capable because we were girls. But it wasn't the last.

And two of them are girls.

Those comments followed us from Mites all the way through Bantams, and they got worse as we got older. Boys harassed us—and their parents jeered from the stands as if we were going to prevent their kids from doing their best. Our dad taught us to respond with our play and to ignore the noise.

MONIQUE

When Dad was on the ice in practice, he was always toughest on the two of us. He never wanted other parents to think we were favored because he was a parent coaching, and he especially didn't want anyone to think he took it easy on us because we were girls. He didn't have that "easy" gear, anyway. At practice, he told us to practice hard—and we knew he expected nothing less. When he put us through drills, he told us to do the drills as fast as possible. "If you don't put your best foot forward, why bother?" he said.

As we got older, we started to understand that if we wanted to make significant improvements, we had to put in extra work. It wouldn't be enough to show up to practice and work hard; that was expected of everyone. So we started by shooting pucks and doing stick-handling drills in the garage in the summer, and soon we were training five days a week. Our dad had this quiet way of letting us know that if you wanted to make it to the next level, you would always have to put in the extra work. "Just know," he said, "there's always someone else out there trying to get better today."

Our brothers were the best role models we could have had. They did drills every day with a single-minded purpose of getting in peak shape, perfecting their skills, and improving their weaknesses. We did the same thing. Conditioning? Check. Stick-handling drills in the garage? Check. Agility drills? Yup. In the summer, we shot hundreds of pucks every day. Our dad taught us to take pride in the work we put in day in and day out because that's what it took to get great at something. At that age, we had no way of knowing if we would accomplish our goals, but we would not be outworked.

He and our mom instilled in us a sense of where we should set the bar, along with an expectation that we'd keep raising it. And not for them. For us. Because we knew we could continue to improve, and we'd be cheating ourselves if we didn't work toward that goal. Mom focused on character, and Dad gave us context. One spoke to us about desire, and the other one taught us about drive. One was about will, and the other was about way. If you have the will, you can find the way.

We saw these lessons brought to life in 1998 when women's hockey debuted as an Olympic sport in Nagano, Japan. Unlike most of our second-grade classmates, we understood everything about the significance of the '98 Olympics for women's hockey and got caught up in the progress of the U.S. Olympic Women's Ice Hockey Team as if we were part of the team ourselves. We were inspired by that team. We identified with its captain and star player Cammi Granato, whose hockey career and personal story foreshadowed our own.

Cammi came from a large, hockey-playing family in Illinois. Her oldest brother, Tony, was a star in the NHL. Growing up, she was always the only girl on her team. She put up with the inconvenience of changing separately from her teammates and being targeted by opposing teams whose players tried to take her out just because she was a girl. She also was berated by the parents of boy players, who should have known better. Unfortunately, all this would be way too familiar to us as we got older.

But there was hope. After college, Cammi competed with the national team from 1990 to 2005 in nine World Championships and two Olympic games. Watching Cammi and her teammates accept their gold medals in '98 and stand together while the national anthem played gave girls like us role models she didn't have at the same age. Jocelyne and I could set our sights on playing for the US in the Olympics. We had a team. Not only that, we had a superstar of our own—a whole team of them—and when our teammates pretended they were Lemieux, Gretzky, or Messier, we could picture ourselves as Cammi, Jenny, Ang, and others.

We could even picture ourselves playing alongside them one day.

4

PLAYING AGAINST BOYS

⭐

"Who we played didn't matter as much as how we prepared ourselves to be our best."

JOCELYNE

Between the ages of ten and eleven, we moved up to the still-all-boys Squirts, where the competition was more serious and games were played in and around North Dakota and Minnesota. For the most part, our teammates appreciated our athletic ability regardless of our gender. Of course, winning helped.

But many parents thought it was high time for us to admit we were girls and realize that we had no business playing against their sons in a game where, as they pointed out, checking would become legal when we moved up to PeeWees. "It's going to get rough," they said. "It's going to be different when they get hit. And the risk is going to be theirs." Those were the same kinds of comments Cammi Granato, Angela Ruggiero, Jenny Potter, and the rest of the '98 team heard when they were our age and playing against boys, and as we well knew, they would never have won gold in the Olympics if they had paid attention to them.

MONIQUE

When we were ready to move up to PeeWees, for the first time, we had to try out in front of real coaches rather than parent coaches who handpicked the teams themselves. This was a sign of how much more serious the play was at this level—on the ice, on the bench, and in the stands. On the day of tryouts, we got to the rink early, as we liked to do (and still do) and went through that transformation that has become so much a part of our lives. We breathed in the smell of the rink, heard the sounds of skates digging into the ice and pucks exploding off the boards, and we got psyched to play.

Our goal was to make one of two A-level teams that would travel around the state for league play and also to weekend tournaments throughout the Midwest. Only the best players made it. The rest were put on the B teams. "It's not good enough that you just barely make it," our dad said as we stood next to the glass, watching the others on the ice. "When the coaches are looking at all the players, you probably won't make it if you're on the bubble. You have to be way ahead of the curve on this. It's important that you make a statement."

We knew that there were coaches, players, and parents who thought we did not belong. When tryouts were over, we had to leave no doubt that we would be difference makers on whatever team we ended up on.

Dad turned toward me. He said that the coaches were probably going to do a one-on-one drill where one player picks the puck up and swings around the net and up the ice, while the defenseman moves up the blue line, skates forward, and then transitions backward, playing one-on-one defense. "If this happens, give him the outside lane," he said. "He'll take it, I guarantee you, and he's going to think it's clear sailing because he's up against a girl. But once he starts to make his move, I want you to turn and take him out into the boards as hard as you can."

I nodded.

"But you have to choose the player you do this against," he continued.

Dad said his name, and the two of us nodded. He would be one of the best players, and we had played against him growing up.

"I don't care if you have to butt in line to match up with him," Dad went on. "He'll be the first guy to go because he's the best player. Pair yourself up with him and then...you put him on his ass."

Just as Dad predicted, that kid got up first, and I did as instructed. I lined up opposite him. As soon as the whistle sounded, he came in and made his move, and I followed my dad's instructions and "put him on his ass." He went down on his back, which ended the drill, and I skated away to get back in line. Mission accomplished. According to my dad, who watched from a balcony above the action, he saw three coaches watching closely, and when they saw what I did, they looked at each other and started writing notes.

Jocelyne, who was trying out as a goalie, had been picking up extra practices for Mario and Pierre-Paul's teams for the last two years. Developing her goalie skills against older boys, all while playing our own hockey schedule. She really loved playing between the pipes and convinced Dad that goalie was the position for her. Regardless of the position, though, we knew we had to be among the best, not just good enough.

JOCELYNE

We made one of the two PeeWee A teams, the GF Wheatkings. Our coach, Brandon Lunak, appreciated our coachability and work ethic. We were two of the more physical players on the team, if not the most physical players, and he appreciated that too. Plenty of parents took exception, though, and encouraged their sons to be physical against us. All season, we heard jeers like "knock her over" and "check her," but we ignored them, put our heads down, and played hard.

We beat Grafton 7–2 that year in Devil's Lake to win the state championship. Monique scored twice, and I played goalie the first two periods and then played defense in the third and scored my own goal. While driving home the next year after we lost a close game in the finals, my dad suggested that I stop playing goalie. "You're as good as Monique when you skate," he said. "But you never practice those things. How many years of repetitions have you missed? Imagine how good you could be if you had practiced them."

Although he didn't say it directly, he was thinking down the line to college and perhaps the national team, where it was unlikely I would be big enough to play goalie, and he knew I needed to make the transition now. I agreed, and the timing worked out. That spring, for the first time, Monique and I played on an all-girls' team. Even though we were much younger, we also played on Team North Dakota's nineteen-and-under team that took on the girls prep team from Shattuck St. Mary's, a top private school with a reputation for excellence in both sports and academics.

After our game, we took time to visit the Shattuck St. Mary's campus, which looked to us like the Hogwarts School of Witchcraft and Wizardry in *Harry Potter*. We liked it a lot, along with the student who gave us the tour, our future teammate Laurel Simer, who later confided that she'd been told to make sure we enjoyed our visit. We did!

High school didn't start until ninth grade, which was still over a year away, but it wasn't too early to start exploring our options. Much of our passion today for helping the next generation of girl hockey players stems from having been there ourselves. We remember being young, looking up, and believing our dreams were within reach if only we worked hard, despite the harsh realities of parents who heckled us, players who didn't want us on the ice with them because of our gender, and limited opportunities because those doors hadn't been created yet, never mind being opened.

MONIQUE

Dad got a call from Dwayne Schmidgall, who was the father of Olympian Jenny Schmidgall (now known by her married name, Jenny Potter). They were from Edina, Minnesota. He was putting together a team for a summer tournament in Minneapolis, and he wanted to know if we'd be interested in participating. The tournament was for high school and college players, and he also planned a scrimmage for college and national team players, as well as Olympians like his daughter, and he invited us to play as well.

We couldn't have been more excited to play, especially the chance to scrimmage with Jenny, whom we'd watched win a gold medal in the '98 Olympics, and other players of her caliber. Dad agreed. Not only would the skill level be high, but it would also be a good benchmark for where Jocelyne and I were in our development. We were good in our small pond, as Dad put it, and this would give us better perspective.

And so it did. At the tournament, Jocelyne and I weren't the best players on the team, but we were in the middle of the pack and maybe even better. Even though we were thirteen-year-olds playing against players who were five to eight years older than us, our strong, aggressive style of play helped us fit right in. We played hard and asserted ourselves physically, as our dad had taught us, which maybe wasn't the best approach to take when transitioning to a game that no longer allowed checking, but we wanted to show that we belonged.

While we were on the ice, Dad spotted the head coach of the women's hockey team at the University of Minnesota sitting in the stands. He introduced himself, pointed out the two of us, explaining that we were his twin daughters, and asked if she thought we had a chance at playing in a D1 school like Minnesota. She said NCAA rules prohibited her from talking to the parents of players from the tenth grade on. When she heard we had just finished the seventh grade, she looked both stunned and amazed. "Does that mean they have a reasonable shot?" Dad asked, to which she responded, "Yes, it does."

On the day after the championship game, we played in the afternoon scrimmage with college and national team players, as well as a few Olympians, including Jenny Schmidgall and Natalie Darwitz, a national champion at the University of Minnesota and the leading scorer in the recent 2002 Olympics. Jocelyne and I were in the locker room, getting ready, when Jenny—or Pottsy, as we now call her—walked in, threw her bag down, and said, "Who are these two French-Canadian twins I've been hearing about?"

Jocelyne and I weren't saying much to anyone in the locker room, especially a celebrated veteran like her. It seemed as though she knew almost everyone in the locker room, so I half raised my hand and quietly said, "Oh, that's us—and we're American." During the actual scrimmage, we were astonished by the speed at which she and Natalie played. Both are fast in a national team setting, but they seemed on a whole different planet that first time we were on the ice with them. "Holy crap," I remember saying to Jocelyne. "They're so fast."

Even when we were teammates with them in the 2010 Olympics, there would be moments where both of us would think, "Good thing I'm not chasing them."

At the end of the day, we felt good about our own play against some of the world's best, as well as girls who were heading off to play Division I hockey at top-end schools, and as we rode home in the car, I turned to Jocelyne and said, "We should be able to do this." It was an important moment of comparing our ability and potential with the reality of who was out there playing at the highest level. Then, a second later, we each had the same afterthought. It wasn't *we should be able to do this*. It was, *we can do this*.

5

SETTING PRIORITIES: FAMILY, HOCKEY, AND SCHOOL

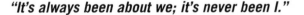

"It's always been about we; it's never been I."

JOCELYNE

Hockey was always our number one priority, but once the season ended, we turned to our other passion, soccer. As thirteen-year-old seventh graders, we asked to play on our local high school's team, an idea that would've seemed unrealistic to most girls our age. Except we didn't play like most girls our age. The coach at Red River High said no, but the coach at his crosstown rival, Central High School, invited us to try out. By the end of the season, we were among the leading scorers in the state, named all-conference and all-state, and helped Central into the state tournament.

Our packed days were carefully choreographed to let us fit in all our activities. We went to school, then walked across the street to practice; rode home with our teammate Alys in her beat-up, old beige Chevy pickup truck; ate dinner; did homework; and went to bed. This was our normal routine until it was interrupted, and we were forced to ask, "What's going on?"

I remember the day. We were playing West Fargo, and our mom told us that morning that my dad, my brothers, and she would be there to watch. This wasn't unusual—even though all of our schedules were equally packed, we always tried to show up for each other's games when we could. But when I ran across the soccer field on a beautiful spring day, I noticed that Jacques was not there with the rest of our family. That got my attention.

After the game, we got in the van, and our mom explained that Jacques was in the hospital. When we asked why, she said he was sad and needed help. The somber tone of her voice indicated there was more to the story than Jacques being sad. And indeed, although Monique and I wouldn't know the details for another year and a half, Jacques was suffering from severe depression.

A few days later, our entire family visited him in the hospital. Bristling with anger and eager to get out, he clearly wasn't himself. We knew Jacques was a perfectionist. We could only guess that he felt so out of control of his life and so low—even desperate—and he hated it. Obviously something was very wrong. Seeing him like that, and in that sterile, clinical setting, unsettled us. After eight days of treatment and observation, though, he returned home and appeared to slip back into his own routine, albeit one carefully monitored by our parents, while we returned to ours.

Nothing was discussed in front of us—we were only in the seventh grade. So we really didn't understand everything that was going on. At the time, we didn't even know what anyone else in the family knew.

MONIQUE

Jocelyne and I always had each other. We always looked out for each other. It was always about we—the two of us—it was never about me—either one of us. As our grandmother once said, two are better than one. We never knew any different.

We were fast on our feet and blessed in so many ways, but we were also taught there were times when it was necessary to slow down and pay attention to those who struggled and needed help. Once again, Mom put it best. When the kids played team sports, who to root for was easy—the team we played on. But when Jocelyne and I ran cross-country, Mom always rooted for the one behind, the slower of the two of us. Which basically meant she was cheering for me since Jocelyne was faster. And when our brothers swam against each other in meets or played against each other in tournaments, she told us, "I cheer for the one behind."

She applied that simple but profound philosophy to everything, not just the sports we played, and we grew up doing the same thing—cheering for the one behind. In sixth grade, I sat next to a boy with Down syndrome. His name was Justin, and he was a good-natured kid who did his very best to keep up. Occasionally, his needs distracted him or led to behaviors that needed to be addressed. They didn't cause major interruptions to the class or slow anybody down, but they were enough to deal Justin a tough hand during the day's most difficult period, lunchtime.

The entire sixth grade had lunch at the same time. We sat at large, round tables of ten, and Justin was usually at a table by himself. It was sad. It also struck me as unnecessary. One day I realized that I could do something to change that situation. Between periods, I walked over to my classmate and was met by a look of curiosity that quickly turned into a friendly smile. "Hey, Justin," I said, "do you want to come sit with Jocelyne and me at lunch?"

He nodded. "Yeah, I'll come sit with you."

He sat with us every day—Justin and nine girls. He showed up early and waited for all of us to arrive. We even made sure he ate all of his food. Gradually, he became a little more outgoing at the lunch table. He participated more in class. Our classmates also did a better job of including him—even inviting him to sit at their lunch tables. Any barriers or fears that existed before disappeared and were replaced by inclusion and friendship.

I didn't think anything of it, and neither did Jocelyne. Being friendly and reaching out to a classmate who was being left out was just the way we were raised. We never mentioned it to Mom and Dad. So we were sort of surprised when our teacher sent a note to our parents, expressing her appreciation for our kindness. The best part of the note was our teacher's observation that we had made a big difference in Justin's life. That's the ultimate benefit and joy of cheering and advocating for anyone who is being left behind.

JOCELYNE

As we entered eighth grade, I had a boyfriend named Curran. We "dated" for about a month, but I didn't think I had time for him once hockey started. Dad had told us that as student-athletes, we had three things on our plate—academics, sports, and social life. But we only had enough time in our day to do two of the three things well, so we had to choose. Typical of my age at the time, I had a friend deliver a note to Curran, saying that we had to break up because I was too busy.

My priorities were clear: hockey and school. The two were completely linked. Not performing well in school could be a limiting factor in where we would be able to play college hockey, and that in turn could impact potential national team opportunities. As such, this last year of middle school was like a showcase for us. We turned fourteen and moved up to Bantams from Pee-Wees. We stayed on the same team, the Wheatkings, but that was one of the only things that remained unchanged from the previous two years. Some of the boys were pushing six feet in height now and were twenty to fifty pounds heavier than us.

You'd think their parents would have grown accustomed to us, if only to set an example for their sons. But most were even more opposed to us being on the team than before, and it wasn't because they were worried about us getting hurt. As the only two girls on the team, the locker room was off-limits to us, not that we shared it before. The biggest issue was that we frequently missed out on the talks our coaches gave before and after the games and, of course, any chance at better camaraderie with our teammates.

If we were playing at home, we knew which locker rooms, coaches' rooms, or refs rooms we could use, as well as knowing all of the rink employees, so finding a place to change was easier. But if we were out of town, we had to get to the rink even earlier just to look for a place where we could change. It wasn't easy. Often the rinks had only four locker rooms, and all of them would be occupied if there were back-to-back games. When that was the case, Monique and I took turns looking for the rink manager to help us find a spare locker room or unlock a ref's or coaches' room. More often than not, we searched for a restroom.

On the ice, we faced other challenges. Some of our teammates refused to pass us the puck, including one teammate who was so obvious about it that our coach eventually said something to him. One dad yelled at Monique from the stands to pass every time she touched the puck. His heckling reached the point where one of our teammates' stepdad actually spoke to him and told him to stop. Then there was a game early in the season where Monique and a player from the opposing team slammed into each other in the neutral zone after a play was called dead. As they faced off, Monique felt someone grab her shoulder from behind and shove her. It was one of our teammates. "Did that really happen?" she asked me, shocked.

Some of the boys took runs at us just because we were girls. Others probably had different reasons. It reminded me of a story Cammi Granato told in *Sports Illustrated* of getting steamrolled by a boy who then apologized and said his dad had told him to do it. Monique and I never got hurt, but we took our fair share of hits and had to learn to keep our heads on a swivel to make sure we protected ourselves—and each other.

MONIQUE

Later that year, Jocelyne and I played in an invitational tournament in Fargo. We were on Team North Dakota, which was composed of all of the best players from the state in our age group—which happened to be all boys other than us. The girls' side didn't have a team for our age group. We'd grown up playing with or against most of these guys, and sadly some of their parents viewed our being on the team as taking away two opportunities from boys who might get chosen to go to national development camps.

It was pretty clear which parents welcomed us and which ones didn't, and unfortunately, that found its way onto the ice. In a game against a team from Minneapolis, Jocelyne ran into one of our opponents and knocked him down. He got up and shoved her, and then she thought it was over, only he didn't let it go. Early in the third period, they collided again, and he found more opportunities to push her after play continued. Soon another player joined in and punched Jocelyne. All of a sudden, it was two against one. As soon as I saw the situation, I flew in from the blue line and joined in. If you picked on one of us, you had to deal with both of us. Right away, the Minneapolis goalie jumped into the fray. And our teammates? They were in the vicinity—sort of. Watching.

It never sat well with us that our teammates just stood there. There is a code on the ice. You always jump into the mix with your teammates. You make sure it's even. This one wasn't. Our coach kept us on the bench the rest of the game. It was the first and only time a coach hasn't put us back on the ice for our own safety. I still remember sitting on the bench, fuming, and thinking we could handle ourselves, without realizing the coach sat us for our own good.

By the end of the season, and in spite of all the obstacles we had to face, we still had fun and continued to get better, but it was clear our future in the sport wasn't going to be in boys' hockey.

Besides looking ahead to high school, the next phase in our career began early that summer with our inaugural trip to the National Festival at the Olympic Training Center in Lake Placid, New York, where we competed in the 15/16 National Development Camp. Future Olympic teammates Hilary Knight and Kelli Stack were also among the players invited, and we enjoyed being on the ice with them. It was our first real exposure to female players and coaches in a national setting—and their first real chance to see the two of us. Nobody at that level had really seen us play. Nobody really knew who we were.

That changed quickly. In the last game, Jocelyne sped down the side with a defender pasted onto her jersey. Without ever letting up, she pulled the puck into her feet and flipped it over the other girl's stick, then cut to the middle, shot, and scored. Eyes were opened. It was an electrifying finish to an exciting week of high-level hockey. We didn't think we were the best out there, but we knew we brought things to the table that others didn't; at the least, we were in the conversation.

A difficult year of challenges on and off the ice was behind us, and although some issues, like Jacques's health, were still not entirely clear, we were ready for high school and whatever else was next. We knew we could handle a lot, so long as we had each other.

6

NOTHING LESS THAN OUR BEST

⭐

"To those whom much is given, much is expected."

JOCELYNE

The stately stone arch at the front of Shattuck St. Mary's was intended to give all those passing under it the sense they were entering a unique environment with a long tradition of higher learning and achievement. It certainly had that effect on us. The Shattuck St. Mary's campus, dating back to 1858, was in Faribault, Minnesota, a six-hour drive from our home in Grand Forks. Our journey there had begun six months earlier when the new girls' hockey coach, Gordie Stafford, phoned with news that the school had increased the financial support it could provide us. Although it was still a stretch for our parents, the extra financial aid made it possible for us to accept.

In addition to playing hockey, Monique and I were both straight-A students, and the promise of challenging academics, along with the school's commitment to its girls' hockey program, made it a perfect fit. Over the summer, we tackled the suggested reading list and shopped for clothes that met the school's dress code of gray, black, white, or maroon polos and black or khaki pants. The day we drove under the school's stone arch was full of emotion. Our brothers had all moved away to pursue their hockey dreams, but this was a first for us.

We wondered if we'd fit in as our dad parked our white Chevy Astro van next to much fancier Range Rovers and black SUVs. We checked in at the upper school, dropped our gear off at the hockey rink, and then got the keys to our new dorm room. At first, we were handed keys to two different rooms. Alarmed that we weren't sharing a room, we quickly said we needed to room together, explaining we shared half our stuff.

The administrator helping us, Mrs. Carpentier, said she could make some changes and move us in together since none of the other students had arrived. She explained there were four other sets of twins who were living in the dorms, and none of them wanted to room together, so they had assumed the same about us.

With that crisis averted, our parents helped make our beds and watched as we unpacked our belongings, including a poster of Oregon runner Steve Prefontaine that Mom had given us to put up on the wall. Similar to the one we had at home, the quote on it said, "To give anything less than your best is to sacrifice the gift." She also gave us a small book of daily inspirations and a framed essay titled "Winning Isn't Normal." We also both received a card-sized, Linda-laminated picture of two girls, one helping the other up, that said, "Two is better than one." We still have that card today.

Unexpectedly, our dad was more emotional than our mom. As we finished unpacking the majority of our stuff, he got very quiet. His emotions threatened to trigger our own waterworks. The two of us put on a brave face and tried not to cry. We got ready to walk our parents to the van and say our big goodbye, when suddenly the prospect of watching them get into the van and drive away was too overwhelming. Instead, we asked if we could say goodbye in our new dorm room. Dad shed a few tears as we hugged him and said goodbye. Mom was much more stoic. We couldn't believe she held it together.

We even brought it up the next time we spoke to them on the phone. We were surprised that Mom didn't cry. "You weren't in the car on the way home," Dad said. "She cried the whole time."

MONIQUE

As soon as they left, Jocelyne and I sat on our beds and bawled our eyes out. It was the profound realization that we weren't going home, that everything was new and different, and that we now had to make our own way. We didn't know anyone. We didn't have any routines. We didn't have a cell phone, either. There was a phone in our room, but we were told that service was cut off every night at 9 p.m. We were all alone, except we had each other. Which meant a lot. As our grandmother said, we were the same, there were just two of us.

We also knew our parents wouldn't have left us if they didn't think we could handle ourselves. Deep down, we knew we could do it. Once we had a good cry, we looked up at each other and knew that we'd hit the wall. We were bored. "We can either stay here and cry some more," I finally said. "Or we can get up and go figure this out."

We wandered downstairs to the lounge and began to make friends. Out of three hundred students in the entire upper school, our incoming ninth-grade class totaled fifty students, ten of whom were girls, and out of them, six played hockey. The six of us lived in the dorm, which was located in the lower school, and so in a short time, we were trading stories and talking about hockey and where we'd played and who we knew in common.

It was an exciting time to be there. Shattuck was renowned for its boys' hockey program, a national powerhouse known for developing standout D1 college players, as well as a growing number of NHL players. The girls' program had lagged behind, not quite as an afterthought, but definitely as a stepsister to the boys' team. Coach Stafford had taken over the program after years on the boys' side, with the stated intention of building a girls' program that would carve out its own national reputation.

Recruiting the two of us had been Coach Stafford's top priority in turning around Shattuck's girls' program, and we were fully on board in wanting to win championships. It was his first year coaching a girls' team and our first full season playing on one. The timing was perfect. Just like the Steve Prefontaine poster we'd hung in our dorm room, Jocelyne and I were ready to give it our all. Nothing less than our best, starting from day one.

Tryouts began the next morning with testing—typical agility and endurance drills, although there was nothing typical about the way the two of us aced the mile run. But rather than stop after crossing the finish line, I cut across the track to run with another player who was struggling to finish. I ran with her until she completed her mile. It was our way of cheering for the one behind and encouraging and helping others to reach their full potential, which made our entire team better.

For our first ice session, Jocelyne and I arrived early, as we still do to this day. We were, in fact, the first two players there. Coach Stafford says we were literally the first two girls he ever coached on the ice because when he came out that day, he found us already sitting on the bench, waiting for practice to start. We wanted to prove we could make the prep team as freshmen, even though he obviously had that in mind when he recruited us.

But we didn't take anything for granted. We were eager to show him that he was right about us and that together, we, along with the other players he recruited, were going to turn the girls' hockey program into a national contender. Ironically, we'd never formally met. We went through the entire first practice looking for an opportunity. Finally, at the end, after he finished addressing the team, we introduced ourselves. He hopped down from the bench, and we all shook hands. We let him know that we were excited to be at Shattuck.

JOCELYNE

Coach Stafford understood us from the get-go. He realized that we enjoyed the daily grind, that we were workers who thrived on the monotony and challenge of working out, trying to improve, and being good teammates. We loved putting on our skates and being at the rink. We loved playing the game—and he loved the game too.

Hockey helped ease our transition into student life. Our days began every morning at six when we hurried out of our dorm in our sweats, with our bags filled with a change of clothes and books, and piled into assistant coach Jennifer Kranz's waiting Jetta. Not counting Coach Kranz, there were five of us in the car; Monique and I usually shared the passenger seat in the front, one of us sitting on the other's lap on the short drive to the rink.

The social aspect of being on an all-girls' team was a really enjoyable change for us. Just being in the locker room with our teammates made a huge difference. We were part of the team! We sat in the corner next to three seniors. We didn't say much initially, as we studied the dynamic and learned the way things were done. Before our first exhibition game, for instance, we noticed the way our teammates hung up their jerseys as soon as they got in the locker room and put them back in their bags immediately after the game rather than leave them on the bench or hanging them on a hook. The respect our teammates had for representing the school, the program, and each other stood out. Not every program or team is like that, but above all else, Coach Stafford preached a simple message to us: Just be a good person. Crush the opposition. Win the game. And be a good person too.

Our team had twenty-one players—four of whom were freshmen: the two of us plus Sasha Sherry and Amanda Castignetti, a.k.a. Duckie. The team's seven seniors embraced us, especially team captain Allie Johanson, who silenced anyone who might've griped about us being ninth graders on a U19 team. As far as she was concerned, we could have been ten years old and she would have been fine with it so long as we helped win a championship.

Our schedule typically consisted of three or four games a weekend, with an occasional weekday game. It seemed like we were always taking a long bus ride somewhere. Before games, Monique and I had our own routine, which has evolved over the years, but there has always been a routine. After the team warm-up, we tucked ourselves in a corner behind the bench and kicked a soccer ball back and forth. Before leaving the locker room, our team blasted Van Halen's anthem "Right Now," and then we were ready.

As the season began, we played on a line with Allie. It was the first time Monique and I had been on the same line together since Mites, and we loved it. Without saying a word, we both knew what the other was going to do, but we constantly communicated anyway. It was a twin thing, and we used it to our advantage. Although checking wasn't allowed, we were still aggressive and physical. The refs were hard on us. Coach Stafford was always quick to defend us. "Hey, you can't penalize them for being strong!" he repeatedly yelled, but sometimes we brought it on ourselves.

There was one game when I came down the side with the puck and heard the opposing coach shouting at his defenseman, "Take her body! Take her body!" She swept in, as instructed, only I skated right through her and left her sprawled on the ice. Her coach was irate and demanded a penalty. "What are you talking about?" Coach Stafford snapped, incensed himself. "Our girl had the puck!"

On and off the ice, we thrived at Shattuck. At night, we called home and eagerly told our parents about the day's news: a test score from biology, the way our algebra teacher, Mr. Irby, seemed to end every period covered in chalk dust, or something Coach Stafford had said during practice. Too often, we were in mid-conversation when the line went dead at 9 p.m. That was frustrating but good. There was something wonderful about not ever having enough time to share all the good things that had happened and knowing that when there were problems, we could figure things out on our own.

7

JUST THE START

"The best players have their biggest games in the big games."

MONIQUE

It's true that most days were carefree and problem-free—but very focused on classes, hockey, and homework. We had almost no free time to engage in more typical high school activities like surfing the internet, going to parties, and socializing. Most of our social interactions were with teammates who had as little time as we did. Somebody needed help with a math problem. Somebody else broke up with a boyfriend. One of us liked a boy but wanted to know more about him. Who was making a new CD for the locker-room boombox? Who were we playing the next week?

Were we going to win playoffs?

Yes!

Were we going to win Shattuck's girls' team's first national championship? Damn right.

Then one day, about two months into the school year, Jocelyne and I checked our mailbox and found a letter from home that shook us to our core. Inside was a short note from our mom along with a copy of a newspaper article reporting on an essay our brother, Jacques, had written about his battle with depression. She also included a copy of the essay. At the time, Jacques was in his senior year of high school in Bismarck and playing in his second season with the Bismarck Bobcats.

Jacques had wanted and needed a fresh start, and by all accounts, he was thriving on and off the ice as he worked toward his dream of attending the Air Force Academy. He wrote the essay for an English class and sent it to the *Grand Forks Herald* at the suggestion of his teacher. It was a harrowing account of his descent into a bottomless pit of sadness and despair just two years earlier.

Jocelyne and I cried as we read and reread his story. While we sort of knew about Jacques's "depression," we didn't know any of the details he described—the intense anguish that swept over him, the pressure he put on himself to be perfect, the frustration that none of his accomplishments was ever good enough, the emptiness he felt inside despite growing up in a loving home, the loneliness he felt despite having five siblings and dozens of friends and teammates, and the breakup with his girlfriend that left him seemingly beyond repair.

"No one knew about my problems," he wrote, which was true. As described in his article, over the previous Thanksgiving—almost exactly a year earlier—Jacques had driven to a parking structure in downtown Grand Forks, parked his car on the fifth floor, placed a suicide note on the dashboard, and walked to the ledge off which he planned to jump and end his life. As he contemplated that finality, the dark thoughts in his head were replaced by the many warm memories he had of all of us, his family, and the fun he had skating on the pond. Those feelings, that sense of joy he felt at that moment, were powerful, like a light that showed him a path out of his depression. He stepped back from the ledge, suddenly wanting, as he wrote, to "put all the bad memories behind him" and live.

Mental health issues are typically difficult to discuss, especially among teenagers, and when you factor in that athletes are trained to conceal their pain, you can begin to understand how Jacques got to a crisis point without anyone knowing. At the time, Jocelyne and I shared our concern with each other, but we didn't really know what was going on with him or grasp the seriousness, except to know that our brother was hurting, which led us to wish for ways to help or make his life easier. Even that was hard. What do you do as a seventh grader when you don't really know what is going on?

It was so courageous of Jacques to go public with his story, considering the stigma around mental illness and the very real prospect that it would nullify his chances of getting admitted to the Air Force Academy. But Jacques did it as part of his own healing process and also to help other people. With the suicide rate in North Dakota four times higher than the national average, he knew there were many others out there like him, suffering in silence, ashamed of admitting their pain, and fearful of asking for help. He wanted to change, lift the veil, change perceptions, open discussions, and let those feeling helpless know there was hope.

We spoke with our parents, who assured us that Jacques was good. Still, learning the details about all that he went through for the first time hit us hard. His story wasn't the kind of thing we could read, cry about, and have it be over, like a sad current events article. Jacques was our brother. This had happened in our house while we were there. How could we not have known? How could we have missed the signs? How could we have not asked more questions?

In his story, Jacques mentioned how he had once taken our dad's shotgun out of its secure hiding spot, brought it with him into his bed, and contemplated pulling the trigger. Fortunately, he was frightened enough by his thoughts that he climbed the stairs to our parents' bedroom and asked them for help before he hurt himself. As I read that, I remembered seeing my dad put his shotgun in the back of his truck and explain that he was getting rid of it. That must've been the next day, and at the time I didn't think anything of it. Again, I asked myself how I didn't know. And when I told Jocelyne, she had the same reaction. How didn't we know?

Was there anything we could have done? Should have done? We second-guessed ourselves and felt guilty. How could we feel otherwise? We worried about Jacques too. How was he now? Our parents assured us that he was feeling good and was pleased with the reception his article was getting not just in Grand Forks, but also across the state. Indeed, over the next few months, Jacques would be invited to speak about depression and mental illness at numerous schools and corporate events where, he hoped, he could make a difference, inspire discussion, and very likely save lives.

Jacques was so admirable, and we were extremely proud of our brother. Championships and statistics are one thing, but he was taking the lessons we were taught at home about what it meant to make a difference and be a winner to a whole different level, which didn't surprise us. That was the way all of us were raised. Still, nothing would comfort us like being able to see him with our own eyes—and confirm that he was really okay.

JOCELYNE

Coach Kranz, who was also my freshman-year advisor, recognized the effect the article had on us. She had most likely read it before talking to us about it. She drove us to practice in her car every morning, so she had a close-up view of the two of us as we processed all that new and disturbing information. Coincidentally, Jacques's team, the Bismarck Bobcats, had a game that coming weekend in nearby Blaine, and Coach Kranz drove us there so we could watch him play and see him in person.

We couldn't have been happier or more relieved. Seeing Jacques play with all his usual flash and skill was reassuring—then talking to him afterward comforted us in a way that was a thousand times more convincing than any phone call. Jacques felt good about what he had shared and about his life. The pain and despair he experienced was impossible for us to understand, but we did have a clear sense of the impact he made by showing how you can turn your weaknesses into strengths.

That visit was enough to hold us over until Shattuck's Fall Family Weekend. It arrived a few weeks later, and with it came a welcome visit from our parents. Seeing our mom and dad was just what we needed. As a surprise, they brought our grandma Edith too. We had plans to show them around the school and introduce them to our friends and teammates. We also had a game against Culver Academy, one of our big rivals from Indiana. But soon after they arrived, I started to feel sick. By dinnertime, I had a bad stomach flu, and all of our carefully arranged plans were put on hold.

Mom and Dad picked me up at the dorm and took me to their hotel. I couldn't keep anything down, including water. At 10 p.m., they took me to the emergency room at the local hospital. I was hooked up to an IV for fluids to deal with dehydration, which helped.

I finished the night back in my parents' hotel room, slept late, and met Monique at the rink the next morning before our game. "You don't need to broadcast that you were sick," my dad said. "If you decide to play, no excuses if things don't go well." I was reminded of when I played in a girls' tournament in seventh grade with a broken thumb and a cast from my hand to my elbow, which made it hard to hold my stick. But Dad had said, "If you're going to get on the ice, don't bring any excuses."

None was needed. I scored in my first shift, and our team won handily, a perfect cap to the family weekend. Dad enjoyed Coach Stafford, and this time both he and Mom were smiling when they said goodbye and drove away.

I don't know how they kept up with everyone. Philippe was a freshman at UND. Jacques was in Bismarck. Pierre-Paul was playing with the Red Deer Rebels in Alberta. Mario was in Nebraska. And we were here in Minnesota. They needed four different sports sections to stay updated with all of our games. Their kitchen was like the ESPN newsroom. In addition to dispensing advice and pep talks to all of us, they provided updates to all the grandparents.

At Christmastime, Shattuck hosted a fancy holiday dinner and dance. Monique and I had never before had an occasion to dress up or do our hair and makeup. This was a first. A couple of the older girls, Jenny Porter and Danielle Hirsch, helped us get ready and showed us how to put on makeup. Our mom was someone who never went out of the house without looking perfect, and when we told her that we'd dressed up for the formal and sent her photos, she was thrilled.

MONIQUE

We got to the end of our first season, losing only a handful of games. Jocelyne and I were the difference makers Coach Stafford had hoped for, tallying over a hundred points each for the season. Coach Stafford remarked to a local journalist that we were "a pretty good one-two combination." His understatement fit our sensibility. Individual statistics were nice, but they weren't as important as a national championship, and that's what our goal was for Shattuck.

Shattuck had never gone further than the quarter finals—and Jocelyne and I had never been to a national tournament before. But we made it to the championship game, further than any Shattuck girls' team had been before, and we felt pretty confident this team could make history and bring back the first girls' national championship for the school.

This championship was the biggest game we had ever played in up to that point. On the way to the rink, Jocelyne and I listened to Tracy Chapman's "Fast Car." We shared a blue iPod mini that we got for Christmas and used an earphone splitter so both of us could use our own headphones. I thought about how our dad had once told us that the best players have their biggest games in the big games. We didn't have to wait long to see if he was right.

Early in the game, Jocelyne and I rushed down the left side. She made a drop pass to me and ran interference on the defender, giving me time to set up and step into a slap shot that flew under Jocelyne and straight into the net. I don't think the goalie ever saw it. I jumped up in the air and did the ugliest three-hundred-and-sixty-celebration ever. Luckily, I got two more chances to redeem myself before the game ended on my way to a hat trick, with Shattuck winning 6–3, to capture the girls' hockey team's very first national championship.

Our team's celebration was exhilarating, and Jocelyne and I got to share it with our grandparents, who made the trip from Alberta. We were thrilled about coming through for our teammates, especially our graduating seniors, and most importantly for Coach Stafford, who had fought to bring us to Shattuck.

With this first national championship, Shattuck's girls' hockey program had skated out of the tall shadows of the boys' program and into the spotlight. The standard of excellence didn't just apply to the boys' program anymore. "This is hopefully just the start," Coach Stafford told the local paper. We felt the same way.

8

TEAMWORK

★

"You can't Hulk Hogan through everything."

JOCELYNE

September 2005. Monique and I sensed that our sophomore year was going to be fun. And why not? We were returning as defending national champions. We had the confidence that comes with experience. We knew our way around the school. We enjoyed our classes and had the same group of friends. The only problem we had really wasn't a problem, not for the two of us anyway. It was that Coach Stafford couldn't tell us apart.

We figured this out during the first week of practice. We were just back from summer break and had joked with him that our summer job at our local Barnes & Noble bookstore, where we unloaded boxes of books and placed them on shelves throughout the store, had kept us immersed in literature. He laughed, but he did so while looking at us with a confused expression that we knew all too well. He had no idea whether I was Monique or Jocelyne.

The reason was that I'd come to school the previous year with a pretty visible scar on my forehead, the result of a bad collision on the soccer field that had resulted in two dozen stitches. Now that scar had faded and wasn't so obvious—and Coach Stafford didn't have a mark to help him tell us apart.

After a couple weeks of being around us, though, he claimed that he could recognize us without even looking at our numbers (I wore twelve and Monique wore twenty-one). Our temperaments were different, he claimed. According to him, I was fiery on the ice, and Monique possessed a slower-burning intensity. "But don't get me wrong," he added, as a broad grin spread across his face. "You're both killers."

In his first speech to the team, Coach Stafford promised this season was going to be a lot tougher than the previous one. Last year, the goal had been to raise the profile of the women's program and win as many games as possible. This year, he said, our goal was to win another national championship. But, he warned, getting to the top was one thing. Staying there was altogether different—and harder. Every team we played was going to bring its best game in an effort to take our place as champions.

It wasn't going to be easy for them. We were determined to not lose—not a game, and certainly not the national championship. It might look like we were unbeatable, thanks to the arrival of super-talented freshman Brianna Decker, a future Olympic teammate of ours, who added power to an already-loaded lineup that included five seniors heading to D1 programs. By mid-December, we were twenty games into the season and enjoying what the local paper called "overwhelming success." It was fun. The team played at a high level, and Monique and I were among the leaders in nearly every category—including penalty minutes.

As Coach Stafford pointed out, the team didn't benefit in any way if we were in the penalty box, and our opposition had an advantage on the ice. "I'm not going to tell you to play any less physical," he said. "But you need to understand how to be physical within the realities of the teams we play and the refs who work the games. The rules don't change, but each game is different, and you have to be able to read that and make adjustments."

Coach Stafford was a great teacher. He could get deeply philosophical about the game, sometimes sounding downright mystical, and other times sounded endearingly old school, like our dad. He frequently spoke about the hockey gods. Listening to him sometimes made it seem as if those gods lived up among the wooden beams and light fixtures in the school's old rink (they finished building a new one that year), gazing down on us in judgment as we went through our drills in practice.

We respected him in a way that probably ruined it for most of our future coaches. Both his knowledge and temperament opened the door for him to speak to us with an honesty that we knew was intended solely to make us better hockey players and people. He took advantage of it. One day, following a game that we had won, but not in a way that pleased him, he said, "You guys just want to Hulk Hogan through everything, and that's not the way it works."

He saw that we didn't understand his reference, but he continued anyway. "You can't Hulk through it. You can't do it all yourself. You have teammates for a reason. You can't dismiss what they bring. Trust them. Use them."

Although we considered ourselves consummate team players, it was maybe too easy for us to occasionally slip into a pattern of play where we relied on each other, as we'd done all our lives. With us, we always knew what the other one would do or where she would be. It was intuitive, and it was definitely an advantage. But Coach Stafford wanted us to understand that this "twintuition" had its limits. Looking for our teammates would create even more opportunities. As Michael Jordan once said, individuals can win games, but teamwork is the only way to win championships.

MONIQUE

We won the state championship in front of a good-sized crowd in Bloomington. As we did the previous year, when we were presented with the state championship trophy, the captains accepted it, we took a team picture with it, but none of us touched it. That wasn't the trophy we wanted. Just like we had seen NHL teams do in the playoffs for so many years, teams would win the conference title, but no one would touch the trophy. Instead, they looked forward to what was next, a chance to hoist the Stanley Cup.

We felt the same way. A state championship was great, but that wasn't our ultimate goal. All of us were focused on nationals and another run at *that* championship—and that trophy.

Right before we traveled to upstate New York for the tournament, though, we had a terrible practice, one where no one was fully dialed in, and we made simple mistakes. A few of the girls were involved in boyfriend issues or breakups at the time, and their lack of focus sort of rippled through everyone's concentration. Coach Stafford blew up. With all of us looking, he spun around and smashed his stick into the glass. "We leave for nationals in a couple of days, and you guys are playing like a bunch of girls," he hissed.

We were stunned. I turned to Jocelyne and muttered, "Holy shit, he's mad." Coach Stafford never lost his temper like that, and he never fell back on our gender when he coached us. But he wasn't finished. "You aren't girls," he continued. "You're athletes. You're hockey players. Out here, you need to perform like hockey players. You need to be athletes. You can't act like a bunch of girls." And I think what he also meant to say was, "Don't act the way other people *expect* you to act because you are girls."

We knew what he meant, and I honestly don't think anyone took offense at his remarks. It was so out of character, in fact, that we had to hold ourselves back from laughing nervously. We knew where we stood with him. We'd heard him often enough tell local reporters that he didn't coach us any differently than he did boys. He treated us like athletes, period. We respected that about him and responded accordingly.

What hurt us more than anything was that Coach Stafford, in his outburst, said that he was also canceling the rest of practice. It was the cliché of, "I'm not mad, I'm just disappointed," and it left us no opportunity to redeem ourselves. But it did get us ready as hell to prove ourselves in the tournament.

JOCELYNE

We arrived in Buffalo to play for another national championship. We cruised through our round-robin games and also the quarterfinals. The semifinal game posed our biggest challenge of the year. We went into double overtime against the Connecticut Polar Bears, whose team included future Olympian and teammate Hilary Knight, and we managed to come out on top after tying it up late in regulation. We still remember it as one of the most thrilling games we had ever played.

The game didn't end until late in the evening, and so in theory, we should've been tired before heading into the championship game, which was early in the afternoon the next day. But once we got to the rink, our adrenaline kicked in, and everyone was fired up. We played Assabet Valley, a U19 team from Massachusetts, whose program had won national championships at every age level. Assabet Valley also had an ace goalie, Molly Schaus, another future teammate of ours on two Olympic rosters. We played another nail-biter, and with less than two minutes to go in a tied game, Emily Kranz on our team scored, and we won our second consecutive national championship.

"The girls won it on heart and soul and guts," Coach Stafford told the *Faribault Daily News*. Our celebration on the ice and on the trip back to school felt that way too. As a team, we had heart and soul and guts. Deep down, I was disappointed in myself. I didn't feel like I had performed my best when it mattered most. But I thought back to what Coach Stafford had said eight months earlier about not trying to Hulk Hogan everything, and then I looked around at my smiling teammates and knew he was right, and I shouldn't beat myself up. Hockey was a team sport. No one person won or lost the championship. Whatever the outcome, in this case, it was mighty sweet, and we did it together as a team.

MONIQUE

After we got back to school, we headed into the gym for our workout, as we did every afternoon. Except we didn't even get a chance to set our stuff down before strength and conditioning coach Eaves spotted us and from across the gym yelled, "You two, turn around and leave and don't come back for two weeks. Take time off."

I think we took a week off, but we very quickly got bored. We were still too young and inexperienced to understand that sometimes less is more, and besides, as sixteen-year-olds, we didn't have an off button. We had just helped Shattuck's girls' hockey team win its second national title, and yes, while we had finals, boyfriends, and various school events on our calendars, it was wholly in keeping with our personalities that we were already working toward the next championship.

9

PERSPECTIVE

★

"The final score only tells part of the story."

MONIQUE

We knew our junior year was going to be fun, but we didn't know how much fun until after we moved into our room in Clapp dorm. We shared a triple with Brianna Decker, and other teammates were kitty-corner from us and downstairs. From the day we all moved in, we got into prank wars with each other, the most outrageous being when I watched a few of the girls sneak into our room and Saran Wrap Jocelyne to the bed while she slept. Somehow Jocelyne never woke up. The whole thing was unbelievable.

Our year was like that, too—unbelievable. We had six girls returning from our first national championship team, several more from the previous year, and we added freshman Amanda Kessel, another future Olympian and teammate. Our power play consisted of four future Olympians and another who would play on the national team. Our assistant coach, Nicki Del Castillo, said we were the closest to a perfect team she'd ever seen.

Then, in our season opener at the Bison International Tournament in Winnipeg, the unthinkable happened. We were upset in overtime by Team Manitoba. With all the talent on our team, it was *unbelievable*. We blamed it on overconfidence, buckled down, worked harder, and only lost a handful of games the rest of the season.

We had several college coaches calling and inquiring if we were interested in their schools. We narrowed down our choices to Harvard, Minnesota, and Wisconsin—all places where we would continue to be challenged and grow as athletes and people. All three were great schools—all were college hockey powerhouses—and all would position us well to make the 2010 Olympic team. Both of us knew that sports has a way of teaching the lessons that you need to learn to succeed in life—hard work, discipline, teamwork, and sportsmanship. For us, it was also gratitude. Fortunately, these schools were offering scholarships, so we could make our decision solely on athletics and academics without having to consider the financial burden of student loans.

In October, we visited the Wisconsin campus, and shortly thereafter Wisconsin's coach, Mark Johnson, invited Jocelyne and me onto the national team competing in the Four Nations Cup. It was a thrill to be on the U.S. Women's National Team for the first time. After the Olympics and the International Ice Hockey Federation's World Championship, which took place every April except during Olympic years, the Four Nations Cup was the next most important event in women's hockey.

Four Nations took place every November and brought together the four best women's hockey teams in the world. In fact, the various training camps that USA Hockey, the sport's governing body, held throughout the year, were geared around ensuring the national team's roster included the strongest players for each tournament, especially the Olympics. It's a process that we've geared our lives around since that first invitation to the Four Nations Cup.

But that first time was particularly special. We were the new kids coming up, and we were excited to be part of the team. That November, we flew to Kitchener, Ontario, the site of that year's tournament, and we tried to fit in as if it were no big deal—except it was. Putting on red, white, and blue USA jerseys for the first time gave us goose bumps. We were back on the ice with Jenny Potter and Natalie Darwitz. We had come a long way from the "French-Canadian twins" Jenny thought she was meeting when we were thirteen years old. Angela Ruggiero and Julie Chu mentored us as we prepared the best we could for our first big opportunity with the national team.

What helped us settle in, even as rookies, was the sense that we were among athletes just like us—they'd grown up playing against boys, ignored the insults and jeers, honed their skills, and turned their dreams into reality. They'd followed their passion from all over the country to this very place. We were in our element, but more so as we realized that we belonged there—but maybe not our sticks, as we were the only players who still used wood sticks. We were quite aware that our teammates here were not only among the world's best female hockey players. On any given day, they were *the* best.

There was a lot of watch-and-learn, and we did our best to take it all in. The intense focus of the players. The enormous crowd filling the arena. The deafening roar that greeted Team Canada, especially Canada's star forward Hayley Wickenheiser. And the action. We lost our opening game to Canada but came back to beat Sweden and Finland, which put us in the finals against Canada again. Unfortunately, we lost the rematch too. Jocelyne and I had limited ice time, which taught us another lesson about what it means to be a great teammate. You may not get all the opportunities you want or think you deserve, but when the puck drops, you still need to be ready when you step on the ice. And we were sure that this was only the beginning of a long tenure on Team USA.

JOCELYNE

While we were enjoying the experience of playing with the U.S. Women's National Team, our brother, Jacques, was persevering like a champion through tough times as he chased his own dream of attending the Air Force Academy. After applying to the school with top grades and even getting recruited by the hockey coach, he was rejected. They cited his past battle with depression. It was a devastating blow to him and the future he had always seen for himself. This was one of those moments where it was necessary to pause our own lives—pay attention—and recognize that Jacques was going through a challenging time.

As siblings, we have always supported each other. In success, we are happy for each other and hope it continues. At times like this, when one of us confronts a rough situation, we live and feel that struggle with them, and we rally around each other like teammates. So it was no coincidence that our mom sent each of us a copy of the famous Cliff Cushman letter she'd taped to our refrigerator as we were growing up.

"I know I may never make it," Cushman wrote. "The odds are against me, but I have something in my favor—desire and faith. Romans 5:3–5 has always had an inspirational meaning to me...'we rejoice in our suffering, knowing that suffering produces endurance, endurance produces character, and character produces hope, and hope does not disappoint us.' At least I am going to try."

And Jacques did the same thing. He enrolled at Northern Michigan and channeled his disappointment into determination. After his freshman season, he reapplied to the Air Force Academy at the end of the year. In addition to his accomplishments, his application was accompanied by numerous letters of recommendation that spoke of his character and courage, and this time he was accepted. Two years later, he led the Air Force Academy and the entire Atlantic Hockey League in scoring, earned All-American honors, and was nominated for the Hockey Humanitarian Award for his work with youth in lifting the veil on depression and mental illness.

Jacques just refused to be stopped. He refused to give up or quit trying. In persevering, he embodied the spirit Cushman had in mind when he challenged the youth of Grand Forks by writing, "I dare you to look up at the stars, not down in the mud, and set your sights on one of them that, up to now, you thought unattainable. There is plenty of room at the top, but no room for anyone to sit down."

MONIQUE

Back at Shattuck, we debriefed with Coach Stafford and played in a handful of games through mid-December before receiving an invitation to Team USA's so-called Christmas Camp, a weeklong tryout for the team that would play in the World Championships in April. The camp was at the Olympic Training Center in Lake Placid, New York, a place we already had grown accustomed to.

Participating in camp meant missing a tournament Shattuck was competing in at the same time, also in Lake Placid coincidentally, but Coach Stafford understood and gave his blessing. Decker and Kessel still gave Shattuck plenty of firepower. But after a night game at the national camp, we learned that the next day's game had been canceled. So in the morning, we headed to Shattuck's rink and suited up in our school colors for the semis. "It's okay, you can take a break," Coach Stafford said.

"No way," we replied. "We're good to go."

Our teammate, backup goalie Laurel Simer, an inspiration in her own right in that she played despite an inoperable brain tumor that she'd lived with since early childhood, was delighted to see us there in our uniforms. Our opponents, Lawrence Academy, were not as happy. "You should've seen the look on the faces of some of those girls from Lawrence when they saw the two of you on the ice during warm-ups," Laurel said. "It was like, oh God, they're here."

In January, the national team was announced—and we found out we did not make the team by reading the list online. We would later learn that it is far less devastating reading a list without your name in the privacy of your dorm room than it is being in a room with your peers and being sent home. Although we were disappointed, we took some consolation in knowing that we were at least a part of the conversation and that we were very young and would have more chances in the future. Besides, between school, the rest of Shattuck's season, and the swirl of talk about colleges, we had plenty of other things to focus on. We put this setback behind us pretty quickly.

One weekend, we made an unofficial visit to the Minnesota campus that coincided with a two-game series the Gophers had against Wisconsin, the country's top-ranked team. The head coach, Laura Halldorson, who was recruiting us, was the same coach our dad asked if we had a chance at playing Division I hockey when we were in seventh grade. We also chatted with assistant coach Brad Frost, who made us feel like we could play a major role in the school's effort to win another national championship. Wisconsin may have won the game, but in the third period, I looked at Jocelyne and said, "This is a program we want to be a part of."

She agreed. "I see us going to college here," she said.

After the game, Coach Frost asked what we thought of the game. It was too early for us to make an official commitment, but we grinned and unofficially asked if he thought they would have our numbers, twelve and twenty-one, available in two years. We had made our verbal commitment to play at the University of Minnesota.

Although we each made our own lists of pros and cons as if we were making an individual decision, we always had an unspoken understanding that we were going to attend the same college. I'm not sure if coaches recruiting us ever viewed us individually, but we knew our strengths and weaknesses and how they complemented each other. Most of our coaches had trouble telling us apart, which honestly didn't bother us, at least when they were getting to know us. But to know us would mean to know our differences, and we appreciated the coaches who took the time to do so.

JOCELYNE

On the surface, it would seem that our preference for the University of Minnesota would have been seen as treason within our family, where we had deep family ties to our hometown school, the University of North Dakota. Our dad and two of our brothers attended the school and played on the hockey team. But everyone understood that the UND women's program was struggling and not the right fit for us at the time.

We had the rest of our season to focus on, anyway. Over the next three months, we went on an incredible run, winning forty-one straight games, breezing through the playoffs, and qualifying for another trip to the national tournament. The team chemistry and camaraderie was something that we had never experienced before. We were confident but not overconfident as we arrived in San Jose, California, the site of the U19 National Championships. Before taking the ice before every game, we put on the Donna Lewis pop hit "I Love You Always Forever" and sang and clapped together through the chorus. It kept us loose and relaxed.

As we got ready to play our first game, Coach Stafford gave us a memorable pregame talk about the psychology of the game, a favorite topic of his, particularly the concept of attrition. "Think about boxers," he said. "You've got two guys in the ring, and they're throwing punches at each other. One guy goes for the knockout and swings wildly, while the other guy repeatedly sticks it to his opponent's body, wearing him down and watching for signs of weakness, knowing the body can only take so much until there's an opening. When he finally sees that opening, it's then that he goes for the knockout.

"It's the same with the teams we face. They come in wanting to win. But if you put enough force and pressure on them, never letting up, you will see a point where their will starts to fade. If you keep it up, you can take that will away and eventually knock them out. It's something you can feel. Then you can literally see it. And then the game is yours." He clenched his fist and cocked his arm like he was ready to bop someone on the head himself. "Their daubers are down, and BOOM, knockout punch."

MONIQUE

After winning games Friday night and Saturday morning, we were nearly eliminated in the semis later that afternoon by Michigan's Belle Tire when our 2–0 lead was erased by three successive Belle Tire goals in the third period. But we kept our composure, focused on the game plan, and fought back. I scored the tying goal on the power play, and Amanda Kessel delivered the OT winner within ten seconds to put us into the finals against Assabet Valley.

The finals were played the next day, which happened to be Palm Sunday. Jocelyne and I and a few others woke up early and decided to go to church. None of us was particularly religious, but we had chapel once a week at Shattuck, and it seemed like a fitting way to start the day. On the way back to our hotel, Laurel Simer, one of our goalies, said to us, "Prayer is good. But I get more of a sense of calm from knowing both of you are going to be playing in the game."

The championship game between Shattuck and Assabet Valley was close, and notable for the lack of scoring. But we never lost faith. Jocelyne scored toward the end of the first period off a pass from me for a 1–0 lead. Coach Stafford came into the locker room, looked at each of us, and instead of a big talk, he simply informed us that Shattuck's boys' prep team had won their national championship game. Then he walked out, leaving us to think about what we were going to do.

Those few words were all that needed to be said. About three minutes into the third period, I slammed a shot into the net to put us ahead 2–0, which was where the score stood when time ran out. The game was ours and, unbelievably, so was our third straight national championship. "It's like Mo just picked up the puck and said we are going to win this game NOW," Coach Stafford said. "Then, BOOM. She went hard to the net, pulled the goalie out, and slam-dunked it. It was like, sorry, OVER."

Lots of celebrating followed, but fittingly our mom was more proud of the two letters she received from our faculty advisers. "She's an excellent role model" and "sets a fine example," my advisor wrote. Jocelyne's added, "So many people are so proud of your daughter. She understands the joy of hard work. The academic excellence and the team leadership aside, Jocelyne is a fine human being." Even with the way hockey dominated our lives and was starting to bring us notoriety, our achievements and behavior off the ice gave our parents more gratification than anything we did on the ice. We would understand this more with the perspective of age and time, but specific wins and losses and even championships generally fade from memory, and what people remember is effort, desire, and character. They remember you not just for when the times were good. They remember how you behaved when the times were tough. They remember whether you were a good person.

10

GRADUATION

"High school is about building dreams,
not giving up on them."

MONIQUE

We weren't invited to try out for the U22 national team in August, an omission that surprised us. That decision likely meant we weren't going to make the team that would play in the next Four Nations Cup. It was frustrating to end the summer this way, and neither of us could make sense out of how we could go from playing in the Four Nations Tournament the previous year to not being invited to try out for the U22 team the following year.

But we arrived at Shattuck determined to enjoy our senior year. Coach Stafford told us not to waste our energy fretting about the reasons we were not invited. "You're ready for that team," he said. "You'll get there too. But you and I aren't in the shoes of those making the decision. They have their own ways of doing things, and we aren't going to know what they are. So let's focus on what we can control. Let's play hockey."

He was right. It would have been easy to go down the rabbit hole of potential reasons why we did not get invited to camp—reasons we would never get—and drive ourselves crazy to the point of distraction. Instead, this was a moment to learn and grow from the adversity we faced and focus on the things we could control, something we have reminded ourselves to do ever since.

Knowing Coach Stafford was in our corner and believed in the two of us as much as we believed in each other was important. The confidence he had in us meant a lot, and his advice, as always, was a steadying influence. As seniors, we knew this was going to be a special year on and off the ice, and it was. We enjoyed our friendships. We had boyfriends and finally had our own cell phones. We had been sharing one between the two of us since our freshman year. We cheered for our classmates in their games, concerts, and performances. Given that we had accepted scholarships to the University of Minnesota and would officially sign later in the year, we probably could have been more social. But we worked hard to maintain our straight-A averages, something that we were proud of and worked really hard for.

A five-day trip associated with the Carlson School of Management took us to Minneapolis, Chicago, and South Bend, Indiana, and enabled us to participate in community service projects in each city. The effort, a gratifying reminder of the importance of cheering for the ones behind, leveling the playing field, and helping those who needed an extra hand, foreshadowed the community work we would do years later with the Ed Snider Youth Hockey Foundation and Comcast—and with our own foundation.

Our great grandmother was then one hundred years old. She volunteered at an assisted living facility and used to tell us she helped out at the old people's home, even though she was older than every one of them. She was an inspiration. As a child, she left school after sixth grade to help out on her family's farm, and she told us how she used to stand at the kitchen window and cry as she watched her friends walk to school. "I wanted to go with them," she told us. "I wanted to keep learning." She left us with a simple message. "Take advantage of every opportunity that life gives you. You don't want to miss out."

The timelessness of her words was, in fact, suited perfectly for our final season of hockey at Shattuck. With virtually the same team as our junior year, we blew past our opponents. Our biggest game was a November exhibition against the Minnesota Whitecaps, a professional team started by Jenny Potter's father. It didn't count in the standings, but the Whitecaps roster included a handful of players from the national team, and for that reason, we treated it with a significance that made it all the more satisfying when we won.

We took on new roles as team captains, a responsibility we embraced as part of our development. At Shattuck, no teams put a C or A on the captain's or assistant captain's jerseys as most teams did. It was assumed that the qualities that made you a leader would be obvious, and you would stand out by the example you set for the entire team. We always let our actions speak for themselves.

Coach Stafford put sophomore Kathleen Rogan on a line with us. She came to Shattuck the same year as us, but as a seventh grader, and she'd go on to play D1 hockey at Minnesota State, but as the season started, she was still a little green and nervous about playing with us. Each week we played together, though, her confidence grew, and she became a better, stronger player, and it had a positive effect on the entire team. Obviously, that was what Coach Stafford had in mind from the beginning.

It had an effect on us too. Playing on a line with Kathleen helped us understand that each person had her own unique strengths and approach, and it was worth the time to learn about each other and create our own chemistry as a line. For Jocelyne and me, the things that made us tick were different than most people. Not all athletes operated the way we did when it comes to training and practicing and doing all the other little things we believed were necessary to ensure we were at our best.

But that was the point. You want different attitudes, mindsets, and opinions in the locker room so long as, at the end of the day, everyone is working toward the same goal.

JOCELYNE

In March, our Shattuck team wrapped up another great season by winning the state championship again and qualifying for the nationals. Only a couple weeks before that tournament, Monique and I were invited to Team USA's final camp before the World Championships in Harbin, China. Since the two events were at the same time, we would have to miss Shattuck's try for a fourth straight national championship if we made the national team, and we were terribly conflicted about what to do.

Coach Stafford helped us reconcile the two opportunities, all but telling us we could not pass up the Team USA camp. But we were still battling our conflicted feelings as we left for the Olympic Training Center in Colorado Springs, Colorado, where we were among twenty-seven players battling for the twenty-one spots on the final roster before the team departed for China the next week.

Even though it was tough going into camp knowing that cuts would have to be made, as it always is, we believed that we had a very good chance of making the team. Behind the scenes, Coach Stafford had heard the same thing. It was, I thought, the reason we were invited to camp on relatively short notice. At the end of camp, we had a team meeting after breakfast. We knew that the roster was going to be announced this morning, so we had gone to bed the night before feeling anxious. No one ever gets a good night's sleep going into these meetings. Everyone took their seats silently as we filed into the meeting room, which was filled with nervous energy. There was very little small talk. Coach Jackie Barto, the head coach of the women's hockey program at Ohio State, entered the room and got right to the point. I don't remember what she said, but she then proceeded to list the names of the players that did not make the team.

Monique and I were the last two names she read. In these moments, you are almost holding your breath until you get confirmation that you have succeeded, then you get to exhale. Except, in this case, our moment to exhale never came. Instead, our hearts wilted like deflated balloons. This time was clearly harder than our first camp—it really hurt. But while all of this was happening internally, we refused to let it show outwardly, and we stood up along with the other three players who got cut and left the room. A brief meeting with each of us followed, and Monique and I both received the same feedback: you need more experience.

We didn't really understand that explanation. It seemed like the ultimate Catch-22. In order to get international experience, we had to make the team, but that didn't happen. We accepted the explanation, however, and vowed to ourselves that we would be back the next year and make the team.

Our moment to exhale came when we returned to our rooms to pack up our clothes and prepare to leave. With it, came a release of tears and the inevitable feeling that we had failed. We took our brief moment to let it out, to be disappointed and mad, and to feel sorry for ourselves. With our bags packed, we headed to the airport and prepared for what was a disappointing and somewhat embarrassing return to Shattuck. Getting sent home by being directly told you weren't good enough is starkly different and more painful than reading a roster without your name on it in the privacy of your own room.

But we were determined to return to Shattuck with a positive outlook. We were able to get back to school and join our Shattuck teammates on the trip to West Chester, Pennsylvania, for nationals. The team had practiced the past week as if we weren't going to be with them, but the adjustments required by our return were seamless from having played together the past eight months or longer. We were happy to be back and participating in nationals with our teammates. It gave us something to compete for.

We would have been even happier with a different outcome. Our chance to bring home a fourth straight national title came to an end in the quarterfinals against the Connecticut Stars, and it had nothing to do with changes in lines, power plays, or overall team rhythm. It had to do with the Stars' goalie. She was just lights out in what was probably the greatest game of her career. We outshot Connecticut 42–11. Nothing got past her. She was a brick wall. It was the first and only time in the two years Monique, Brianna Decker, Amanda Kessel, and I were on Shattuck's team together that none of us had a single point.

When I called home and said we'd lost, my dad thought I was joking. It was the most heartbreaking defeat we suffered during our four years at Shattuck.

MONIQUE

For the last two months of the school year, Jocelyne and some of our team-mates played on the lacrosse team. Minor wrist surgery sidelined me from the action, but I served as equipment manager and cheered Jocelyne as she picked up the new sport quickly. We wished we'd thought about playing lacrosse a few years before, but luckily for us, when it was time to look back on our years at Shattuck, we had no other regrets.

As for the disappointment of not making the national team twice and missing out on the World Championships, we knew Coach Stafford was right—we'd get there. High school was about building dreams, not giving up on them. Our future was still ahead of us, and as bright as we believed it could be.

As our high school careers were coming to an end, we reflected on our senior speeches, a requirement that all seniors had to share in front of the student body. I spoke about the way our hundred-year-old great grandmother still reminded me to take advantage of every opportunity I was given, and then I added a challenge of my own to all the younger students in the audience. "Whether you are here at Shattuck for academics, performing arts, or athletics, take advantage of everything the school has to offer, including the opportunity to learn from each other."

Jocelyne reflected on all four years at Shattuck, and she spoke for both of us when she concluded, "I've never had to wonder who to turn to if I was at a crossroads in any aspect of life. I've never had to wonder if I will have an ally on a team or someone who will inspire me to do better and reach for my best. I've always had Monique. And I felt like through our four years at Shattuck, we found in our classmates, people like that: lifelong friends who will always be there to sit, talk, listen, and inspire."

Our entire family—except for Jacques, who was unable to leave the Air Force Academy—showed up for graduation. It was a beautiful, tradition-filled ceremony, with the boys attired in blue blazers and the girls in white dresses and carrying a dozen red roses each. In addition to making the honor roll, Jocelyne and I were awarded the Williams Cup, which recognized us as the school's best athletes. It was the first time the award had gone to a girl—or in our case, two girls—and it paved the way for the next generation of girls at Shattuck to dream as big as any of the boys, if not bigger, and know their accomplishments would be recognized. Since then, over half a dozen girls have received the cup.

We'd been recruited to help put the girls' hockey program on the map—and four years later, the Shattuck St. Mary's girls' hockey team owned three national championships. Our legacy was to set the stage for those coming after us to win more championships in the future, which they have done—ten more to be exact. We had made a difference, and we were moving on with the knowledge the school had also made a difference in our lives. We were ready for the next chapter.

Part 2

TEAM USA

★ ★ ★

11

ONE IS BETTER THAN NONE

★

"Do the little things well, and the rest will take care of itself."

MONIQUE

After a long, busy summer spent training, working as counselors at Shattuck's hockey camp, attending a weeklong training camp in Lake Placid, and playing on the U22 national team in a three-game series against Canada, it was time to start our college career.

On the day we drove to the University of Minnesota, our dad joked that there would be no wearing any Minnesota Gopher gear within the Grand Forks city limits. Such good-natured barbs had been plentiful for most of the summer, but our parents and brothers, and others we knew with deep ties to UND, understood why we chose Minnesota over our hometown school. They agreed with us.

The hardest part of moving in was carrying a heavy bench our dad had made out of hockey sticks we had broken over the years, as well as some of Philippe's broken goalie sticks. The bench wasn't even comfortable—at best, it was a conversation piece. Otherwise, the move was easy—and so was saying goodbye to our parents. Clearly, we'd grown up since our first day at Shattuck. We lived with two other freshman teammates, Sarah Erickson and Kelly Seeler. In this new arrangement, Jocelyne and I each had our own room for the first time. But we still talked to each other all the time—through the air vents.

Our first hockey practice began with conditioning tests, including a grueling "Four Corners" run up and down and around the ten-thousand-seat Mariucci Arena, which was a large, bowl-shaped arena. We had to run two laps, going down and up the steps in each corner, as fast as we could. Besides the concentration it took to go fast down the steps without falling or tripping, the burn you felt in your lungs and legs was beyond painful. Jocelyne and I ran neck and neck but in different groups and finished one and three, with other freshmen right behind us. Everyone knew the kids were here to play.

Brad Frost had been promoted from assistant to head coach, and he tapped Natalie Darwitz as one of our assistant coaches. We liked the team's mix of experience and youth, talent and tenacity. Three of our teammates had been on the U22 National Team with us, and along with team captains Gigi Marvin and Melonie Gagnon, we saw the potential for a winning season and lots of fun.

Then came a quick reality check. We lost our regular-season opener 3–2 to Robert Morris, a team we should have beaten easily. It was a huge upset. We outshot the Colonials 65–10, but goalie Brianne McLaughlin, an Olympian in 2010 and 2014, stood on her head. We could not score on her. It happens. At least all the shots we had taken left Brianne exhausted the next day when we played Robert Morris again. This time, we won, and the victory almost put the huge egg we laid in the first game behind us.

We went on to win the next five games before facing off against number one–ranked Wisconsin. It was our biggest test of the season, and we split the series. While every loss is a disappointment, we knew we had fought hard and played unselfishly as a team, even if we had been outplayed in one of the two games, which happens when you go up against the best. Every situation, good and bad, offers you something new to learn.

JOCELYNE

Monique and I had rarely experienced anything other than success, and on the couple of relatively recent occasions when we didn't make the national teams, at least, we didn't make them together. Whether celebrating or dealing with disappointment, we always had each other. So when the new U.S. Women's National Team coach, Katey Stone, who was also head coach of the women's hockey program at Harvard, called to congratulate me on making the Four Nations Cup team, I assumed Monique was going to make it too.

That's just the way it had always been.

But not this time. Coach Stone hesitated when I asked if I should grab Monique and said that she would be making the rest of the calls throughout the day. Monique didn't get a call—and didn't make the roster. That sucked. It really sucked. There was no other way to describe it. She said having one of us on the team was better than neither of us making it, which was the same thing I would have said if the situation was reversed. But it was still a really painful blow—for both of us, but especially for Monique.

In November, a few weeks after our split with Wisconsin, I packed up and left for Lake Placid, the site of the Four Nations Cup tournament. I wasn't the only one from our team that went. Gigi Marvin, Rachel Drazan, Anne Schlepper, and Natalie Darwitz were also on the roster, and Coach Frost was one of the assistant coaches. None of this helped Monique. She was amazing, though, and showed her maturity as she wished everyone good luck.

Once we were there, I missed Monique, and others acknowledged her absence. "Oh sad," Meghan Duggan said as we walked through the Zamboni area before a practice. "You're used to having Monique here." I called Monique every day, and we talked through everything that happened in our games against Sweden, Finland, and Canada, who we beat in a tense shootout in the finals. It was a great accomplishment for the team and my first championship with Team USA, but it was certainly bittersweet.

MONIQUE

While Jocelyne was away, I used the time between classes to think about the situation. I realized that we had a perception problem, one that would linger throughout our entire national team careers. The coaches who worked with us for short periods of time in camp settings saw us as the same player, almost the same person—or as our grandmother more lovingly said, the same person, except there were two of us.

But that wasn't the reality. Yes, we were alike in many ways, and we lived and played with a sixth sense that was unique to us, but it was the way our differences complemented each other that made us better together, especially on the ice. Jocelyne was a little craftier with the puck, more willing to try fancier moves, while I was the tougher power forward, willing to lower my shoulder and take the puck to the net. And on defense, which Jocelyne didn't play, I understood the position with a very offensive point of view.

Going forward, we had to make sure that we each stood out on our own and played in such a way that it would be impossible for coaches to not put both of us on the team. Our dad always said to focus on the little things, and the rest would take care of itself. Coach Stafford reiterated that same message. Years later, Doc Hacker gave virtually the same advice. "Control the controllables," she said. In other words, only worry about the things within your power to affect. Are you moving your feet? Are you executing your passing? Are you a good teammate? Do you have a good attitude? Are you responsible with the puck? Are you focused on the next shift, or are you worried about your last mistake?

I checked all the boxes throughout the rest of the season. I finished as Western Collegiate Hockey Association (WCHA) Rookie of the Year and the conference-scoring champion. I was also a second-team All-American and a top-ten finalist for the Patty Kazmaier Award as college player of the year. Those individual honors were nice, but our season ended in a heartbreaking loss to Mercyhurst in the NCAA semifinals. I would have traded any of my individual recognitions for a shot at the national title.

At the end of March, we tried out for the US team going to Worlds. There was an abbreviated two-day camp in Lake Placid, and we were part of a talented group of younger players—Meghan Duggan, Kacey Bellamy, Hilary Knight, Kelli Stack, Erika Lawler, and Jessie Vetter—looking to carve out spots alongside veterans like Angie Ruggiero, Natalie Darwitz, and Jenny Potter, who were eager to defend their 2008 world title.

At the end, head coach Mark Johnson called all the players together and read the names of those on the final roster. Jocelyne and I heard our names, right between Hilary Knight and Gigi Marvin. We had made it! The two of us. Together. We managed to contain our smiles, but both of us felt a huge measure of satisfaction and relief!

Within a week, we were on our way to Finland. We left on a Monday and arrived in Vierumäki, Finland, on Tuesday. We really felt the jet lag. After three days of acclimating, we departed in the morning for Hämeenlinna, the site of the event. Jocelyne and I, known for being compulsively early to every-thing, set the alarm on our iPod, as we always did, and we woke up the next morning on time—or so we thought.

On my way to get breakfast that morning, the team manager saw me moseying along in my sweats. "Hey, we're leaving in a few minutes," she said. What? Back in our room, I discovered that our clock had reset the time with-out us knowing it. We were late. A mad scramble ensued as we packed our stuff and hurried out to the bus. Fortunately, we were soon able to laugh it off as one of the only times we have ever been late to anything.

JOCELYNE

In our first three games, we outscored our opponents, Japan, Russia, and Finland, 23–0. We had never been a part of a team where scoring was so balanced, and each player on every shift was a threat to score. The firepower was endless. The next day, however, Canada beat us 2–1 in a game that our coach termed "friendly" because, no matter the outcome, we were set to play each other again in the championship final.

Of course, that game was anything but friendly, like all of our games against Canada, and it was obvious the final was going to be even more intense. We were defending the title, but Canada owned the reputation as the world's number one women's hockey team. As we walked out of the locker room, Angela Ruggiero banged her stick against everything she passed. She was a one-woman drum corps, and the bang-bang-bang of her stick set the tone. Moments later, we jumped out to a 1–0 lead when Caitlin Cahow scored on a nice pass from Jenny Potter. In the second period, I fed Meghan Duggan streaking through the slot for another goal. Caitlin put us up 3–1 in the third, and Hilary Knight added an insurance goal in the final seconds. We won 4–1 and claimed the World Championship.

We all hugged each other and reveled in the euphoria of the win. Our celebration reflected the way we had made this whole tournament about the team. The play was unselfish, supportive, and something everyone contributed to equally. It was hockey the way it's supposed to be played, and it made everyone proud. We weren't trying to knock Canada off the pedestal as much as we were climbing up there with them. We wanted Team USA to be seen as equals—and with back-to-back World Championships, we deserved it.

During the trophy ceremony, Monique and I stood with our teammates on the blue line. We shared one regret—that this special moment didn't last longer.

But that only made us want more, and as both of us knew—in fact, as our entire team knew—the end of this World Championship tournament began the official countdown to Vancouver and the 2010 Olympics.

12

THE SPIN MOVE OF ALL TIME

"If you're going to bet on someone,
don't you want to bet on yourself?"

MONIQUE

With Worlds behind us, we spent the rest of the spring like most college students. We took our finals, packed up our apartment, and put books and furniture in storage to await our return as sophomores. Before going back home, we even signed a lease with several teammates on a condo for the following year. Then came the big surprise, what the local Minneapolis paper called "the spin move of all time." We decided to transfer to UND.

Our decision was not premeditated, as some assumed. In reality, it caught the two of us off-guard as much as everybody else. One day shortly after returning home for the summer, we were working out at the gym when an acquaintance of ours casually asked which would be more meaningful, winning a national championship with the Minnesota Gophers or the UND Fighting Sioux. We didn't have to think about it. "The Fighting Sioux," we said.

That response, and the speed with which we said it, gave Jocelyne and me reason to pause and reflect not only on our answer, but also on the whole past year. As we did, we realized that, despite an outstanding, exciting freshman year at Minnesota, our hometown roots ran very deep, including our ties to UND. UND's new head coach, Brian Idalski, had taken the team to a .500 record after winning only two games the season before. While he had a ways to go before the Fighting Sioux would be in a position to compete for a national championship, we saw an opportunity to be part of UND's rebuilding effort. It didn't hurt that we'd be close to home too.

Nervous about what it would mean to change schools, we went to our brother, Pierre-Paul, for advice. He had dated one of our roommates earlier in the year, so we had seen him more than the others recently, and he had a solid, sensible perspective on most things. After hearing us out, he suggested we speak with Greg Lotysz, a family friend who had played in the NFL and was on the verge of becoming a starter on the New York Jets offensive line when he tore his ACL—and then developed a life-threatening infection following surgery.

At six-seven, Greg was an imposing figure and even more inspiring when he told how, while debilitated by the extreme pain of his infection, and with his wife in recovery from cancer and pregnant with their first child, he filed a lawsuit against the NFL. Even though he didn't want to, he had to fight for himself, and it turned out to be the right move. So he knew something about making changes and taking risks as an athlete.

He listened to our reasons for wanting to transfer and then told us to go for it. He even offered to speak to Coach Idalski on our behalf. "If you two are going to bet, don't you want to bet on yourselves?" he added. "Whatever it is that you want, have the confidence that you're going to make it happen. Bet on yourself to do it."

Encouraged by his advice, we told our parents. When we asked if we could talk to them for a few minutes, a look of panic spread across our mom's face. "What's going on?" she asked. "Is one of you pregnant?" We laughed, relieved, knowing that whatever we said after that was going to be okay.

"It sounds like you've thought this through," our dad said. "You have my support."

As for our mom, she had the upcoming Olympics on her mind. "Is it going to affect anything with the national team?" she asked.

We didn't think so, and Coach Idalski confirmed this when we met with him to go over the details. According to WCHA rules, as transfers, we could enroll in classes, but we had to sit out a full season of competition. That wasn't a problem since we would need to miss the 2009–2010 season if we made the 2010 Olympic team.

The hardest part was breaking the news to Coach Frost. Extremely surprised, he was nonetheless gracious and respectful and granted our release from Minnesota's program. We also called our closest friends on the team, wanting them to hear the news from us before they read about it in the newspapers. The story broke at the end of May. Within a week, we signed with UND. Coach Idalski was thrilled and told reporters he looked forward to adding our "winning mentality and swagger on the ice." We did too.

JOCELYNE

We spent the summer working out with UND's men's hockey team. Pierre-Paul was coordinating video for the team that season, and since we were home, he suggested we train with the men's team until tryouts for the national team at the end of August. Former assistant coach Brad Berry gave the go-ahead, and starting every morning at eight, we practiced and trained with about fifteen guys, a group of UND players, but also a few alumni who were between pro seasons, getting ready to try to make the national team going to Vancouver.

The Olympic tryouts were at the National Sports Center in Blaine, a vast complex with eight rinks that illustrate why Minnesota is known as the "State of Hockey." We were among the forty-one top women hockey players who had been invited to camp, and we showed up in the best shape of our lives. We also felt prepared mentally. It was a good thing, too. In this Olympic year, the level of play was at an all-time high. The talent pool was a mix of Olympic newbies like us and veterans like Angela Ruggiero and Jenny Potter, both of whom were looking to play in their fourth Olympics.

Monique and I were on the same tryout team, which in all our years of playing had happened only a handful of times. We had a few practices and three games. After the last game, we got off the ice feeling like we did what we needed to do to be put on the roster, but at the end of the day, you just never know what is going to happen. As Coach Stafford always cautioned, you can't read the coach's mind, so don't try to even guess.

Coach Johnson didn't make us wait long. With everyone assembled in a meeting room, he read the names of the initial twenty-three players on the 2009–2010 national team. Two players would have to be cut at the end of December. Monique and I sat next to each other. Going by position in alphabetical order, we heard Knight, then M. Lamoureux, and then Marvin. Our hearts dropped. He didn't call my name, and our hearts sank. Not again.

A second later, though, he said, "J. Lamoureux." For whatever reason, Coach Johnson had messed up the alphabetical order. But I made the team —which explained the huge sigh of relief that came from me—and a few others, including Erika Lawler, who turned toward us and said, "For a second, I thought how could that be?"

It's hard to describe the exhilaration we felt. Yes, making the national team was awesome, as it is each and every time. But this national team was going to the Olympics. We were going to get our shot at winning an Olympic gold medal. Together. And that little alphabet glitch reminded us how important that was to both of us.

VANCOUVER 2010

★

"You don't win the silver medal."

JOCELYNE

Monique and I were early risers, always the first two up in the five-bedroom house that we rented with Meghan Duggan, Erika Lawler, Kelli Stack, and Kacey Bellamy for our six-month residency in Blaine as we prepared for the Olympics in Vancouver. As usual, we had our routines, including breakfast. We didn't want to wake any of the others with the loud Bullet blender we used to make our morning smoothies, so we would run the blender in the garage.

After our smoothies, it was the quiet before the storm. By 10:00 a.m., we were on the ice for our daily practice. Workouts were in the afternoon. Monique and I spent our free time taking a full load of online courses at UND, satisfying our academic requirements as sophomores, leaving us very little free time. Before we had left for the year, our mom had given us a classic Linda-laminated pink note card. On it was printed former UCLA basketball coach John Wooden's Seven-Point Creed, which apparently his father had given him as a child.

1. Be true to yourself.

2. Make each day your masterpiece.

3. Help others.

4. Drink deeply from good books, including the good book.

5. Make friendships a fine art.

6. Build a shelter against a rainy day.

7. Pray for guidance, and give thanks for your blessings every day.

I kept the card in the little kit that sat in my stall at the rink and looked at it when things seemed to be in a rut or were not going as well as I hoped. The list put things into perspective for me—and for Monique. Were we being true to ourselves, helping others, being good friends or teammates, and so on? If those things were the focal points of our day, and we reminded ourselves they were what really mattered to us as human beings. We could be confident that everything else would fall into place.

As the residency intensified, we continued to develop relationships with veterans like Julie Chu, Angela Ruggiero, and Jenny Potter, and we deepened friendships with the younger players, like our housemates. That was the special part of being on the national team. The rivalries between our schools went away. Age differences disappeared. In their place, a bond developed. We worked as a unit. We pushed each other. Helped each other. Laughed, cried, celebrated, and dreamed together. We wore the same uniforms, with the USA crest on the front, all working toward the same goal.

I practically grew up with Hilary Knight. We were born only ten days apart and raised in different parts of the country. In the beginning, our paths mostly crossed when our teams were facing off against each other in high school and in college, but as our national team careers started, we found the things that made our lives different paled in comparison to the gold-medal dreams we pursued together.

A full schedule of exhibition games during the six-month residency ensured we built chemistry on the ice. We had no trouble beating a mix of colleges and all-stars from the WCHA and the ECAC. But we were less successful against Canada on the seven-game Qwest tour. Between October and December, we played our northern rivals five times and lost all five games. Canada played nearly twice as many games as us and played a more competitive schedule. We weren't daunted or intimidated; if anything, the challenge of beating Canada motivated every single one of us. "We're making progress," Coach Johnson said. "We're continuously learning." We sensed the gold medal in Vancouver was going to come down to our two teams. We could lose every exhibition game to Canada. They didn't matter. The only game that counted was the Olympic final.

MONIQUE

In mid-December, we returned to Blaine after playing Canada in Calgary. As we unloaded our gear, Rachel Drazan and Angie Keseley got pulled off to the side to meet privately with the coaches. Maybe the older players knew what that meant, but it took a while before those of us with less experience figured out that two teammates who had been a part of this team and shared the same dream about playing in the Olympics were not going to be on the final roster. Everyone sympathized with them, but unless you have been in their shoes, it is almost impossible to understand fully the extent of their disappointment.

At the same time, it meant that Jocelyne and I had both made the team and would be going to the Olympics together. This was confirmed that afternoon in the locker room in Blaine in a team meeting. Two days later, the twenty-one women's hockey players who would be representing the United States in Vancouver were introduced to the media at the Mall of America. The two of us and Hilary Knight were the three youngest members of the team. It was surreal to think we would be playing alongside women like Angela Ruggiero and Jenny Potter, who had inspired us as members of the first US Women's National Ice Hockey Team when the sport was introduced to the Olympics in 1998.

We shared the good news with our family over Christmas, and from then on, it was a march to Vancouver. On January 1, we played Canada in Ottawa, losing 3–2 in a shootout. A month later, on February 4, we beat Finland in our final tune-up. The entire team contributed, and everyone was excited and ready for the challenge ahead of us. Three days later, we traveled to Vancouver and checked into the Olympic village.

The thrills started immediately. Each of us had our picture taken, was issued our credentials, and then entered a giant conference room, where we literally took a shopping cart and went from station to station filling it with official USA Olympic outfits, special apparel, and gear. It was like Christmas, but way better. Jocelyne and I shared a room, along with Kelli Stack and Kacey Bellamy. We were in the corner on one of the top floors with a beautiful view of the nearby bay.

If any place captured the Olympic spirit, it was the cafeteria, where all the athletes from all countries and sports ate their meals. Normally, we would sit with teammates if we could find an open table. If there wasn't an opening, we looked around for people wearing Team USA jackets, joined their table, and made immediate connections with other athletes.

Participating in the opening ceremony was a magical experience. All of the USA athletes walked together to the B.C. Place Stadium in our matching Ralph Lauren outfits. As we waited our turn to enter the stadium in the carefully choreographed procession of international teams, Jocelyne and I looked at each other and shared a smile that wordlessly recognized the long, determined journey we'd been on to get to this moment. We thought back to our grade-school dream. Now we were here. And we were here together. Becoming Olympians was a big part of our dream, and we had officially accomplished that. The next part was becoming Olympic champions; that part would have to wait.

JOCELYNE

Our mom, who ignited our Olympic dream when we were little kids through her own passion for the Olympics, texted us that she and our dad were on their way from the airport, but running late. We told her not to worry. She hadn't missed anything. She was determined not to miss seeing us in the opening ceremony, in addition to the competition and hopefully on the medal stand. Once Mom and Dad arrived at the venue, however, there was a problem. Mom had left their tickets to the opening ceremonies in her luggage, which was in the car of the friend of our dad, who had picked them up at the airport and dropped them off.

I can't imagine the way she must have frantically searched her bag before realizing what had happened, but from the account she gave us later, I know that she burst into tears in front of the security guards, explaining that her daughters, identical twins, were on the U.S. Women's National Team, and she and my dad had just arrived from the airport and had left their tickets in their luggage. Knowing my mom, I am pretty sure she also filled the guards in on her passion for the Olympics and emphasized that this was a once-in-a-lifetime thrill for parents to see their children in the opening ceremony. Could they imagine the disappointment of missing it?

Whatever she said, it worked. Without tickets or credentials, the security guards allowed our parents to go inside. I guess they could tell an honest parent when they saw one. The crisis averted, our mom and dad got to their seats moments before we entered and saw us walk in with the entire US contingent of athletes. Amazing. And when we finally took our seats, we turned around to look for them and there they were, sitting only a few rows behind us.

Our opening game was played on Valentine's Day, February 14, and we looked like the world's number one–ranked team as we overpowered China 12–1. Monique set a US record with four assists, and I scored in the second period with a flashy move that Mom didn't see because she was at the concession stand getting a coffee. Even though she missed the highlight-reel play, Pierre-Paul, Jacques, and our childhood friend Alyssa replayed the moment for her. Our next couple of games were also lopsided wins—a 13–0 win over Russia and then a 6–0 victory against Finland in which Natalie Darwitz passed Cammie Granato for most points by a U.S. Women's hockey player in the Olympics. We made it through pool play easily, as expected.

Canada, ranked number two in the world, was seeded number one in Vancouver and played like it. As expected, both of our teams landed in the semis—Canada against Finland and us versus Sweden. Four years earlier, Sweden had knocked the US out of contention for the gold in the semifinals, and the US went home with a bronze medal. It wasn't just a ticket to the gold-medal game that our team was looking for. This semifinal game represented redemption for the players who lost in Torino—our pride as Americans was on the line. We wanted to leave no doubt that we belonged in that final game.

This time, we overwhelmed Sweden 9–1 in an excellent team effort, with nine US players finishing the game with more than one point, including Monique's hat trick. The win put us in the gold-medal game against Canada.

After the game, we met briefly with Sweden's head coach, Peter Elander, who was joining the UND women's hockey coaching staff the next year. He wished us luck in the finals against Canada, which had enjoyed an easy 5–0 win in its semifinal against Finland. Both of our teams appeared to be firing on all cylinders, although such lopsided games can leave you less sharp than closer, harder-fought games.

The Canadians took advantage of two free days before the finals with a secret scrimmage against a top local boys' team. We practiced as scheduled. Any signs of nervousness were kept at bay as we approached the biggest game of our careers. The next day, there was no denying the special atmosphere inside the arena. The air was electric, like nothing we'd ever felt. Nearly twenty thousand people were in the stands, including Canadian Prime Minister Stephen Harper, and millions more watched live on TV.

Once the game started, both teams delivered the type of high-level play that you would expect from the two best teams in the world. The play was extremely close and physical. From the outset, it was apparent that both teams' goalies, Jesse Vetter for the US and Shannon Szabados for Canada, were exceptionally sharp. Szabados made that clear when she had to do the splits to make a stretched-out glove save off Monique's point-blank scoring chance. In any other game, that was a goal. In these Olympic finals, it was a save for the highlight reel.

Canada got two goals from Marie-Philip Poulin in the first period, after which Vetter was perfect the rest of the game. Even with two five-on-three power plays, we could not capitalize on any opportunities. I glanced over at

Angela Ruggiero and Jenny Potter and tried to summon even more determination. This was their fourth Olympics, and they'd come up short in the last two. Knowing this might be their last Olympics, we wanted them to get one more gold medal.

Monique felt the same way. She fired two shots in the third, including one just four feet out from the goal, but Szabados didn't give an inch, and that hot hand of hers was the difference in the game. Canada won 2–0 and, with that, took home the gold medal.

MONIQUE

After the game, we were on the ice for thirty minutes, watching Canada celebrate and waiting for Olympic officials to set up for the medal ceremony. It was gut-wrenching. We spent another thirty minutes on the ice as bronze medal–winning Finland came out. Finally, we all lined up for the actual ceremony. Even with the Canadian fans cheering for us, we were unable to hide our disappointment. Watching the Canadians get their medals drove home a harsh Olympic reality. You don't win a silver medal. You get one by losing the gold. Our team thought this was going to be our turn, and it wasn't. It hurt—and still does to this day.

I was pulled for a random drug test and missed Coach Johnson's postgame talk. When I finally made it back to the locker room an hour or so later, Jocelyne and Meghan Duggan were there, still trying to process their disappointment. I had the same anguished expression on my face. "That didn't just happen. I want a do-over," I said, falling onto the bench next to them.

Jocelyne nodded. "We had the opportunities. We had two five-on-threes. We just didn't capitalize on them."

Later that night, all the players and their families met at the Team USA house. Our mom and dad and brother, Pierre-Paul, along with our godfather, met us outside. Noticing that we were holding back tears, Pierre-Paul pulled us to the side and gave us a much-needed hug. As he let go, our parents were waiting; they embraced us and gave us shoulders to cry on, exactly what we needed before going inside. We sat with family and teammates, and before the night ended, we were at a table with Kelli Stack, Meghan Duggan, Kacey Bellamy, and Erika Lawler, vowing to be back in the finals four years from now.

That's one of the ways sports mirror real life. Even after a devastating loss, you look ahead to the next day, another game, and another chance to create a different outcome, no matter if it takes four more years.

14

STARTING OVER

★

"The best athletes are always working to improve."

JOCELYNE

I don't know if we were ready for the attention that followed us back home, but when UND asked to celebrate our Olympic silver medals at one of the UND men's hockey games, we felt obligated to say yes. Only a couple weeks had passed since we returned home from Vancouver. Up until that point, our focus had always been on getting to the Olympics. We had never really thought about life after the games. We were also much more comfortable fighting for a puck than the spotlight.

At the game, we signed autographs and performed the honors at a ceremonial puck drop. We waved to thousands of people who gave us a standing ovation. This was not a crowd of anonymous fans. They were our friends—our neighbors—people who had supported us throughout our careers. The reception was beyond special. Although we didn't realize it at the time, that evening marked the start of the next chapter in our lives.

Coming out of that extraordinary reception, Monique and I began to ask ourselves what our medals were for. What did it mean to be an Olympian? A medal winner? We answered those questions with more questions: How can we use our notoriety to help people? Can we share the lessons that got us to the Olympics—like cheering for the one behind and making a difference—with other people in a way that they can use in their own lives? We shared these thoughts with the UND Alumni Association, which had helped raise money to offset costs for our parents and brothers to attend the Olympics.

This wasn't easy or natural for us. We felt a bit awkward and a bit shy delivering such a message publicly. But these basic questions have continued to guide and motivate us to this day—with an even greater sense of urgency—and no doubt will continue long into the future.

At twenty years old, it seemed so odd and unnatural to be the center of attention when we still had so much to figure out about our own lives. Competing in the Olympics was only part of our dream. Winning a gold medal was still an unrealized and really important part of that dream, and we had every intention of making that a reality in 2014.

More immediately, we wanted to get to know our new UND teammates. Coach Idalski let us join the team for the remainder of spring training. We used it as an opportunity to bring an increased level of intensity to team workouts and to set a new expectation as a team, leading into next season.

Apparently, we weren't the only ones who felt that way. Before everyone left for summer break, Coach Idalski informed us that we were going to be the team's cocaptains when we returned, along with current season MVP, goalie Jorid Dagfinrud. Believing that he'd made the appointments, we said thanks but no thanks, explaining that we only wanted to be team captains if we were voted into the roles by our peers. "I have the votes right here," he said, smiling as he pulled an envelope from his desk. "I'll show them to you if you want."

MONIQUE

That wasn't the only change in our status. Over the summer, I got married. That might come across as a shock, and that's pretty much the way it was received by friends and family. As a high school senior, I had started dating Taylor Kolls, whom I met through his sister, Madison, a classmate of ours at Shattuck. After graduation, Taylor joined the Marines and was initially stationed in California, and then transferred to Hawaii, while I went off to college. We kept things going long distance, which was convenient for both of our busy lives.

Before Taylor deployed to Afghanistan in 2009, we got engaged. It was one of those decisions driven more by emotion than common sense. Both sets of our parents hoped our engagement would be a long one; they believed we were too young to be talking about marriage, and, of course, they were right. But we didn't listen. While I competed in Vancouver, Taylor was deployed in Afghanistan. He rooted for me, and I constantly worried about his safety.

As a machine gunner on patrols, his safety was a serious issue that added a sense of immediacy and emotion to our relationship and made marriage seem like the right thing to do sooner rather than later. As we told ourselves, who knew if there would be a later? We were faced with serious, real-life decisions at age twenty. It's hard to wrap your brain around designating your next of kin on medical forms when you are barely an adult.

That summer, Taylor came home on a two-week break, and we got married. Ignoring the advice of those close to us, we thought we knew better. Then, within days of becoming husband and wife, Taylor returned to active duty, and I resumed my routine of working out with Jocelyne and our teammates to get ready for the upcoming season.

Since very little changed other than the addition of a hyphen to my last name, making it Lamoureux-Kolls, I could say, "See, not a big deal." And it wasn't. For the next two years, Taylor was stationed in Hawaii, and we saw each other only a few times. My life went on as it always had—until, of course, it didn't, and I had to make a change.

JOCELYNE

That same summer, I began dating Brent Davidson, the man who would ultimately become my husband. He was a teammate of my brother Mario on the UND men's hockey team. Standing six-four, he was described in the school's press guide as a big man with a heart. Before the Olympics, we had crossed paths at the rink and in the weight room. Mario called him Davey, a shortened version of his last name, and I did, too, always saying, "Hi, Davey," and I didn't think anything more since we were both dating other people at the time.

After Vancouver, we reconnected through our mutual friend, Greg Lotysz (who had advised us about our decision to transfer to UND), and I learned his name was actually Brent. Once he found out I wasn't dating anyone, we started hanging out. We tried to keep things low-key, but one day he left his sandals outside the front door of the off-campus house I rented with my teammates and a couple friends. Our roommates, Max and Margot, noticed his sandals were team-issued and also had his number stenciled on them. After a quick search of team rosters on the internet, they discovered his identity.

It was pretty funny, but our relationship was no longer a secret. I told Brent that he needed to speak with Mario. As both of us knew, there was an unwritten rule about dating a teammate's sibling. If I screwed things up between us, it wasn't going to impact my relationship with my brother. He'd still be my brother. But if Brent did something stupid, it had the potential to hurt their relationship as teammates on and off the ice.

It took Mario a little time to warm up to the idea of his teammate dating his younger sister, but eventually he was okay with it. From then on, Brent was free to park his sandals wherever he wanted without worrying about who might see them.

MONIQUE

With the return of hockey season, we settled back into our familiar routines. In August, we participated in the national team's annual weeklong summer camp. We played on the U22 team in a three-game series against Canada, where we had a less-than-stellar showing, losing all three games. We then headed back to Grand Forks to start the school year and a new hockey season. Without meaning to sound boastful, we brought a new and different energy to the team and an expectation that we would compete to win every single night.

In our first exhibition game, we cruised to a 9–0 victory. Jocelyne gave fans a taste of things to come by scoring three straight goals in the second period. But our goal wasn't to, as Coach Stafford might have said, Hulk Hogan through everything. We wanted to raise everyone's level of play, and I think we did. To begin the regular season, an attendance record was set, and we split the opening series against number six–ranked Boston University. Then we did the same the following weekend against number one–ranked Minnesota-Duluth. Next on the schedule was a two-game series in Minneapolis against our original college team, number three–ranked University of Minnesota.

The day before we left for Minneapolis, Jocelyne and I were making up a test we were going to miss. Jocelyne had been complaining of nagging stomach pain all morning. During the test, I noticed she was very uncomfortable and actually sweating. She finished the test by circling all Cs down the last column and left abruptly, telling me that she was going to see the trainer immediately. Soon after, she ended up in the doctor's office and was diagnosed with a kidney stone.

When I came home a few hours later, Brent was in the backyard gagging as he was cleaning out Jocelyne's puke bucket. It was one of those times where I was so happy Jocelyne had a boyfriend around. I knew he was a keeper.

As sick as she was, Jocelyne still traveled with the team, expecting to play. Pain medication was not allowed eight hours before competition, so Jocelyne lay on the training table with a heat pack until it was time to put her gear on and go on the ice. Her toughness had an effect on the entire team.

Energized by the string of great games from the previous two weeks and motivated by Jocelyne's grit, one of the most heroic displays of getting through pain I've ever seen, we won both games. It was the first time in the history of UND's women's ice hockey program that the Fighting Sioux had beaten the Gophers. It was also the first time Minnesota had ever been swept in its home opening series. All of a sudden, UND women's hockey was ranked as one of the top teams in the country.

JOCELYNE

Just a couple months earlier, at the start of the season, Peter Elander had asked both of us to have coffee with him. Peter had coached Sweden in the Olympics and was our new associate head coach. We met him at the bookstore café, where, after a pleasant catch-up, he said, "What do the two of you need from me in order to become the best players in the world? I know you want to be on top. I see your drive and talent. What can I do to help get you there?"

We weren't just impressed and appreciative; we were blown away. No coach had ever asked us anything like that before. Either we had followed instructions or been on our own. He read us correctly. We weren't satisfied with our games. We wanted to turn our weaknesses into strengths and make our strengths even stronger. Peter also knew that was only part of the challenge. After Vancouver, the whole four-year Olympic cycle began again. We were starting a new quad, with the goal of making the national team for the 2014 Olympics in Sochi, Russia.

Between UND's schedule and traveling every two to three months for USA Hockey camps or tournaments, it was going to be a long, tough, competitive haul. So his offer resonated with us. *What can I do to help you get there?* Throughout the UND season, Peter came out on the ice with us one or two times a week and ran us through extra drills. Mostly skill work. We realized how much he cared about us.

In November, we competed in the Four Nations Cup in Newfoundland, where the US team breezed through early rounds before losing the final to Canada in a tense contest that was decided in overtime. Except for that "break," we put everything we had into UND's season. It became the school's finest to date. Between mid-December and the end of January, we put together a seven-game win streak. Altogether, we won twenty games, the most in the program's history.

We had home-ice advantage for the first-round matchup against Bemidji State in the conference playoffs. Our appearance in the playoffs was so unexpected that the men's team already had games scheduled, so our three-game series was relocated to Purpur Arena, where we had first learned how to skate. The smaller arena was full, loud, and a perfect atmosphere for the exciting series. We split the first two games, and the deciding third game was one of those electrifying events that seem to happen only in small towns like ours. Everyone was talking about the game.

The arena smelled like hockey—ice and cold, and years of blood and sweat hammered into the boards. It was the longest game in UND's history, ending in double overtime. The UND press guide captured the deciding goal in the game: "In the nail-biter, Monique Lamoureux took the puck from her own end, skated through the neutral ice, faked a shot to get around a defenseman and buried a backhand in front of the crease for the series-clinching goal."

Unfortunately, our season ended in the next round when we lost to Wisconsin, the number one seed and eventual NCAA champs. Coach Idalski termed the season a positive step forward, setting team history bests in every category. Both Monique and I received several individual accolades, but for us, the most important accomplishment for this season was how much our team improved. We went from finishing in last place in the WCHA the previous season to fourth—and beating top-ranked teams in the process.

MONIQUE

We had three weeks between the end of the college season and the start of camp for the World Championships. Peter went out on the ice with us every day. He ran us through practices and drills, teaching us different skills that he made us repeat hundreds of times until we could perform them with ease. Some of these drills required four tires that were lined up along the ice, which we tagged "Highway Patrol." He at least gave all the shots fun names, including "Oops, I Did It Again," the one Jocelyne would use to score the winning goal in the 2018 Olympic final. But these drills were not always fun. This was work—hard work—and these days were tedious and sometimes frustrating, especially the way Peter gave meticulous feedback after every single shot or drill and then said, "Let's do it again."

As a result, we showed up at camp more prepared than ever before. The team was named, and we were soon on our way to Switzerland for our second World Championship. Heading into the tournament, we had been on the ice twelve days in a row before getting a day off, including the day we left for Switzerland and the day we arrived. The intense work schedule seemed to take a toll on everyone, and I ended up pulling my groin right before our day off, which caused me to miss the first two games of the tournament.

I hated being on the sidelines, but as we rolled past Slovakia and Russia, it was pretty clear that something special was happening with this team. A bunch of us were stepping into our own at the same time and making an impact on the national team together. So much of that depends on a chemistry developing among players. It either happens, or it doesn't. It can't be manufactured. We had it—that chemistry where you play for each other, not yourself.

We liked each other. We had fun. We laughed and kept each other loose. You could hear it in the daily banter and the nicknames we gave each other. Hilary Knight was Knighter. Meghan Duggan was Dugs. Jennifer Potter was Pottsy. Molly Schaus was Schausy. And from playing on a line with Kelli Stack, Jocelyne and I went from being known as the Lampops and then the Lamsicles to the Stacksicles.

We started out sluggish in our semifinal game against Russia, but soon that chemistry kicked in as if it were an extra player, and we hit a groove where a bunch of us scored—I twice, Jocelyne, Kendall Coyne, and Brianna Decker once each—for a 5–1 victory that sent us into the finals against Canada. As always, whenever our two teams met, the only safe prediction was that it wouldn't be easy, and this final was true to form. Jocelyne scored the game's first goal, but we gave one up at the end of the first period. Jenny Potter put us up 2–1 in the second, and we stayed that way until Canada tied the game late in the third on a power play. We didn't let that deter us—we dug in harder.

It was one of those situations—four-on-four, sudden-death overtime, the score tied 2–2, championship on the line—that have come to belong to Hilary Knight and her cool-under-pressure disposition and laser-sharp marksmanship. Nearly eight minutes into OT, she put the puck in the net to give the US its third straight World Championship. Not to be overlooked, Jesse Vetter had fifty-one saves. We were all ecstatic. The win helped put Vancouver behind us and let us begin looking ahead to Sochi. We knew it was a long way off, and there was no telling what might happen in the three years until then. Only that we would be older and even hungrier to win gold.

1 5

HEART AND CHARACTER

"Facing the worst is the best way to come back stronger than ever."

JOCELYNE

September 2011. At the start of our junior year, our expectations were high—as high as the championship banners hanging from the rafters inside the Ralph. The women's hockey team wanted a banner of our own, and we thought this was the year we might accomplish that feat. Peter helped recruit a handful of dynamic players from Europe, including forwards Josefine Jakobsen from Denmark and Andrea Dalen from Norway. Sophomore Michelle Karvinen, who played for Finland's 2010 Olympic team and was, in our opinion, one of the best forwards in the world, was also eligible after redshirting the previous season.

"This is just the place you want to go if you want to play some good hockey," she told the school paper when explaining why she chose UND. She described the kind of atmosphere we had hoped to create when we transferred—a program with a winning tradition and a culture that expected everyone's best day in and day out. On our bench, we often heard two or three different languages being spoken at the same time—and occasionally I needed to ask for a translation to make sure I followed what was being said about the game. But we were all saying the same thing. We wanted to win.

After struggling with some early season matchups against powerhouses Boston University and Wisconsin, we settled into a winning groove leading all the way into the break for the Four Nations Cup. We hated to interrupt our momentum, but being part of the national team brought us a step closer to the Olympics. Also, the tournament was being played in Nyköping, Sweden, and it gave me the opportunity to see my boyfriend, Brent, who was playing professional hockey there and living only a couple of hours away. After being apart for several months, it took traveling halfway across the world for us to reunite.

My major logistical challenge in Nyköping was circumventing the team's strict no-visitors policy. But with an assist from Monique, we squeezed Brent's six-four, two-hundred-and-twenty-pound frame through the window of our hotel room. Between games, there wasn't much to do in Nyköping, except walk around the small town or go to McDonald's, and I was petrified the whole time that Brent and I would be caught, and the coaches would think I was distracted. It was the first time I had to make a conscious effort to balance my personal life and hockey.

It wasn't a problem until Brent had to leave, which happened to be the day before we played Canada in the finals. We spent our entire day off plotting how to sneak him out of our hotel. Monique constantly checked to see if the coast was clear because the team's coaching staff spent all day working in the lobby. Finally, we snuck Brent out the hotel window, the same way he had entered, and no one ever found out.

As for the championship game, it followed a familiar script. Our two teams ended regulation play tied 3–3, and then Hilary Knight added another dramatic headline to her résumé by slamming home a goal in a shootout to put the US on top. Jesse Vetter cinched the win by stopping the Canadians' last shot. Monique was named player of the game, and our team celebration was an acknowledgment of each other's effort. We weren't just the best team in the world on the ice. In terms of character and all the other qualities that define what it means to be a winner, this group of women was unbeatable off the ice too.

MONIQUE

Our UND season resumed the following weekend. With Michelle Karvinen, Jorid Dagfinrud, and Andrea Dalen all returning from their national team obligations, like the two of us, our Fighting Sioux roster looked like a Four Nations Cup all-star team. Even though you play on the same team for four years in high school and college, every year, the team is slightly different in its makeup, and the different dynamics and skills our international teammates brought to this team made it that much more fun for us.

We were lucky enough to play on a line with Michelle until I made the move back to defense. Josefine Jakobsen took my place on the line. I had spoken with our coach and suggested that I might help the team more on D since we were too often struggling to break the puck out, and we had the talent to at least try the shift. It seemed to work. Going into Christmas break, our team was ranked fifth in the country, an all-time high for the UND women.

In mid-January, we waged a fierce battle against top-ranked Wisconsin, losing the first game and beating them in a shootout in the second. Our team's passion and determination were never more evident. We closed the regular season with a third-place finish in the conference, surpassing the records set the previous year. In the WCHA playoffs, we lost in the second round of the conference finals to Minnesota.

The next day, we found out we would face off against Minnesota for the sixth time that season in the first round of the NCAA tournament. Getting that far was another first for UND women's hockey. Unfortunately, our season ended there, while Minnesota went on to win the NCAA championship.

It took us a while to get over the disappointment of falling short of our goal to bring a national championship to UND. Whether or not it was realistic in the face of the competition, we believed it was an achievable goal, and belief is what fuels athletes. We were also playing for respect—the respect we believed the women's hockey program deserved as it ended its first decade at UND. Like most women's programs across the country, no matter the talent we put on the ice or the excitement we generated, we always felt the shadow of the men's program, as if only by their effort were we able to exist.

The individual successes and achievements that Jocelyne and I accomplished were nice, but did not make up for falling short of our team goals. Jocelyne tied for number one in the nation in total points and number two in goals. I was sixth in points nationally and in the top twenty in goals. Both of us were Patty Kazmaier top-ten finalists, and Jocelyne was named to the top three. She was also named UND's Grace Rhonemus Female Athlete of the Year and the WCHA's scholar-athlete of the year. Jocelyne's perfect GPA earned her Academic All-American honors.

These accolades were nice. But we would have traded all of them for a championship.

I was also experiencing problems in my marriage, which I had been trying to conceal. Months before, Taylor and I had purchased a house together, which I shared with a roommate. That spring, in preparation for his four-year military commitment coming to an end, we began to talk in earnest about building a life together. In the process, I realized we had grown apart—that is, if we had ever really grown together.

The truth was painful. The longest we'd actually spent together was five weeks—the summer we got married in 2010. I would ask myself, how well do I know him? Is this really the person with whom I want to have a family and spend the rest of my life? I didn't want to admit that our parents were right, and we probably should have waited. So I didn't. I kept everything inside and avoided addressing these issues until they were unavoidable. In April, Taylor completed his service and flew from Hawaii to Vermont to watch me compete in the World Championships.

"It's one of those love stories that never gets old," wrote ESPN in a story about his homecoming. Headlined "Monique Lamoureux-Kolls Has No. 1 Fan," the article chronicled our relationship, although a careful read between the lines revealed that we had barely spent any time together. Taylor was on one side of the world, and I was on the other. Publicly, I pretended everything was great. I spoke about returning with him to Grand Forks and living as a married couple. But privately, even as I said those words, I knew that was a mistake. I was scared to let anyone know how I really felt, except Jocelyne.

JOCELYNE

I've never seen anyone handle as much as Monique did during our time in Vermont. She was going through a major life event off the ice and playing magnificently on it in one of the world's biggest tournaments. In our preliminary game against Canada, a 9–2 victory, she had six points and was named player of the game. After our next game, a 9–0 win over Russia, she led the team in total points. In the next outing, an 11–0 rout of Finland, she and Kelli Stack both scored three goals. Her mental toughness was incomparable.

No one suspected anything, even as we went into the final against Canada. The matchup was another classic. We clawed our way back from a 3–1 deficit, went into overtime with the score tied 4–4, and then lost when Canadian Caroline Ouellette connected on a pass out from Meghan Agosta and scored. Kendall Coyne, Brianna Decker, and Gigi Marvin scored for our side. "We showed a lot of heart and character," said Julie Chu, our team captain. None more so than Monique, I thought.

MONIQUE

Within a week of returning home, I recognized the profound difference between a long-distance relationship and the day-to-day reality of building a life together with a husband who I didn't really know, never mind love. One was manageable, while the other was impossible. I blamed myself for being in this situation, and the feeling it gave me was totally unfamiliar—thinking that I was a failure.

Unsure of what to do, I did nothing. I buried myself in books and term papers and studied for my final exams. I worked out. Going to the gym was my one escape. It was where I turned off my phone, stuck it in my locker, and forgot about everything else for a few hours. I knew that I couldn't keep this up forever, but gradually the routine gave me a sense of control. After two weeks of this, as well as quiet contemplation of my options, I decided my only choice was to admit the truth, face the consequences, and move on.

I moved into my parents' house on a Sunday night with finals coming up.

On Tuesday, Taylor moved out of the house. On Wednesday, a family friend helped put it up for sale. On Thursday, we opened it up to prospective buyers. I will never forget how, as Jocelyne and I sat on the curb out in front, I cried the last of my many tears, dried my eyes, and said, "I'm not going to let this define me. I have too many things I want to do and accomplish, and I won't let this stop any of it."

By the time our house sold, I was ready to turn the page. I still had a lot of healing and maturing to do. I went to bed those nights like most people. When my head hit the pillow, my mind was filled with questions. I wondered why I had been rash and ignored advice that was so obvious now. I wondered how this would affect my family. I wondered if they thought any less of me, even though they assured me with their words and hugs that they didn't. With the UND season ahead of us, I wondered the same about my teammates and coaches. Were they disappointed? Did I let anyone down other than myself? I wondered if I owed anyone an apology. I wondered if I could fully forgive myself.

I resolved to learn and grow from the experience. After six weeks of living with my parents, I rented an apartment in Jocelyne's building with one of my teammates. I continued to train with Jocelyne and our team throughout the summer. I let them pick me up when I was down and keep my spirit afloat. I carried on. I didn't give myself an alternative. I had to find my own strength, confidence, and more importantly, my own happiness. You can't get those things from other people.

I knew what I was going through and what I was feeling would be temporary, but I also knew that I had to self-reflect in order to learn from the experience.

This was an important and complicated time in my life, the same as many people go through at some point. It's an experience that has influenced the person I am today. I faced a less-than-ideal situation in my life, but I learned, I came out of it a little wiser, and ultimately, I was willing to let someone else in when the time was right.

TRIPLE OVERTIME

"Certain athletes want the pressure, they want to be difference makers."

JOCELYNE

Our senior year was about to start, although we had actually completed our undergraduate academics the previous year as a result of the online courses we took in 2010. We understood the confusion that created for some. But there was no confusion on the ice. We entered our final season with the Fighting Sioux ranked number five in the country and got off to a solid 4–2 start thanks to the most talented team our coaching staff had put together in our three years at UND.

In addition to Michelle Karvinen, the previous season's WCHA Rookie of the Year, Andrea Dalen, and Josefine Jakobsen, we also added players from both Canada and USA's U18 teams. The attitude was exceptional and reflected the kind of program we'd hoped would materialize while we were there. Players came in with the expectation that we would work hard and win often.

For Monique and me, there was a desire to help in the community, too—one that we were so pleased to see our teammates join. I would have moments where I was reminded of Coach Stafford's, "Just be a good person," and now, in his place, Peter would tell the team, "It's nice to be important, but it's more important to be nice." Through Brent, Monique and I had gotten involved with our local Special Olympics. One weekend, Special Olympics sponsored a dance, and a whole group of our teammates attended with us. The Special Olympics motto—"Let me win, but if I cannot win, let me be brave in the attempt"—fit in with our own approach to competition as did the smiles we always saw at Special Olympics events and reminded us that these games we played with such seriousness were also supposed to be fun.

I also saw that motto reflected in Monique, who was back to her old self. Since finalizing her divorce in September, she flew around the ice like she was having fun again. Not that she ever didn't. But she could finally take a deep breath with a weight being lifted off her shoulders, and at the same time, my load, being inextricably bound to hers, felt lighter too.

For us, the biggest test of the new season came in late October when Minnesota, the defending NCAA national champions, came to Grand Forks for a two-game series. Ranked number one again and off to an 8–0 start, the Gophers brought with them a lethal roster led by Finland's superstar goalie Noora Raty, plus Amanda Kessel, Megan Bozek, Hannah Brandt, and Lee Stecklein—all future Olympics teammates. We played hard in both games, but Minnesota was just too strong, and the Gophers went home with their unbeaten record intact.

By midweek, we were refocused and preparing for the next series. This is how sports work. Win or lose, there is always the next game, the next season, the next medal. Monique and I were feeling the pressure to win. We had transferred from Minnesota to UND and just got swept at home by the Gophers. There was never a time we regretted our decision, but there were moments where we felt the pressure of having set big goals for ourselves, the team, and the future of the UND program. And we weren't giving up on them.

We prepared for the following weekend of games against the number four–ranked team, Clarkson. We split the series, before going on a seven-game win streak right to Christmas. In the middle of that streak, Monique and I traveled to Finland and helped win the Four Nations Cup, before going on Christmas break.

MONIQUE

At home for Christmas, we enjoyed the family time. There was also much looking ahead to the last half of our senior year, which would surely be emotional—expectations around the playoffs, then the Worlds, and even further down the line was the big event that was like the bull ready to roar out of the gate, the 2014 Olympics in Sochi. There was a lot going on, but we did our best to stay present, which is the healthiest way to be—in the moment, dealing with whatever is directly in front of you.

Going into the second half of the season, we were focused, but we didn't forget to have fun. One day Monique was able to get Coach Idalski's car keys before practice. She, along with teammates Mary and Tori, waited for Coach to arrive at the rink, and then they got in the car and drove it down the bus ramp and through the Zamboni doors and parked it at center ice. We kept the lights off in the rink until Coach Idalski came out onto the ice. Without cracking a smile, he firmly said, "Practice still starts at eight." We hurried to get the car off the ice, unsure if he thought this prank was funny.

We closed the regular season in second place in our conference, the best finish in the team's history. Over three years, we had finished fourth, third, and now second. We played our last regular-season home game at the Ralph over senior weekend. Our team included eight seniors—Jorid Dagfinrud, Ashley Furia, Megan Gilbert, Allison Parizek, Jordan Slavin, Mary Loken, and the two of us. A senior tribute video played as the eight of us stood with our arms around each other. Our parents, Grandma Edith, and brother, Pierre-Paul, were in the stands for the emotional event. Video highlights from our careers were played on the Jumbotron. The local paper called our career statistics "absurd"—a combined 229 goals, 304 assists, 533 points. Our favorite tribute came from Ohio State coach Nate Handrahan, who shook our hands and said, "I'm so glad we don't have to play against the two of you anymore."

Again, for us, individual statistics took a back seat to wins and team accomplishments. And we still had our conference finals, the Frozen Faceoff, the furthest our team had gotten in program history. No matter that we were going up against our old team and frequent opponent, the Minnesota Gophers, who had gone through the season undefeated and were in the midst of an incredible win streak that would make them the greatest women's hockey team in collegiate history. We believed we could beat them. It turned out that we lost in the finals 2–0, but we rallied ourselves for a rematch the next week in the opening round of the NCAA tournament, convinced that whichever team won was going all the way.

We still talk about that game, which was one of the monumental games of our careers. Played at Ridder Arena in Minneapolis, our two teams battled into the last minute of triple overtime. We led 2–1 early in the second period of regulation before Minnesota tied the score 2–2, which is where the score stayed seemingly forever. The intensity heightened minute after minute, while players somehow found the energy for one shift after another.

Between overtime periods, players were swapping out socks, blow-drying gloves, and changing their undergear because everything was soaked in sweat. The benches were shortened, and we rolled every other shift. It was the kind of game with the kind of moments that we trained for. That we lived for.

Jocelyne, who totaled an amazing fifty minutes on the ice, nearly gave us the win in the first overtime when her quick deke opened up the net, but her shot hit the post, and her expression of astonishment and exasperation was shared by all of us. A few minutes later, I took a shot, and in my mind, I saw the puck going in the net. But it hit a post too. Really? Was that even possible? What cruelty were the hockey gods handing out?

Finally, the Gophers broke the logjam, putting a shot past our goalie an astounding sixty-two minutes after the last goal had been scored in regulation. Minnesota got the victory, 3–2, and went on to win the entire NCAA championship again, finishing the season undefeated and justifiably earning the accolade of being the greatest women's hockey team in NCAA history.

It was a bittersweet end to our college careers, a great game to be a part of, and one we would never forget. It just didn't end in our favor. We were emotionally and physically drained after the game. Two of our brothers—Philippe and Jacques—were in the stands that night. For Philippe and Jacques, it was the only game they ever saw us play in UND jerseys, which made it truly special for us.

After the game, we walked up to the concourse level to see them, and I was hit by a wave of exhaustion. I could barely stand. My back and feet ached. Jocelyne and I crouched down, so sore from the game that we couldn't stand up straight. When we got to our phones, we saw that we each had a voice mail on our phone from Mario, who was in California playing in the ECHL but had followed the drama online. "I'm so proud of both of you," he said.

As tough as this loss was, it reinforced for us the overriding importance of family. And for us, making our family proud was just as important as a victory in any game.

Before the night ended, we got one more chance to be difference makers. When we boarded the bus taking us back to Grand Forks, we found our dinner—pizzas. Having been delivered about four hours earlier, timed for the game to end in regulation, they were no longer warm and not very appetizing. No one wanted them. From my seat in the back of the bus, I asked if people were hungry. "Starving," they said. I walked up to the front and asked Coach Idalski if we could stop at McDonald's. A short time later, we pulled up in front of the golden arches. Everyone cheered, and I ended my college career by making an impact.

JOCELYNE

A few weeks later, we went to Ottawa, Canada, for Worlds. It was early April, and by now, this tournament, like the Four Nations in November, was as much a part of our calendar as birthdays and holidays. We circled the dates and planned our lives around the trips, although, as we learned over the years, nothing was ever guaranteed. For instance, Kelli Stack tore her ACL the previous December; that put her out for eight months and marked the end of the Stacksicles. It also meant the coaching staff had to figure out where we fit in.

Not that we worried—too much. We were a fast, scrappy team, and we fit right in, as was apparent in Ottawa. Although we dropped our opening game to Canada 3–2 in a shootout, we settled down once round-robin play started, cruising past Finland 4–2, topping Switzerland 5–0, and then besting Finland again, this time 3–0 on excellent all-around team play, to reach the finals against Canada. These tournaments had the feel of big Hollywood movie franchises. *The Matrix, The Matrix 2…The Matrix 4.* You knew the characters and the story line. The only mystery was how it would turn out at the end.

This time, we beat Canada 3–2, after Amanda Kessel broke a tie with a bullet that whistled through the smallest opening between the net and Canada's goalie Shannon Szabados. "We all showed up and played great, and it paid off," said our coach, Katey Stone. That fact was undeniable. An unselfish, all-around team effort got us the title. But something else about her statement—*we all showed up*—hit home with me.

I might not have fully realized the connection then, but I spent my free time in Ottawa finishing my literature review for my master's thesis, "Should Girls Play Hockey with Boys: Perspectives from the USA Women's Olympic Hockey Team." I would end up interviewing my teammates and hearing their stories, many of which were similar to Monique's and mine. They underscored the importance of *showing up*, so to speak—maybe not as Coach Stone meant it, but of serving as a positive role model, opening doors, and sending a message to younger generations of girls that they didn't have to limit their goals or measure themselves against boys. Young girls could be better than boys, as many of us were, even if they weren't physically bigger than boys. And they could dream big, as all of us had.

My thesis took a data-driven, quantitative approach to answering the question, but underlying the numbers were stories of passion and perseverance. Those stories were similar to Monique's and my own—with struggles and negative experiences that were overshadowed by the successes and rewards of playing against boys until physical differences made it impractical and dangerous. At that point, girls played hockey against other girls, and in the process, found others like themselves: talented, driven, goal-oriented, uncompromising, and passionate. They could feel accepted and, most importantly, be themselves.

I wrote that, by and large, the "participants reported positive effects from playing with boys on skating, shooting, stick-handling, passing, positional play, as well as confidence, competitiveness, leadership, and enjoyment."

I found the number of girls playing competitive sports was on the rise and continuing to grow. However, according to the Women's Sports Foundation, there were 1.3 million fewer opportunities for girls to compete in organized sports than for boys. Besides the obvious inequity, the disparity showed that sometimes—or perhaps oftentimes—playing on a girls' team is not a possibility. Playing on a boys' team might be the only option. It was a fascinating window, not only into gender differences but also into the qualities of character that drive some to compete simply because something inside drives them to be the best.

Gigi Marvin, whose grandfather is in the Hockey Hall of Fame, played against boys and even grown men as she honed her game in Warroad, Minnesota. Kendall Coyne and Megan Bozek grew up in Chicago, playing on boys' teams. Kendall's parents started her in figure skating with the other girls while her older brother played hockey with the boys. After a week, she wanted to be on the ice with her brother, racing around with a stick and shooting the puck. "What it came down to for me was growing up playing with the boys," she said years later. "There were no limits."

Legendary NHL skills coach Kenny McCudden was all for girls playing with boys and believed there was something special about those who did. "If I see a ponytail out there playing with boys, I stop," he said. "I'm really, really excited to know who she is, where she comes from, and why she is playing boys' hockey."

Work on my thesis made me feel the same way. I felt like I was onto something. I realized that our stories weren't unlike so many female athletes who came before us, like Billie Jean King, Cammi Granato, Venus and Serena Williams, and the 99ers.

MONIQUE

A few days after we got back, we received an unexpected honor from the mayor of Grand Forks, Michael R. Brown, when he declared April 15 as Jocelyne and Monique Lamoureux Day. We didn't give it too much thought but later learned that it was a big deal. At the time, it was something our parents took more pride in than we did as they stood off to the side while an official proclamation was read listing our accomplishments as Olympians, All-American collegiate athletes, and students whose GPAs earned Academic All-American honors.

The discomfort we felt standing there was worth it for the way the honor made our mom and dad feel. All that time spent in the van driving to practices and games, picking us up at school, waiting in the drive-thru—and now, there was the mayor proclaiming it Jocelyne and Monique Lamoureux Day in Grand Forks. A few weeks later, I was named UND's Grace Rhonemus Student-Athlete of the Year, the same award Jocelyne had won the previous year. In both cases, Jocelyne and I were referred to as trailblazers, groundbreakers, and role models for other girls in our community.

Although it wasn't our intention, we knew we could be a positive influence on those around us and on those following us, and we embraced that role and responsibility. It's the way we were raised. Also, you couldn't put on a USA jersey and play for the national team without understanding that representing your country came with a responsibility. Standing at attention during a medal ceremony, while the national anthem played, always brought that home and reminded us what it meant to be Americans.

The next stop, we hoped, was making our second Olympic team—and going to Sochi.

1 7

SOCHI

★

"When you think you've given your all, give a little bit more."

MONIQUE

In June 2013, we were in Lake Placid, participating in the seven-day camp that would determine the twenty-five players who would train together up to the 2014 Winter Olympics. In most ways, the camp was like so many others we had been to over the years. Those in charge—Reagan Carey, the director of women's hockey for USA Hockey, and head coach Katey Stone—were familiar. So were the players, from veteran Julie Chu, who was hoping to go to her fourth Olympic games, to Hilary Knight, Meghan Duggan, Kacey Bellamy, and Jessie Vetter.

But there were some not-so-subtle differences that made this camp unlike any other we'd been to in the past. First and foremost, the pressure to win gold in Sochi. You didn't have to be adept at reading tea leaves to realize the staff had been given a mandate. Coach Stone made that clear when she told *USA Today*, "There has been tremendous talent in this program, but the results have not been satisfactory."

In other words, having taken first place in five of the last seven World Championships was great, but in this Olympic year, only one thing mattered, winning gold, which the U.S. Olympic Women's Ice Hockey Team hadn't done since 1998. Anything other than gold would be considered a disappointment.

The message was relayed to us at the start of camp. Coach Stone compared making the final roster to the most competitive job interview any of us would ever have. Nobody had an easy path onto the team. There were no guarantees, gimmes, or sure things, even for those of us who had been on the national team in previous Olympics or World Championships. That was relayed to Jocelyne and me in a separate aside, where we were reminded that we had to make the team as individuals. We weren't a package deal, we were told, although it felt otherwise when coaches clearly couldn't tell us apart on or off the ice.

At the end of camp, the roster was announced, and both of our names were listed among the twenty-five players who would be training together for the next six months. In August, we moved to Boston to begin the six-month residency program. We had just graduated college, didn't know the Boston area, and couldn't really afford rent. So a group of us decided to move in with billet families—folks who were gracious enough to take us in for six months. It turned out to be a positive experience for most of us and a way to feel settled away from the rink.

Every day felt like a tryout. In practices, we were constantly reminded that no one's spot was guaranteed. Maybe that was due to a lack of imagination or the fact that there was very little that had to be said to motivate the best women hockey players in the country, all type-A overachievers who had dreamed their entire lives of winning an Olympic gold medal. I remember leaning against the boards, sighing to Jocelyne as this familiar message was being delivered, "We know. No one's spot is guaranteed. We got it."

What was already a stressful environment was exacerbated by hearing this same message repeated over and over. It was exhausting and ultimately counterproductive. As a player, you're always aware that cuts still have to be made. It's the big elephant in the room. As players, our preference is to back channel that anxiety and instead work on a good, healthy, cohesive team dynamic that brings out our best. I don't know for sure, but it could have been that the coaches were feeling their own stress, and this was the way they compensated for it.

In our experience, fear is not usually the best way to motivate people. It has a shelf life. It may work for a little while, and you may get results for a short period of time, but eventually, performance will suffer. I think this was the case in November's Four Nations Cup, where we finished a surprising and disappointing third place.

The tournament was in Lake Placid, and as a team, we were in a rough place. There was tension between the staff and players. One of those tension points related to social media. The coaches thought it was a distraction—so much so that social media use started to be restricted. What they didn't understand was that some of us had sponsors and were contractually obligated to post.

Social media was still new at the time. What wasn't new, though, was the limited opportunity we had as female athletes to earn outside income from our sport, and we had to capitalize whenever possible.

Without any warning or suspicion, I was scratched in our game against Finland, which we lost. It was the upset of the tournament. No explanation was ever

Our two-year-old portrait (*Left to right*: Monique and Jocelyne).

Getting the two of us and our four brothers all together for any picture was a challenge. To get us all to look at once was even more difficult. (*Left to right*: Pierre-Paul, Monique, Mario, Jacques, Philippe, and Jocelyne).

About to head onto the Eagles Arena ice at age seven for practice with our dad after he just finished coaching our brother's team. (*Left to right*: Jocelyne, Pierre, Monique, and Pierre-Paul).

Our Shattuck-St. Mary's School senior class during picture day for the hockey program. (*Left to right*: Lauren Rogalsky, Julie Pesta, Jocelyne, Emily Johnson, Margot Miller, Sammy Phillips, Amanda Castignetti, Barb Bilko, and Monique).

Our last game at the Ralph Engelstad Arena as seniors for the University of North Dakota. The school eliminated its women's hockey team as we were leaving for the 2017 World Championships. The eight of us took a moment to enjoy the senior tribute video. (*Left to right*: Ali Parizek, Jorid Dagfinrud, Jordin Slavin, Ashley Furia, Megan Gilbert, Jocelyne, Mary Loken, and Monique).

Brent and Jocelyne enjoying speeches during their wedding reception, June 20, 2014.

Monique and Anthony exchanging vows on their wedding day, May 13, 2016.

Celebrating our fifth World Championship in 2016 that was hosted in Kamloops, British Columbia, with a 1-0 victory over Canada in overtime. (*Left to right*: Jocelyne, Kelli Stack, Meghan Duggan, Kacey Bellamy, and Monique).

After the entire 2017 World Championship roster and player pool threatened to boycott the World Championships, USA Hockey and players met in Philadelphia at the Ballard Spahr office to negotiate. Negotiations lasted over ten hours, and this would be the beginning of what would become a historic four-year agreement for the women's national team. On March 20, 2017, players took a photo with the Ballard team knowing this would be a groundbreaking day. (*Top row, left to right*: John Langel, Esq., Gigi Marvin, Jocelyne, Kacey Bellamy, Meghan Duggan, Diane Spagnuolo, Esq., Mary Cate Gordon, Esq., Ashley Wilson, Esq. B*ottom row, left to right:* Hilary Knight, Kendall Coyne, Kelli Stack, Monique, Brianna Decker, Kim Magrini, Esq.).

Celebrating our sixth World Championship victory in Plymouth, MI, with another overtime win in 2017, following our near boycott and successful negotiations with USA Hockey. (*Left to right*: Jocelyne and Monique).

The gold medal–winning women's ice hockey team posing with our medals in PyeongChang before heading to closing ceremonies with the rest of Team USA.

Brent and Anthony threw us a surprise welcome-home party with family and friends after we returned home from the post-Olympic victory tour. Coach Stafford came for the occasion, and we couldn't have been more thankful. (*Left to right*: Monique, Coach Stafford, Jocelyne).

Our mom ignited our Olympic dream when we were six years old. Celebrating a gold medal with her was a dream come true. (*Left to right*: Jocelyne, Linda, Monique).

In Philadelphia with Avery Hakstol, showing her a couple of our World Championship rings. This was just weeks before announcing our threat to boycott the 2017 World Championships in Plymouth, MI. Avery sent us a "keeper" text after the negotiations, thanking us for standing up for girl hockey players. (*Left to right*: Jocelyne, Avery, Monique).

Sharing our medals with kindergarten students in Boston during their first day of school. One young boy asked if they were big coins.

Enjoying an Internet Essentials event with Jackie Joyner-Kersee, one of our most important Olympic idols.
(*Left to right*: Jocelyne, Jackie, Monique).

Nelson and Mickey on the ice with us in Pittsburgh, PA, at our second USA Hockey event since their birth.
(*Left to right*: Jocelyne and Nelson, Monique and Mickey).

The Davidsons' Easter photo from 2020.

Mickey's first birthday party in 2019.

Mika Brzezinski, along with David Cohen, introduces the two of us as Comcast's new ambassadors for its corporate values initiatives, making us the face of the company's programs to encourage volunteerism, diversity/inclusion, and close the digital divide. This event took place in the famous 30 Rock, and David surprised us by sneaking our parents into New York City to witness the announcement.

Speaking at TEDx Fargo in 2018 in front of a sold-out crowd where we received a standing ovation.
(*Photograph courtesy of J. Alan Paul Photography*).

given to me; I was just told that I wasn't suiting up. It was the first time I had been a healthy scratch for a national team game—or any game for that matter.

It was new territory for me, and it was territory I didn't like being in, watching from the stands when I was perfectly fit and capable of playing. But I needed to manage my irritation and keep my head in the game. I had to continue to be a good teammate and have a good attitude. When things are not going right, or you are in a slump, having a bad attitude usually keeps you going in the same direction for a longer period of time. So I cheered from the stands and then played hard when I returned to the lineup, but the third-place finish in the tournament was a bummer for everyone.

When we arrived back in Boston, two players were released from the team. As the rest of us knew, two more players still had to be released before the roster would be finalized on January 1. With about two months to go before Sochi, it felt like we had hit rock bottom. In terms of our spirit, there was no question, we were at an all-time low. But this was when the friendships and respect we had for each other from the past four years, or in some cases much longer, became so important.

We recognized it was time for us as a group of players to decide which direction we wanted to go. We could keep going in the direction we were going, and that direction would not get us the results we wanted, or we could get back to work, ignore the noise outside of the locker room, and change the course we were on.

JOCELYNE

After Four Nations, the team made a bit of a turnaround. Forward lines and defensive pairings started to become set. Monique and I played on a line with Meghan Duggan. The team got some much-needed consistency and stability. In December, we played four exhibition games against Canada, the ultimate test of our readiness. As a measure of the heights this rivalry between our two teams was taking women's hockey, NBC Sports Network and the Universal Sports Network televised all four games, which had never been done during a pre-Olympic tour before.

We gave fans a show, starting on December 12 in Calgary, where we won 5–1. A week later, we met again, this time in our hockey-crazed hometown of Grand Forks. Our parents, Grandma Edith, Brent, and our brothers, Jacques and Pierre-Paul, who was just back from deployment in Kuwait, were among the nearly six thousand screaming fans at the Ralph chanting "USA." Both Monique and I scored in the 4–1 victory, as did Hilary Knight and Brianna Decker.

With the game in hand, our coaches took exception to some unnecessary contact by Canada in the final minutes. As we got tapped to go out on the ice for the next shift, Coach Stone gave everyone the green light to take care of business. At the time, we were trying to keep our physical play in check and play a more responsible game. Still, when the coach tells you to do something, you do it, especially when you're trying to make a roster. A scuffle ensued, after which the refs handed out ten penalties. The crowd roared as the penalty box filled up on both sides. While I didn't love being celebrated for the penalties, I didn't mind the girls in the arena seeing us send a message that you have to stand up for your teammates.

Afterward, we signed autographs for an hour and a half. It was midnight when we got back to the hotel. Despite the late hour, we were told to go right to our meeting room. On the way, the staff pulled two players, Lisa Chesson and Annie Pankowski. All of us guessed, correctly as it turned out, that they were going to be the last two players released from the team. Then the coaches came in and informed those of us in the room that we had made the 2014 U.S. Olympic Women's Ice Hockey Team.

We played two more games against Canada, winning both, making that four straight wins against the Canadians leading into the Olympics. Those games lifted our confidence and put our heads in a positive space. The difference was night and day and where you want to be heading into a big competition. Even the coaching staff acknowledged that we were in a good spot, although Coach Stone cautioned that we still had more than a month before our first game in Sochi and a lot of work to do until then.

MONIQUE

Around that time, we learned that Nike had redone its design of our new Olympic jerseys to include the year 1998 on the collar as a tribute to the women's hockey team's past gold-medal victory. This repaired a major glitch in our road to Sochi. When the original jerseys were debuted to the press a few months earlier, the new jerseys featured the dates 1960 and 1980 stitched onto the back of the neckline as tributes to the two years the men's team won Olympic gold, leaving those of us on the women's team to ask, what about our gold medal in 1998?

USA Hockey also had a player from the men's team at the press event, but no women. Why not someone from our team? For that matter, what about the men's sled hockey team? They won gold in 2002 and 2010.

We accepted an apology, and the remade jerseys were just fine. The oversight wasn't intentional or malicious. It was worse. Here we were, eleven former Olympians, twenty-one World Champions, and five Patty Kazmaier Award recipients—probably with more trophies and titles than any women's hockey team the US had ever assembled—and we weren't even on the radar of USA Hockey. The women's team wasn't even part of the conversation.

It never sat well with the team, and it would resurface in the future as one of myriad examples that were part of a much larger issue.

JOCELYNE

On February 2, following a long flight from Boston to Munich, where we were processed before traveling the final leg to Sochi, we finally arrived at the Olympic village. Unlike Vancouver, where all the venues were scattered, everything in Sochi was clustered within walking distance (except the alpine events, which were in the Caucasus mountains, which rose off in the distance like jagged pylons). Much was made about the security in the village because of terrorist attacks happening in Russia before the Olympics, but we felt safe. We were instructed not to leave the village anyway.

After nearly a week of practices, we opened play against Finland, our first game against the Finns since losing to them in the Four Nations Cup. This time, we won 3–1. Two days later, we added a lopsided victory against Switzerland, 9–0. In the first period, Monique, Brianna Decker, and Amanda Kessel all scored in less than a minute, a record for the most goals scored in a minute in Olympic history. The victory ensured we wouldn't leave Sochi without at least playing for a medal, but none of us was thinking about playing for third place. That wasn't why we were there.

Next up in the round-robin was Canada. Both of us were 2–0 and headed for the semifinals, so the game's outcome wasn't going to determine either team's fate. But every game we played in these Olympics felt like it was for a gold medal. That was what made our 3–2 loss so alarming. We were sluggish and undisciplined. Compared to our previous games and the way we played all through December, we had suffered a lapse. We knew it. The coaching staff knew it. And after the game, we received the thorough chewing out we deserved.

Five days later, we played our semifinal against Sweden. Fired up and eager to prove ourselves, we recaptured the form and fury that had eluded us the previous game. A 6–1 victory landed us in the gold-medal matchup everyone wanted to see.

MONIQUE

In the three days between games, we practiced, watched videos of Canada's team in action against us, tried to relax, and did all the other things necessary to prepare for the biggest game of our lives up to that point. We tried to get a good night's sleep and stick to our routine, going into game day. But there was nothing routine about this contest. Our two teams had met numerous times. Canada had beat us the previous week. We had won four consecutive games against them going into the Olympics. We knew each other's strengths and weaknesses as well as we knew ourselves. And as with every great rivalry—and ours was, and continues to be one of the greatest in all of sports—there was no telling what would happen.

Not much happened in the first period, but we were playing well. In the second period, Meghan Duggan broke the 0–0 tie and launched a wrist shot past Canada's goalie Shannon Szabados. We continued to pour on the pressure for the rest of the second period. Then Alex Carpenter opened the third with a power-play goal that put us up 2–0. I can't explain why, but midway through the third period, our coaches shifted strategy, and it had the unintended effect of slowing us down.

Until this change, we were outshooting Canada, outplaying them, and with a two-goal lead, it felt like we were on our way to a gold medal. But now, every time we crossed the red line, we dumped the puck, sat back, and tried to hang onto the lead. It opened the door to a change in momentum—and luck.

With 3:26 left in the game, Canada got on the board after an errant shot caromed off Kacey Bellamy's leg and into the net. Then, with a minute and a half to go, the Canadians pulled their goalie. Fully expected. Not a problem. We won the draw, we rimmed the puck, and Kelli Stack iced it toward the empty Canadian net. From the bench, I followed her shot as it traveled down the ice. Everyone watched and waited breathlessly—the thousands in the arena and millions more staring at the screen on their TV, phone, or computer.

Those at home almost had enough time to run to the fridge and get another drink. That's how slow the puck seemed to travel. But it looked straight and on target. I was poised to leap in the air and erupt with a loud cheer. We were going to be up by two goals again, with time running out. But then...

Tink!

Instead of going in the net, the puck hit the post and died.

I couldn't believe that happened. None of us could. With only fifty-five seconds left in regulation play, Marie-Philip Poulin tied the game, 2–2, sending us into overtime. On our way to the locker room, we walked past several attendants holding the gold medals in trays in preparation for the medal ceremony. They were clearly still up for grabs—and we wanted them, badly. The locker room was thick with disappointment and tension. Every player knew that we had been so close that we could feel them putting the gold medals around our necks.

Julie Chu clapped her hands and snapped us to attention. It was time to refocus for overtime. We had to manufacture enthusiasm and excitement. "When you think you've given your all, give a little bit more," she said.

We tried—we really did—and when I close my eyes, I see Jocelyne and Hilary in the penalty box, along with a Canadian player, all three of them in there for debatable calls, and I see my teammates digging deep and really straining to kill off a four-on-three penalty. But Canadian Laura Fortino faked a shot and passed it to Marie-Philip Poulin left of the net on the faceoff dot. She had plenty of time to shoot into a relatively open net as Jessie Vetter went down and was not in position to stop the puck. That was it, game over. We had lost 3–2.

I put my head down and thought, *Not again*. I did not want to see what had just happened. I did not want to look up and see our opponents celebrating amid the devastation felt by those of us in the red, white, and blue jerseys. We were the better team for fifty-seven minutes, but those three minutes were all it took for it to slip away. We didn't get it done. Canada never gave up and never stopped believing. That's the beauty and agony of sports: no medal, championship, or victory is ever guaranteed.

We went limp. There we were, on the ice in Sochi, watching Canada celebrate another gold medal, but suffering a whole new level of heartbreak because we had been so close. Some of us had to take a knee as we waited for the commotion on the ice to clear and our tears to finally stop.

JOCELYNE

Monique was pulled for drug testing (again) and wasn't in the locker room with us after the medal ceremony. The coaches came in and talked, but I can't remember a word they said. Only what Amanda Kessel said stands out. Amanda doesn't say much in the locker room, but we were all sitting there in silence, still in our gear, still stunned, still in a fog of disbelief, and she said, "Chuey"—referring to veteran Julie Chu, who had just finished her fourth Olympics and was ending her career with three silver medals and one bronze—"I can't even look at you right now. I am so sorry." That was everything I felt too—everything we all felt.

MONIQUE

It was nearly one in the morning when I got back to the locker room. Everyone but Jocelyne had already left. We didn't say much as I got out of my gear, showered, and dressed. We didn't have to talk to know the way each other felt. A few hours later, I was on the phone with former teammate Angela Ruggiero, who helped us to start putting the loss in perspective. "As athletes, I know you're disappointed," she said. "It's heartbreaking, and nothing will ever take away the sting of that loss. But when you come home and meet other people, they don't give a shit what color your medal is. They just see that you're an Olympian—and they know that makes you pretty damn special."

She was right. As much as it stung to lose that game, and still does to this day, the hurt diminished as time passed, and we came to understand that our impact on the sport and future generations of girls with dreams like ours could be so much greater than any single medal. Even as time has proven that to be true, our dream was always to win a gold medal together. We knew it would be extremely difficult and require hard work and lucky breaks beyond our control, but we never imagined getting so close only to fall short—not once, but twice. We knew we weren't done chasing gold.

Anyone who was close to us, and knew us as people and athletes, understood that we wouldn't end on that note. Retirement wasn't even an option because we refused to let our hockey story end with a silver medal in Sochi.

Part 3

THE BATTLE FOR
EQUITY AND GOLD

★ ★ ★

18

A RECIPE FOR SUCCESS

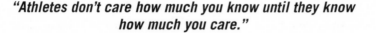

"Athletes don't care how much you know until they know
how much you care."

JOCELYNE

After the Olympics, out of school, and having successfully completed my masters, I was fortunate that I didn't have to do much soul-searching to figure out what was next for me. Grand Forks was big enough to satisfy my small-town values and sensibilities—and enabled me to be close to family and friends. I found a job as a strength coach and worked with the UND women's hockey team while training and competing with the national team.

But first things first. I had been playing through a nagging shoulder injury for a few seasons and took the opportunity to schedule surgery to repair and rehab it. Then I planned a summer wedding to my longtime boyfriend-turned-fiancé Brent Davidson.

After three years, Brent had become the person who knew me better than anyone. He was the first person I called after games and the one I looked to for those all-too-frequent and always-inconvenient airport pickups and drop-offs. Obviously, I am making light of the way our relationship had grown into a deep commitment to each other. Then, in May 2013, right after Worlds, Brent let me know that he was ready to make his commitment permanent with a surprise proposal I still can't believe he pulled off.

One Friday morning, Monique and I went to the Ralph to get our workout in, but this time our close friend Kayla Berg, a college player herself, came with us to skate that day. Monique and I finished our workout, and then the three of us got on the ice together.

Suddenly, Kayla said she forgot her water bottle and dashed off the ice. Monique and I waited for her in front of the net. As soon as Kayla left the ice, though, the lights went out, and we were standing next to each other in the pitch-black arena. A moment later, a video started to play on the Jumbotron, and Monique left the ice, saying that she was going to go check what was going on. *Okay, no big deal,* I thought.

I made my way over to the penalty box, where I saw Monique and Kayla were sitting while still watching the video on the Jumbotron. The opening frame said, "Where we first met," and I thought, *Oh, there must be a wedding coming this weekend.* People often rented the arena for weddings, and I assumed they were testing the video. Except I recognized the house on the screen belonged to our friends Greg and Heather Lotysz. Then there was a picture of Brent and me, and all of a sudden, I was like, holy shit! This was happening…to me!

Monique quickly told me to go back to where I was previously standing on the ice. Once I was there, Brent stepped out from the locker-room tunnel. The spotlight went on and followed him as he walked over to me. After we finished watching the video, he dropped to one knee and asked if I would marry him. Even though I was in total shock, I didn't hesitate to say yes. Our families and several friends, who were watching from one of the private suites, broke into applause, and as I looked up there, I heard UND's men's hockey coach Dane Jackson yell, "What'd she say?"

As surprises go, it was perfect—and so, in my opinion, was our wedding. We married on June 20, 2014, in a traditional ceremony held in the Grand Forks church I attended growing up. It was a beautiful day, and the simple celebration, with family and friends in attendance, came off without a hitch. And since most things that happened to me also happened to Monique, more than a few people that night took a long look at her boyfriend, strength and conditioning coach Anthony Morando, and wondered about the new chapter she seemed to be writing with him.

MONIQUE

Anthony and I met in 2012 when UND played Boston University in Grand Forks. Jocelyne and I showed Anthony around the UND weight room as a favor to Mike Boyle, our strength coach from the national team. But that pretty uneventful, courtesy tour was the extent of our contact until our paths crossed again about ten months later in the Woburn gym owned by Mike Boyle, where we worked out during the national team's East Coast residency leading up to the Sochi Olympics. A Boston native, Anthony had a longtime association with Mike, working with Boston University's men's hockey team and numerous professional and collegiate athletes.

After a few months of seeing him regularly in the gym, I took a stab at wishing him and Boston University luck before one of their weekend series. I messaged him on Facebook, which opened the door to more conversation. Then he asked me out on a date. It was a Sunday, the same day the New England Patriots were play-ing in the AFC championship game, so our date had to wait until after the game.

Anthony and I spent four hours at the restaurant without ordering food. Then we went out for dinner the next night and the night after that, and it was clear pretty quickly that both of us were cut from the same cloth, even though our backgrounds and upbringings were drastically different. His attitude and work ethic matched mine. "Be humble or be humbled," he said.

By the Olympics, we were unofficially a couple. Soon after we returned from Sochi, I decided that I would return to Boston in the spring for an internship, to play hockey, train, to finish my graduate degree—and also to live with Anthony. I was excited about my future with him, but I dreaded putting fifteen hundred miles between Jocelyne and me. Saying goodbye to her was one of the hardest things I have ever had to do.

I left for Boston at the end of a weekend. I was driving back east by myself—twenty hours. I hadn't been in the car very long when Anthony called me to ask how I was doing after saying goodbye to Jocelyne. I muttered something unin-telligible. "I'll call you back," he said.

He understood how hard it was for me to not be around my twin every sin-gle day. Even now, we can spend most of the day together and not long after we get home, one of us will call or text the other. "Weren't you two just together?" one or both of our husbands will ask, and we will nod yeah, and say, "I had a question," or, "It was important," even though it wasn't. We might grow up, and we have, but we will never grow out of all the wonders and invisible ties of being identical twins. Even though I have Anthony and Jocelyne has Brent, we are still each other's people too.

With Anthony, in fact, I got a future husband, and Jocelyne and I both got a coach. To prep for the Four Nations Cup, I trained with him at BU, starting in August. On my first day there, I ran two three-hundred-yard shuttles. I don't remember if he timed me, but he watched carefully. My legs didn't feel great that day, and my times weren't great either. Afterward, I threw up, which wasn't uncommon for me after hard-conditioning days.

My power output was no better. "Okay, we're strong," he said. "We're fairly fit. But there's something not clicking. There's a disconnect. Let's work to find it and fix it."

Jocelyne soon started the same program in Grand Forks. We asked a ton of questions. We always wanted to know why things were going to help us. Recognizing this, Anthony took time to explain everything—why we did certain things on certain days and how he expected us to progress from phase to phase. He realized the more we understood, the deeper we took the exercise.

Outside of hockey, our lives were moving in the direction we wanted them to. Over Christmas, Anthony came home with me for the holiday and asked my dad for permission to propose to me. With Brent, my dad took out a notebook, asked a series of questions, started jotting down notes, and invited my mom to be a part of the conversation. I think they were a little gun-shy with how my first proposal went, but with Anthony, Dad choked up and said, "Welcome to the family," and quickly added, "Let's go tell Linda."

In May 2015, we moved back to Grand Forks. The local hospital partnered with EXOS, a world-renowned fitness and performance company, which hired Anthony as the performance manager in the new gym. Jocelyne was already working for the hospital, and she would be joining Anthony at the new facility. The two of us were elated to be together in the same city again.

Under Anthony's tutelage, our strength and conditioning and overall fitness improved immediately and every year thereafter. He is one of the main reasons we had so much success throughout the four years leading into the 2018 Olympics. In both the 2015 Worlds and Four Nations Cup, played under new head coach Ken Klee, we beat Canada in the finals. At the World Championships, Hilary Knight was the MVP, I was named to the all-star team, and Jocelyne was among the leading scorers in the tournament, even though she didn't play in one of the games.

Although Anthony won't take credit for it, I believe Jocelyne and I were able to take our game to the next level because of him. We'd always worked hard, but with him, we worked smarter. The improvements we made were obvious enough for coaches and staff to ask us what we were doing at home when it came to training. We both increased our verticals by over four inches within two years, which is rare for elite athletes who have been training as long as we have. Our conditioning numbers had never been anything to brag about, as our results always put us in the middle of the pack. But there are moments when your work truly shows. In our three-hundred-yard shuttle test in Colorado Springs, at the Olympic Training Center, Jocelyne and I both finished in the top three—which opened everyone's eyes. Anthony's attention to detail paralleled our type-A personalities. Also, his understanding of us as athletes and as individuals was the secret sauce to our success. He knew how to push the right buttons, when to rein it in, when to push hard, and when to ignore our many questions.

His approach and passion took me back to a time when Coach Stafford said, "Athletes don't care how much you know until they know how much you care." We knew Anthony cared. We knew that we were going to get his best, and he knew that we would give him our best.

In May of 2016, soon after the World Championships, Anthony and I got married. Our wedding day had sleet, snow, and rain, apparently a sign of good luck. We spoke our own vows in a ceremony with one hundred of our closest friends and family there to celebrate. It was exactly what we hoped for—simple, low-key, and fun. I only wish our basset hound, Millie, had been able to attend.

19

INEQUITIES—TIME TO MAKE A STATEMENT

⭐

"The message these issues sent boiled down to one thing—respect."

JOCELYNE

All of us on the national team were looking down the road to the 2018 Winter Olympics in Pyeongchang, but now that many of us were out of college, getting there posed a whole new set of challenges. Monique and I juggled jobs, our daily training, and our personal lives the best we could. As post-grad female athletes, it was harder than we imagined to make it all work without the infrastructure and resources of our school hockey program. USA Hockey provided small living stipends for the six months we spent in residency every four years before the Olympics. Outside of that six-month window, we received a monthly training stipend, which ranged from $500–$2,000 per athlete that was funded by the USOPC (the National Olympic and Paralympic Committee for the United States). Otherwise, we were on our own financially, as we tried to figure out how to maintain our status as elite-level hockey players and keep our gold-medal dreams alive. It was a real struggle.

And it wasn't just the two of us. Kelli Stack signed with the National Women's Hockey League when it launched in 2015—and played for a pittance. Several players considered going overseas to play professional hockey in Sweden and Russia. Meghan Duggan coached at Clarkson University and played in the CWHL/NWHL during the 2014–2016 seasons. Alex Rigsby and Megan Bozek had jobs with flexible employers who allowed them to take time off or work remotely to be at camps and tournaments. Monique and I got jobs, but had to juggle attendance with national camps. We started hockey camps. We coached. We trained. We asked for favors to get ice time.

This was the life of elite women athletes aspiring to play in the Olympics. We picked up odds-and-ends jobs while trying to train at a high level and make it to Pyeongchang. But the grueling schedule wasn't conducive to honing our skills and getting ready to play for our country in the Four Nations Cup, the World Championships, or the Olympics. It was exhausting. I got sick at a rate that I had never experienced before, but I had no choice but to keep burning that candle at both ends. Pathetically, it was what we had to do. It was what the players who came before us had to do. It was the way it had always been.

This grind was a frequent topic of conversation among the players as we traveled between international tournaments and training camps. After practices, in airports, and at meals, Monique and I found ourselves talking with Kelli Stack, Meghan Duggan, and Kacey Bellamy and sharing our thoughts on USA Hockey's relationship with the women's program. This core group of women were training and living on our own, out of college hockey for a season or two, and pushing the limits on and off the ice of what we had to do to maintain the level of excellence to play on the national team.

We loved representing the US in international competitions. We still got goose bumps every time we put on our red, white, and blue jerseys. We'd won the World Championship five of the last six times and had taken home three of the last six Four Nations Cup first-place trophies. Our sport was growing thanks to our success. We were painfully aware that we had not yet realized our dream to bring home an Olympic gold medal, which was why we were getting up before dawn to practice, working, and training late into the evenings after our day jobs to earn money so that we could chase our childhood dreams.

Obviously, Monique and I were on the same page about the inequities we were experiencing, but through our many side conversations, we discovered that our teammates felt the same way. They shared our same frustrations and complaints and our same question: It had always been this way. But did it have to stay this way?

Some of the inequities were big—lack of marketing support for women's hockey, essentially no support for girls' hockey programs, and simply inadequate financial support for national team members in between Olympic years.

Unlike gender-equity battles in other sports (including the women's national soccer team dispute with US Soccer), we were not demanding *equal pay* with the men, who, after all, played in the National Hockey League in between Olympics. Our fight was for *more equitable treatment,* including more equitable compensation:

- Per diems—the women received a per diem of $15 a day, while the men received $50. Were a woman's daily expenses less than a man's?

- Catastrophic injury protection and maternity benefits—the women didn't have any.

- Family fund—the players on the men's World Championship roster received a travel stipend for a family member to travel to the tournament and provided accommodations. There was no such stipend for the players on the Women's World Championship roster.

- Stipends in between Olympic years—we were looking for a fair stipend from USA Hockey beyond the six months of compensation we received just before each Olympic games—not NHL-level pay. This seemed particularly appropriate given that the women had to show up at many more camps and tournaments than the men did.

There were other issues that some might consider "small," like unequal travel arrangements. I remembered Hilary Knight and Monique squished in the last row of the flight back from Malmo, Sweden, as they returned from the World Championships in April. When the men's team traveled, they enjoyed the comfort of business class.

The list went on. Like the fact that the men's world junior team players received the same number of sticks for a two-week tournament that the women received for the entire season, leaving women to ration their sticks to make sure they would have enough for the season. The goalies on the men's U18 or U20 teams always had new pads and freshly painted helmets going into a World Championship. Jessie Vetter's red-and-white Wisconsin pads didn't stick out like a sore thumb during her years with the national team. But compare that to pictures of nineteen-year-old Maddie Rooney tending goal in the 2017 World Championships wearing gold-and-maroon pads from her college, Minnesota-Duluth.

The men and boys received rings whenever they won a championship—not so for the women. Those rings were a sore subject on their own. USA Hockey has yet to present us with rings commemorating our World Championships in 2011 and 2013, and even the 2018 Olympics. Monique and I had played on four of the five World Championship teams by this point and had only one ring. The girls' U18 team had won seven World Championships and received zero rings. By comparison, the men's hockey team and their junior teams got all their rings.

MONIQUE

While rings might seem trivial to some people, they are more than nice pieces of jewelry. Those rings were special. They stood for a lot. They were a constant reminder of what we had worked and trained and fought for on the ice and what we would continue to fight for outside the arena.

The lack of rings also represented the mindset we were up against. No matter what we accomplished as a team, it was not valued on the same level as similar accomplishments by the men's and boys' teams. When you are making the kind of sacrifices all of us did to win, you want to know your governing body is not only appreciative, but also equally committed to you—and the lack of rings was a representation of how we were viewed.

The message these slights sent boiled down to one thing—respect. It was painfully obvious our team wasn't getting the respect we deserved—we were not being treated equitably by USA Hockey as compared to the men's and boys' programs. As the national governing body of ice hockey in the United States, USA Hockey is required by the Ted Stevens Amateur Sports Act to provide equal opportunity to athletes. Legally, this opportunity is not tied to any type of revenue stream that USA Hockey may or may not have.

Importantly, these issues were not confined to our national team. All of us had experienced similar slights and inequities throughout our careers. We were constantly treated like we should be grateful just for the opportunity to play. Even on the national team, which should have been the shining star of our athletic careers, we experienced so many of the same inequities that working women have faced for years.

The players on our team have always been grateful for the opportunity to wear the red, white, and blue. That was not the issue. It became clear that if we wanted to make a difference for the next generation, if we wanted the same resources to be put into the girls' and women's programs that were afforded the boys' and men's programs, we couldn't just be grateful anymore. We had to stand up for what we deserved.

Too many women are conditioned not to speak up or complain, not to ask for what is due to them or what they are worth. But our group was different. We were a different generation. We grew up watching the '99 US Women's Soccer Team sell out the Rose Bowl to win a World Cup. We grew up with the increasing legitimacy of the WNBA and NWSL, and we would watch the 2016 Summer Olympics be dominated by the women of Team USA. This was a new era for women's sports. Why settle for less than?

We couldn't—and we didn't. We dug into the big issues of compensation, support for girls' youth hockey, and marketing and promotional support for the women's game, and we came up with a list of questions. Why were the financial resources devoted to women's hockey so small? In 2014, USA Hockey, which reported revenue of $43 million, spent $1 million on the women's national program—our team, ranked number one in the world. At the same time, USA Hockey allocated $3.5 million to the boys' U17 and U18 national teams—and no comparable amount of money went to a similar girls'/women's program.

These grievances had been around for years, in most cases, since the women's program was started. The women's team had a history with USA Hockey, and it wasn't a good one. We thought that it was up to us to take action and get results. We sensed this was the right time to take a stand. We were the right group of athletes. We were the right age. We had taken care of business on the ice, and now it appeared we had to take care of it off the ice too.

The small group of us having these conversations knew we were representative of the rest of our team, as well as those who'd come before and those who were on their way up. We understood what it took to continue to play after college, and like those who had come before us in women's soccer and women's tennis, we were going to start our own movement.

We needed to stop accepting the status quo and demand more equitable treatment—and the respect that came with it. We understood the impact we could have as female athletes—especially in the current social climate.

As we prepared to look into the best way to effect change, someone gave Jocelyne, Meghan, and me the number for a lawyer who would ultimately change the trajectory of our lives and careers. Once we had more information, we would start bringing more players into the fold, like Kelli and Kacey. We were reminded of what our dad told us when we were starting our first year of Bantams. Make a statement. Find the biggest guy on the opposing team and knock him on his ass. Kelli, Meghan, Kacey, and the rest of our teammates—all of us, in our own way, had done that as we grew up. Our backgrounds had prepared us well.

We might not actually knock anyone on their ass, but the time had come to ask the biggest guy on the opposing team for some changes and, if he didn't take us seriously, well, we'd have to do what we had to do.

We'd have to make a statement.

20

THEY ALL WANTED TO HELP

★

"You sound like the US soccer team in 1999—except you get even less."

JOCELYNE

Most of our small group conversations took place in fall 2015, about two months before the national team would be traveling to Sundsvall, Sweden, to compete in the Four Nations Cup. As Monique and I talked, we decided that we needed advice on how to start, what to ask for, and how to approach USA Hockey. In other words, we needed help to turn talk into action and action into change. I called Brant Feldman, our longtime agent.

Brant had represented players on the women's hockey team since the sport was introduced to the Olympics in 1998. He'd participated in several previous attempts to negotiate new contracts with USA Hockey, without success. With the frustration of someone who knew his limitations, he recounted the way those in charge of our sport's governing body said women's hockey was a money-loser and shut the door on efforts to get more compensation and benefits. End of story.

But Brant had an idea. He gave me the number for Philadelphia-based lawyer John Langel, a partner at the Ballard Spahr law firm, who'd represented the USA's women's soccer team for sixteen years. "You need to call him," he said. "I think he can help us."

Soon I was cold-calling John's cell phone. I pictured him in a suit, sitting at a desk in a fancy wood-paneled, book-filled office; by contrast, I was on the sofa in Monique's basement, wearing jeans and a sweatshirt. The phone rang a couple times, and John picked up. "Hi, is this Mr. Langel?" I asked, in a nervous, higher-pitched voice. I introduced myself, explained that I played hockey for Team USA, including in two Olympics, and said that our team was looking for representation in an effort to get fairer, more equitable treatment and support from USA Hockey. "We know that you represented US Soccer, and we wondered if you'd be willing to represent our team," I said.

John spent the next hour explaining what he and his colleagues at the firm had done for the U.S. Women's National Soccer team after they won the World Cup in 1999. Like most people, I recalled Brandi Chastain whipping off her jersey after she kicked the winning goal, as Mia Hamm, Briana Scurry, Julie Foudy, and the rest of the team rushed toward her in celebration. But I knew very little about their fight with U.S. Soccer for more money and benefits. "It sounds like your hockey team is like the U.S. Soccer team in 1999," John said, "Except you get even less."

I mentioned the upcoming Four Nations Cup in Sweden, and John asked for a rundown of our entire tournament schedule leading into the 2018 Olympics. Going forward, I said we had the 2016 Worlds in Kamloops, British Columbia; the 2016 Four Nations tournament in Finland; the 2017 Worlds in Michigan, and…"Stop," he interrupted. "Circle that tournament. If it ever gets to a point where you guys don't go to a tournament, it will be that one."

I asked what he meant. The United States was hosting it, he explained. It was the last major tournament before the Olympics. That's where the players would have the most leverage, he said, and where USA Hockey would feel the pressure in the lead-up to the Olympics

John said that he was going to put together a team of lawyers to work with us. I knew we couldn't afford John, let alone a team of lawyers at Ballard Spahr, but I needed to at least ask what their fee would be, while simultaneously crossing my fingers and hoping we would qualify for some pro bono work. Talk about awkward. Fortunately, John knew the issue before I could bring it up and addressed it head-on. "After this conversation, I know how little you make, and I know you can't afford us," he said. "And you won't have to. This is a cause we believe in. We're going to handle it."

This was just our first exposure to the incredible generosity of John and his partners at Ballard Spahr, and it made us feel stronger about the validity of our positions. But, in the moment, it left me speechless. I thanked John, exchanged numbers and emails, and after hanging up, I turned to Monique and simply said, "Wow."

After giving Monique a thorough download, I texted Meghan Duggan. "Just had a great conversation with John Langel. I think this is something we should pursue." Then we solicited opinions from Kacey Bellamy and several other veteran players. We knew we needed to build a complete consensus among all the players. And it wasn't going to be only the national team players. All of the postgraduate players had to be on board too. After speaking with everyone, we decided collectively to move forward with Ballard Spahr.

The next day, John walked down the hall to enlist the help of his law partner, Diane (Dee) Spagnuolo. Dee had played hockey her entire life, including through college, and John knew her innate understanding surrounding issues of gender equity in athletics would be an asset in serving us as clients. They immediately identified three associates to approach with the opportunity—Mary Cate Gordon, Ashley Wilson, and Kim Magrini. All three were also former collegiate athletes and were rising legal stars in their own right.

On that day back in late 2015, there's no way those lawyers could have envisioned how this new representation was going to play out over the next fifteen months. While we didn't fully understand it at the time, this was a big statement of support for us. Ballard Spahr believed strongly in pro bono projects, but for young lawyers to volunteer for a major pro bono project that was going to take a lot of their time—and reduce their regular billable hours—spoke volumes about the importance of our equity arguments to smart people who had a little more objectivity than we did.

With our legal team in place, we began exchanging emails and providing information to our lawyers. Tax returns, costs of training and travel, and medical expenses were among their requests. In turn, they educated us about the Ted Stevens Amateur Sports Act, signed into law by President Jimmy Carter in 1978, that obligated governing bodies of national teams to provide equal opportunities and resources to both men and women and girls' and boys' teams, and more to underserved populations.

To further understand what we were getting ourselves into, I contacted soccer legend Julie Foudy, who had been involved in several negotiations as a player with U.S. Soccer. Now a broadcaster for ESPN, Julie had played for the U.S. Women's National Soccer Team from 1987 to 2004, the last four years as team captain, and was elected to the National Soccer Hall of Fame in 2007. I emailed her and introduced myself, reminding her that I was one of the twins on the U.S. Women's National Hockey Team in an effort to jog her memory about a couple of interactions I'd had with her. I explained that our team was looking to work with John Langel and Ballard Spahr, and I wanted to pick her brain on her experience.

We got on the phone and had a long, friendly back-and-forth with lots of helpful advice, including a strong endorsement of the work Ballard Spahr had done for the women's soccer team. But she said the real work was up to us. "You all have to be in it together," she said. "Not just the national team. The Under-22 and Under-18 team. Everyone. You have to be one group, one voice. You have to be unbreakable."

Obviously, Julie spoke from firsthand knowledge, and as time went on and our battle with USA Hockey came to a head, her advice proved to be a key factor in our success.

MONIQUE

In the meantime, we had to remain focused on hockey. In November, we went to Sundsvall, Sweden, and finished first again in the 2015 Four Nations tournament with a 3–2 victory over Canada. Hilary Knight gave us the win with a breakaway goal in overtime, her trademark. If this tournament was any indication of what the future held for us and the adversity this group could endure, it was a great sign. Even though we were deep in the preliminary stages of our work with John and Dee in fleshing out our story and developing our asks, when it came time to play and perform, we left everything else at the door and didn't let it distract us from our competitive mission.

That same team culture helped us with John and Dee. We knew the importance of communication and making sure everyone knew what was going on and felt included and that everyone's voice and opinions were valued and heard. We encouraged people to ask questions, to speak up if they didn't agree, and to add insight that had been overlooked or might be valuable. It was always a group effort. We communicated mostly by email— with frequent updates drafted and sent by Jocelyne and proofread by her secretary—me.

As we moved past the 2015 holidays and into the new year, John and his team condensed our conversations and emails into three main pillars:

1. Fair compensation and related benefits;

2. More programming opportunities for the national team, such as added games and camps; and

3. Development and marketing of the women's and girls' programs.

This battle was about way more than us—one national team in one Olympics cycle. We wanted our sport to thrive and grow well beyond 2018. We wanted a bright future for the next generation of girls playing hockey.

In February 2016, John reached out for the first time to USA Hockey. In a letter, he wrote that Ballard Spahr was representing the women's team and requested a meeting to speak with USA Hockey on our behalf. They met in April, the day after Worlds in Kamloops, British Columbia. The wait for that meeting had been frustrating and fraught with anticipation, but the timing seemed in our favor. For the first time, the NHL Network televised all of our games from the tournament, an indication of our sport's rising popularity. We also successfully defended our title with another overtime win against Canada, this one 1–0. It was our third World Championship in a row and the sixth out of the last seven.

We enjoyed ourselves, too. We had a large contingent of family in the stands, including Anthony and Brent (it was Anthony's first time seeing me compete in a World Championship), parents, a few aunts and uncles, and most importantly, our grandparents, which meant a lot to us as they were getting on in years and we sensed it might be one of the last times they'd get to see us play live.

Our grandparents recognized from a young age our desire to achieve something great. On our annual summer trip to visit them at the family cabin on Moose Lake in Bonnyville, Alberta, they would watch from their porch swing in the mornings as Jocelyne, the boys, and I ran stairs, up and back down, up and back down. We made up a loop that went up the stairs, through the trees up the driveway, down the road to the neighbor's driveway, back down to the other side of the cabin, and flew back down the steps. It would take about forty-five seconds to finish, and our grandpa would be on his swing listening for us rounding the corner… "Here she comes."

At Worlds, a long way from Moose Lake, but with that same look, I'm sure he said to himself, "Here she comes," as we stepped onto the ice. He sat in the stands wearing his Coors Light trucker's hat next to Grandma like they sat on the porch swing. Emily Matheson (Pfalzer) would give our grandpa a big hug after games, and he loved it! So did we. Little things like that, small acts of kindness that make others happy, stick with you. When you go and play in tournaments all over the world, sometimes the only people in the stands are the families. Over the years, you get to know your teammates' loved ones and friends. We become part of a big, extended family. We're all on the journey together.

Two days later, the Ballard attorneys met with representatives from USA Hockey in Colorado Springs, Colorado. It was an introductory meeting—a "feeling out" meeting—where John and Dee reiterated that they were representing post-grad players and explained what we were looking for. The USA Hockey representatives thanked John and Dee and said they would get back to us. There was nothing substantive to report back to the players, although in retrospect, USA Hockey probably thought they could give us a few crumbs, and that would be good enough. No big deal. Just like in the past.

But this wasn't the past. We were a new—and different—group of players. This was a different time. We had a different set of advisers. We were all looking to the future—a different future.

JOCELYNE

By August, we were still waiting to hear from USA Hockey—no reactions, no feedback, no scheduling of a second meeting. Crickets. Nothing had happened, not even enough for tension to start rising. We still believed in the essential fairness of our requests—and that there was plenty of time to make significant progress. In September, the team came together in Boston for a camp, which provided an opportunity to meet with John and Dee face-to-face for the first time in the year since we had retained them.

Unable to find a conference room, we all crammed into a regular hotel room. John and Dee, who came in from Philadelphia, found themselves looking at twenty-five very attentive, interested, and focused athletes, ready to make change happen. Although they didn't really have anything new to report, the two lawyers offered an overview of conversations over the past few months and their plan for moving forward. They reviewed our asks, summarized the information they were waiting for USA Hockey to provide, and reinforced the importance of our lines of communication and the need to be on the same page.

This in-person strategy session was really important. It amplified and fleshed out our email and text communication chains. Questions were asked and answered. By the end of the meeting, everyone was aware that if we didn't make progress, boycotting Worlds was on the table.

A meeting between the two sides was finally scheduled a few weeks later back in Boston. Even though we were on opposite sides of the table, USA Hockey agreed to pay for Monique's and my flights, as they would during the rest of our negotiations. USA Hockey's willingness to do this always gave me a feeling that deep down, our governing body wanted to do something to make it work.

Monique and I took the day off from work and flew into Boston for the meeting, arriving that morning from Grand Forks and leaving later that night. The rest of the Boston-area players attended in person. There were a total of eleven of us. We made a statement by just being there that day, saying without saying it, "We are in this together," with John and Dee by our side.

We sat around the table and talked for six hours without making much progress. It was eye-opening and maddening, especially when we discussed the realities of financial support to help post-grad athletes stay in peak shape. Those of us not in college not only had to get jobs, but also had to give up at least two months of income if we didn't have paid time off saved in order to attend the camps and tournaments for the national team. During an Olympic year, we were paid $1,000 a month for six months while in residency, but that hardly covered expenses in a small town like Grand Forks, let alone those who lived in larger urban areas. As one reporter later noted, $1,000 would barely cover two tickets to the finals in Sochi. But what about the six months preceding the residency? "Training isn't mandatory," one of the executives with USA Hockey said. "It's your choice."

Our choice? Did they really think we could just show up six months before every Olympics and compete for gold? Monique, quiet up to that point, leaned forward and began to paint a picture of what it actually took to play and compete at an elite level. For the two of us, it meant alternating the morning shift at work. Every other day one of us would wake up at 4:20 a.m. to train adult clients at the gym where we worked. While one of us woke up, the other was able to "sleep in" all the way until 5:30 a.m. and head to the gym so that we could get our own daily training session in at 6:30 a.m. We hit the ice after that because of a generous rink manager who made sure we were blocked out on the ice schedule, wrapping up our morning around 11:00 a.m. Then we quickly ate our lunch, premade the night before, and headed back to work. Our days finished between 4:00 and 5:00 p.m. We were fortunate that we had a boss who accommodated this crazy schedule—and let us take time off for camps and tournaments—Monique's husband, Anthony.

These days were long, tiring, and monotonous. And our story was similar to the lives that all of our teammates faced. Early mornings and late nights for training, and struggling to make financial ends meet.

MONIQUE

We all wanted negotiations to move faster and to show real progress. The 2017 World Championships were still far enough away that attitudes were generally positive. By this time, Coach Ken Klee was also aware of our discussions; earlier in the year, we told him that we'd sought out legal representation and were in the beginning stages of negotiations with USA Hockey. He and the other coaches stayed far away from the fire and didn't officially take sides. But Ken seemed supportive, having been through a lockout himself as a player in the NHL. At one point, he gave an approving nod that very much said, "Good for you guys."

Unfortunately, without notice, Ken was let go. After winning the last four major international tournaments, we had a new head coach in Robb Stauber. Unsettled and confused by the abrupt change, we went on to lose the next two exhibition games against Canada that December, leading into the World Championships. Not only were we navigating negotiations that didn't seem to be going anywhere, but we also were trying to figure out what it was going to take to win on the ice, with a new coach.

The clock was ticking now. We were twelve months away from the Olympics in Pyeongchang, South Korea, and less than four months away from Worlds in Michigan. We had a negotiating session scheduled in Denver in February 2017, after which we would get a sense of which direction things were going to go. Either way, Julie Foudy's words would ring true, "One group, one voice, unbreakable."

2 1

ONE GROUP, ONE VOICE, UNBREAKABLE

★

"We understood the importance of women supporting women.'"

JOCELYNE

On February 23, 2017, we sat down for another negotiating session with USA Hockey in Denver—only our third face-to-face meeting. By this time, all of our back-and-forth communication led us to believe that we would have to crystallize a framework for an agreement; waiting on USA Hockey would likely be fruitless. In an attempt to move things along, Ballard mocked up a contract outlining our asks and sent it to USA Hockey before our meeting. We hoped that this document could frame a productive discussion in Denver, and our proposal could serve as a positive framework. Unfortunately, that's all it turned out to be—just hope.

Monique and I flew from Fargo to Denver. We met with Kendall Coyne, who then lived in the Mile High City. The meeting was part in-person and part conference call. Meghan and Hilary were among the players on the phone, as was John, who dialed in from Ballard's office in New Jersey. Dee and Mary Cate from Ballard were with us at the table.

When we looked down our side, we saw all women, something that always gave me a sense of strength and pride. Other than John, the other Ballard lawyers who represented us were women, all of whom played college sports and volunteered to be a part of our team. They understood the changes we were trying to make—not just the substance, but the underlying rationale and importance of those changes. None of us mentioned it directly, but we understood the importance of women supporting women.

And on the other side of the table? All of the USA Hockey representatives, and all but one of their lawyers were men. It was a metaphor for everything that was wrong.

I don't know that anyone else noticed or that it mattered, but the male/female divide at the negotiating table assumed an unspoken significance later in the meeting when discussions became heated. One of the USA Hockey representatives talked about a USAH staff member's daughter and said because of her influence, he was passionate about "the other side," referring to us and women's hockey. I interrupted him. "That is the problem right there," I said. "There are no sides." He apologized. "This is the fundamental issue," I said. "We're all supposed to be on the same side."

MONIQUE

As we discussed compensation, another USA Hockey attorney claimed we should just be grateful for the chance to represent our country. "You get to wear the red, white, and blue," he said. I saw the look on the faces of the players. Everyone was asking themselves, What? Did they not get it? We weren't a bunch of 1950s housewives happy to get a new blouse. I calmly but pointedly explained that we were honored to represent our country, and many of us had done so for years, having dreamt of it all our lives. But this went beyond being grateful. We were talking about being respected and supported as athletes who made sacrifices and put our lives on hold to pursue our hockey careers and represent our country in the Olympics and other tournaments.

The negotiations were harder than any of us imagined—more like lessons in self-control and consistency. Our emotions swung from frustration to disheartened and back. We honestly didn't understand. This was 2017. We were just looking for more equitable treatment. We weren't being greedy. Asking for fundamentally fair treatment shouldn't have been this hard.

It could have been easy to let the frustration get the best of us, but we always kept our end goal in mind. While USA Hockey offered a significant increase in payment for the six months leading into the Olympics, nothing changed about being supported the other three-and-a-half years when we were expected to play without compensation. We focused on all of our key priorities. They represented our game plan, and we stuck with it.

Financial Compensation: We wanted to be paid a livable wage for more than just the six months leading up to the Olympics. We played year-round, in the Four Nations Cup, the World Championships, and numerous exhibitions and camps—we had many times the required appearances as the men.

We trained essentially every day while trying to hold onto jobs to support ourselves. Our ask wasn't going to make anyone rich. It would simply allow players to train without having to juggle other jobs. We believed in the proposition that if you act like it's a part-time job, then you'll treat it like a part-time job. We tried to make the point that we didn't treat it that way. We trained as elite athletes. It was our full-time job.

Equitable Support: Having the same travel accommodations, same per diem, getting rings for championships, and so on. Some of these things may seem small or petty, but when disparate treatment is consistently applied, it makes you feel less than others, and you wonder if the people in charge think of you that way—or if you are even on their radar. But the most important element of our ask in this category wasn't about us. We asked for more equitable funding for our girls' and junior programs, in addition to the women's program, so that the next generation of girls' hockey players would feel valued and supported. Whatever you provided for men and boys, some sort of equivalent had to exist for the girls and women.

Programming and Marketing: We believed that it was in everyone's interest to grow the sport of women's hockey. That required more programming—tournaments and exhibitions—outside the Olympics, World Championships, and Four Nations tournaments—and increased marketing and promotion of our sport. The data showed our growth potential. Our tournaments were being televised. Our games against Canada got the media coverage and respect of other great rivalries in sports. And more girls were going into the sport.

It's easy to be critical of USA Hockey. And in the midst of our negotiations, we were discouraged—and even a little upset, like anyone would be in the heat of the moment. But that's not where we are today. In retrospect, something much more important was at play. The representatives of USA Hockey were relying on fifty years of history. They were, and many still are, to a certain extent, captives of fifty years of culture. They weren't overtly discriminatory. They weren't being deliberately unfair. They just didn't understand that the times were changing, and those of us across the table from them were instruments of that change in women's ice hockey. Coming to grips with those changes in history and culture is what makes movements like ours so difficult for everyone.

A few days later, the entire team convened for a post-grad training camp in Attleboro, Massachusetts, including a clinic for local girls and an exhibition game against a U18 boys' team. These three days were a new addition to the schedule. It was one of the things we had been asking for—more programming—and it was the one ask we had that was accommodated pretty quickly, even while we continued to talk, which we appreciated. But it wasn't enough. It wasn't the "substantial progress" we needed.

On our first night at the hotel, we had a players-only meeting to recap the latest round of talks in Denver. Unable to get a conference room, we gathered in a hallway, which felt like it might burst from the collective energy. It was one thing to communicate by email and another thing to have the entire team packed into one relatively small space and feel the energy of all of us getting on the same page and the solidarity being forged among all of us on the team. We held out hope that we weren't going to need to take action on the date John told us to circle over a year ago, but that date was quickly approaching, and we just weren't making the progress we needed to make to avoid an ugly boycott.

JOCELYNE

I had never looked at a calendar as much as I did at that camp. We started on March 3. The World Championships began on March 31. What was that—twenty-seven or twenty-eight days? It depended on how you counted. Would that one day matter? Possibly. Negotiations were at a stalemate and showed no immediate signs of progressing. At that point, not going to Worlds was a real possibility. As leaders, Meghan, Hilary, Kacey, Kendall, and Monique and I had been preparing mentally for what could happen in March from the beginning. I began to think about it from the first time John said to circle the date of Worlds on our calendar.

It was one thing to be intellectually prepared, but as the pages of the calendar turned, the emotional impact of actually having to pull the trigger was another story. That's why, in meetings and updates with the players, we always made sure to mention a boycott as a possibility so it wouldn't come as a shock if it did happen.

With that possibility only three-and-a-half weeks away and looking very much like it might turn into a reality, we brought it up again in that memorable meeting in the hotel hallway. We wanted everyone informed and to be able to ask questions and talk through any concerns so that we could spend the next few days playing hockey without distractions. We also wanted everyone to know that if we didn't stand together now, things would never change.

One group, one voice, unbreakable.

Everyone understood and was on board. This was a group that was ready to make change happen, to stand up and be bold. We took strength from each other—we were a team in every sense of the word. This group was ready to make history. The opportunity to make change—for ourselves and for the next generation—was on our shoulders, individually and collectively. We were all willing to be a voice for change and stand together—regardless of what it might mean to us individually. The unanimous, collective commitment was amazing—there was no second-guessing.

The farther away we get from those scary days back in 2017, the more we appreciate the selflessness and courage it took for all the players to stand together. All of them. We're still blown away by the trust in the information we shared, by the unity of purpose. The moment wasn't upon us, not yet anyway, but when it happened, we were all ready. After camp, we all went back to our lives. Monique and I returned to Grand Forks, where we trained and managed our jobs and home lives while waiting for something to happen. We benefited from being able to compartmentalize the different areas of our lives. Our dad had instilled that in us: prioritizing, focusing, and executing the task at hand.

Even though we weren't together, communication between and among players and lawyers at Ballard ramped up, as did updates among players. We were preparing to play in the upcoming World Championships but simultaneously preparing for the now-more-likely boycott that was on the near horizon. There was always an understanding among the group that if we wanted change to happen, we had to be the group to do it. We didn't think we were any better than players and teams that came before us. This was just the time for change—and we were the players who held the future of girls' and women's hockey in our hands.

No player ever questioned if we were doing the right thing. The only question was, what can we do as players to help accomplish our goals? The most powerful part of this experience was that the foundation of these conversations was rooted in the unifying concept of more equitable treatment in the future. We all knew that many of these players would not benefit from the selflessness of the whole. Every player knew that her role in this was just as important as the person next to her.

22

BE BOLD FOR CHANGE

★

"We are part of something bigger than ourselves."

MONIQUE

After more conference calls with lawyers and players, working through details and schedules, we landed on the date of Wednesday, March 15, to announce our boycott. It was six days before we were supposed to report for pre-camp at the World Championships. We wanted to give USA Hockey enough time to negotiate with us, come to an agreement, and get us to camp on time. Although very unlikely at this point, we figured it would also at least be enough time to negotiate and get us to Michigan before the first game in two weeks.

Up to this point, word of our negotiations had remained private, known only to those of us involved. The fact that we were able to keep everything "in house" for over a year was key to our strategy—confidentiality was critical to give the negotiations the opportunity to succeed—and the extended period of confidentiality was also a testament to the trust everyone had in each other.

But all that was about to change. We knew if we handled this the right way, our team would be able to create some big waves throughout the sporting world. But we had no idea that it would become national news.

Like soccer, tennis, basketball, and track and field, our negotiations with USA Hockey transcended sports and addressed issues and questions across the entire economic, political, and cultural landscape—issues that were increasingly in the public spotlight. Fair and equitable treatment didn't just apply to women in sports. It applied to women in the working world. It applied to diverse groups of people. It applied to anyone who is not part of the perceived majority—and that fundamental advocacy for equity resonates well beyond women's hockey and sports.

As March 15 approached, Ballard's communications department helped craft a press release and come up with a PR plan. Kendall Coyne and Alex Rigsby were also instrumental in helping execute this plan. Along with Hilary Knight, they came up with the graphics and concepts for all the social media posts. Our graphics were so good, people later asked what PR firm we had hired. It was, in fact, all proudly team-generated, with significant guidance from Ballard's communications team. Our talents went beyond the rink. We are smart, hardworking, educated young women who understood we have the potential to make a difference.

John and Dee emphasized the importance of consistent messaging and recommended having a small group of players handle all interview requests. The three captains, Meghan, Kacey, and I, along with Hilary and Jocelyne, were the designated spokespeople for the team. Other players were always allowed to do interviews if they felt comfortable, but most media would be directed to the five players.

Next, and most crucial to our plan, we needed to contact all players outside of our post-grad group—any player USA Hockey believed could potentially play on a team of replacement players. This pool consisted of about seventy players. We knew that USA Hockey would try to replace us at Worlds and beyond if necessary. We remembered Julie Foudy's warning—we had to make sure we had solidarity through the entire player pool. *One group, one voice, and unbreakable.*

Up to this point, only our post-grads and mainstay college players were aware of what was going on. The timing of when to contact other players—and the strategy of how to do that—were critical. But first things first; we had to contact the three players who had just made their first World Championship team and who were still in college: Kelly Pannek, Kali Flanagan, and Maddie Rooney. These were some of the hardest conversations we held. For these players, it was their first opportunity to represent Team USA at a World Championship—and a year out from the Olympics. All of us knew what that felt like and what it meant. And now we were asking them to trust us and stand with us and potentially give up that opportunity.

Jocelyne spoke to Maddie, and Meghan talked to Kali, and we had former teammates of Kelly at Minnesota talk to her. We also contacted their college coaches and made them aware of the situation. They deserved to know what was going on, and we trusted them to help guide their players in the right direction. The coaches we spoke to were supportive; one of them said, "This is awesome." The players themselves trusted us. Maddie, who wasn't one to say a whole lot, told Jocelyne, "Okay, whatever you do, I'm in. I'm on board."

Then we were off to the races. We grabbed all the camp rosters from the previous year, divided them up, and called all those players. If we didn't have contact information for a player, we found it. I was nervous as I made the first call. I was sweating, my heart thumping in my chest as I paced around in my basement. But every conversation got a little easier and was some version of the following: "Hey, this is Monique Lamoureux. I'm on the U.S. Women's National Team. On the fifteenth, we are going to announce that our team is not going to play in the upcoming World Championships in two weeks if we don't make significant progress in negotiations with USA Hockey about gender equity in our sport. These negotiations have been going on for over a year. Unfortunately, we think USA Hockey leadership is going to respond by calling other players and trying to replace us. I'm calling to ask that you stand with us in this fight. We can't win if all of us aren't on the same team, standing together—and this is about us being on the same team and future teams. Ultimately, this is going to have the greatest effect on the upcoming generation of female hockey players."

Reactions were positive and affirming of our efforts. We recognized the trust these players were putting in us, and it made us even stronger and more determined. This was real—and getting more real by the minute.

On the night of the thirteenth, the captains set up a conference call with all the U18 players and their parents. Cayla Barnes was the captain of the U18 team that year, and I had communicated with her throughout the process. But we waited as long as possible to talk to the larger pool of U18 players. We figured that these players were in high school, and the secret would not be kept for long once we talked to them and their parents. But we laid out the facts and made sure they understood that the headlines they would soon read had more to do with them. "This is going to affect us and our careers for a short period of time," Meghan explained. "But ultimately, you guys are the next group of players, and what we're doing will hopefully change the way you are able to continue your hockey careers. We do not want you to have the same struggles that we have had."

In response, a father spoke up and applauded what we were trying to do. His statement was really simple—something like, "Thank you for what you are doing for our daughters." That really struck a chord with me; I got emotional, something I didn't expect. These parents seemed to understand immediately that this would ultimately change how their daughters could think about their future in hockey—and maybe even in life. Remember, we were among the older players on the team, but we were only twenty-seven years old, and hearing adult affirmation of the importance of what we were doing was really powerful.

JOCELYNE

At 10:00 a.m. ET on March 15, the entire national team announced our intent not to play in the 2017 World Championships. In a coordinated social media blitz, all of us posted the same photo and caption, which said, "The US Women's National Ice Hockey Team will not play in the 2017 World Championships due to unresolved negotiations over fair wages and support from USA Hockey. #BeBoldForChange."

We tipped off Julie Foudy, and moments after our announcement, she posted a story on ESPN's website: BREAKING: US WOMEN'S HOCKEY TEAM TO SIT OUT WORLD CHAMPIONSHIPS DUE TO STALLED CONTRACT NEGOTIATIONS. She reported that we were prepared to stay home "unless significant progress is made," which meant, as Meghan explained, "a living wage and for USA Hockey to fully support its programs for women and girls and stop treating us like an afterthought."

USA Hockey acknowledged our "concerns" to Julie and said they "have communicated that increased level of support to the players' representatives" and looked forward to continuing talks with us.

In her story, Julie wrote how this stalemate had been percolating for two decades since USA Hockey met initial player demands with a lockout and allegedly cut Hall of Fame player Cammi Granato from the team in 2005 when she remained an outspoken proponent for equity and change. Our press release cited "more than a year of stalled negotiations with USA Hockey" to address inequities that violated the Ted Stevens Olympic and Amateur Sports Act and had to do with such basics as equipment, staff, meals, travel expenses, transportation, publicity, and playing more games together.

Later that morning, Cammi Granato responded on Twitter to Meghan Duggan's post. "Standing behind you all!" she wrote.

No other comment captured our sense of duty like that one. "It's hard to believe that, in 2017, we still have to fight so hard for basic equitable support," Monique said at the end of our press release. "But when I think about the women who paved the way for our team—and when I see girls at rinks around the country who are dedicated to pursuing big dreams and look to us to lead by example—it's well overdue for us to speak up about unfair treatment, even if it means sacrificing an opportunity to represent our country. We owe the next generation more than that. We owe it to ourselves to stand up for what is right."

By early afternoon, the news was everywhere. *The New York Times. The Washington Post. USA Today. ESPN. Sports Illustrated.* All the network and cable news shows. Everyone reported the story, most requested interviews, and the five players designated to speak with reporters had a full schedule of calls to relay the same message. It is one thing to be an individual and to stay on message, but with five people taking interviews, a slipup was almost inevitable. But it never happened. If a reporter tried to make the dispute about equal pay as USA Hockey was pitching, we redirected the message to equal support and a livable wage. If a press outlet tried to argue that the men's team brought in more money than the women's team, we educated the reporter and readers that USA Hockey's obligation was to grow the game—men, women, boys, and girls equally. We had a message to share, and that's exactly what we did.

That afternoon, USA Hockey put out its own press release, stating its position. It didn't seem to resonate with the press—or with anyone we knew. By the end of the day, #BeBoldForChange was trending on Twitter.

That evening, Monique and I were sitting around the island of our parents' kitchen, and our dad asked, "What if you don't go? Then what?" I looked over at the fridge, where our mom had taped so many inspirational messages when we were growing up. It was as if I could still see them. "I'll be able to lay my head on my pillow at night knowing we did the right thing," I said. My dad simply nodded his head. No response was needed.

MONIQUE

As we predicted, USA Hockey wasted no time before trying to replace us. We had already communicated to the first layer of players contacted that they could either not pick up the phone when they got a call or politely decline the offer. We wanted them to do whatever made them comfortable. Some players told us that they wanted the chance to personally say no to USA Hockey—to be part of the movement, to exercise their voice, and stand up for themselves. That made us proud. The relatively new professional National Women's Hockey League, where many of us had or still played, issued a statement on its own saying that none of its players would step in as replacements. "We are incredibly proud to have such strong and empowered pioneers in our league," they said.

Jocelyne and I were on our way to the rink to skate while the leadership group was on a call with John and Dee discussing next steps. They heard USA Hockey had moved to the next level of potential players, American-born Division I college players. Jocelyne, Meghan, Kacey, Kelli, Hilary, Kendall, Decker, and I used the list we had already created of all American D1 college players and figured out who we still needed to call. We then divided up the coaches that we needed to contact in each of the conferences, the Western Collegiate Hockey Associations, the Eastern College Athletic Conference, Hockey East, and the College Hockey America Conference. Players with existing relationships with coaches made those calls. Jocelyne and I were in charge of the WCHA coaches.

As our team captain, Meghan felt duty bound to call every single player herself and personally ask for their support, and I think she may well have spoken to everyone. If not, she tried. She was on the phone all day calling players. A lot of these players had already spoken with one of us, but Meghan felt so deeply that they needed to hear directly from her, the one leading the charge. The message she relayed and the one she got back was loud and clear—we were *all* in this together.

This was the kind of determination that won us championships. You weren't going to beat us without a fight. We understood the power of team.

Jocelyne and I decided we would skate for forty-five minutes to an hour and then make our calls. We brought our phones up to the ice with us and put them on the bench and checked them periodically while we skated to make sure we weren't missing anything important. But the calls we had to make were too much of a distraction, and we ended our workout after thirty minutes. That proved to be good timing, as we both received calls from two different coaches on our way to the locker room. Imagine two players in their gear in the hallway trying to find a good service spot in the rink in order to explain everything that was going on.

We spoke to only one D1 coach who was less than supportive but seemingly uninformed. "I'm going to look out for the best interests of my players," she said. "What are you guys asking for anyways?"

Katey Stone and her Harvard coaching staff were on the other end of the spectrum. A letter went out to the Harvard team that said, "We all dream about wearing our country's colors. But today the honor is in not putting the jersey on. The pride and honor is in saying no to this opportunity and standing with the national team." That letter was a keeper.

Meanwhile, as we navigated this chaos, our normal day-to-day responsibilities continued. The world kept turning. We had jobs, workouts, relationships. If one of us in the leadership group was going to work out, skate, or take care of some other obligation, we sent everyone an update. "Hey, guys, I'm heading into the gym, I won't be responsive for the next hour or two." It was not unusual to come back after an hour and have fifty text messages of updates on what had or was in the process of transpiring.

On the morning of the sixteenth, all the players received an email from USA Hockey, asking us to let USA Hockey know by 5:00 p.m. ET whether we were participating in the pre-camp starting the twenty-first. No one responded to the email before or after the deadline. There was more posturing in the press that day and the next leading into the weekend. USA Hockey's intention was clear: our governing body was on the attack and wanted to divide us and break our boycott. Emboldened, we silently challenged them, *Good luck*. During the four years leading into the Sochi Olympics, we had come up with a motto that we said in our huddle before games. It was even more meaningful now.

We are part of something bigger than ourselves.
We are Team USA.
We are team first!

JOCELYNE

On Friday night, we heard that USA Hockey had started to call D3 college players. Eleven of us were on a text-message chain where we talked about how to address this. Meghan Duggan, Brianna Decker, Hilary Knight, and a few others were playing that night in NWHL games. "Play in your game," I texted them. "Monique, Kendall, and I got this." Putting aside our plans, while pouring myself a glass of wine for the evening, the three of us researched websites for all the D3 programs in the country and found contact information for each coach. Finding this information is much more difficult compared to gathering information for D1 programs, but we had a spreadsheet completed with all the information we needed well before the night was over.

We composed a letter to the coaches and also a separate one to the players, who we wanted to speak to directly. That letter began: "Ladies, we are contacting you on behalf of the entire U.S. Women's National Team. As you have all probably seen, we are currently willing to sit out the upcoming World Championships in order to receive equitable treatment from USA Hockey. This has been the hardest decision we have ever made as athletes, but sometimes the hardest thing and the right thing are the same."

Yes, we realized that we were quoting a lyric from The Fray's song "All At Once," and we laughed at ourselves, working late and getting a little punchy, but the line worked, and that's what mattered—getting out the message. "In order to make the change, we must all stick together," we continued to write. "This is bigger than hockey, and it is certainly bigger than the upcoming World Championships. We ask that you join us in this movement." We ended with a quote from Gandhi: "You must be the change you wish to see in the world."

As this was breaking, Team Switzerland was playing Adrian College, a Division III school with a women's hockey program in Michigan. Shiann Darkangelo, who was in the player pool but not on the national team, drove over an hour to that game, knowing that USA Hockey would likely show up to try to recruit players from the Adrian team to replace us. We were right. But Shiann walked into the locker room after the game (she wasn't recognized by the USA Hockey representatives) and told the players what was happening—including that we thought USA Hockey was going to offer the Adrian players spots on the national team to break our boycott. Shiann asked the Adrian team to stand with us—and support the boycott. Which they did. Every one of them.

We realized something remarkable. In just two-and-a-half days, we had reached or attempted to reach every eligible female college hockey player in the country. Even more remarkable, and to this day something that causes us to get emotional—as far as we know, everyone banded together and trusted us. No one broke ranks.

One team, one voice—unbreakable.

23

DARE TO MAKE HISTORY

★

"We banded together with a common goal and an unbeatable resolve."

JOCELYNE

F our days after our announcement, USA Hockey asked for a meeting. It was set for Monday, March 20, in Philadelphia. We flew in for the meeting from Grand Forks—seven other teammates joined us in person: Gigi Marvin, Kacey Bellamy, Meghan Duggan, Hilary Knight, Kelli Stack, Kendall Coyne, and Brianna Decker. News of our meeting had leaked, and we were greeted by a couple of TV news cameras in the lobby of Ballard's building. Dee ushered us past the press and into the elevators to the forty-eighth floor. Once inside, our meeting lasted twelve hours. Besides those of us at the table, everyone else on the team called in throughout the day. Haley Skarupa later sent around a screenshot of her time on the call showing it at just over ten hours.

John and Dee led the meeting. USA Hockey presented a detailed spreadsheet with its interpretation of what the operating costs would be for the women's hockey team under our current requests. It took close to three hours to go through all of those numbers. We didn't necessarily agree with USA Hockey's analysis of the numbers, which I suppose is typical in such negotiations. Everyone's entitled to their opinion. When they finished, I said to myself, "Okay, can we get to work now?"

Which we did. Over the next several hours, we dug into the issues that were important to us—compensation, support, and programming and marketing. Our same three pillars that we had identified at the outset of the negotiations. When you continually come back to the same main points, conversation can seem redundant, but as athletes, we were used to executing a game plan from the start to the final buzzer. It didn't have to be flashy. It needed to be focused and designed to get the desired results.

I think we surprised our USA Hockey counterparts when the talk turned to bonuses for winning medals in Pyeongchang. We were all entering new territory because before 2018, no hockey player had ever received a bonus from USA Hockey; bonuses came only from the USOPC. In order to provide the potential for more compensation for us in the first year of the deal, USA Hockey proposed certain amounts for winning gold, silver, and bronze. Our response showed that money wasn't the sole reason we were there. "If we get bronze, we don't want anything," we said. "Put more into gold and silver." Players' phones buzzed with positive emojis. We were betting on ourselves.

At the eight-hour mark, we were all a couple hours away from our scheduled return flights home. Every one of us decided we were going to miss our flights so that we could stay at the table and hopefully finish a deal. The two parties split into separate rooms to work out new offers to bring to the table before the day ended. Included among the many details in our proposal was the dollar number we wanted USA Hockey to put in the player pool every year, not just an Olympic year, and a requirement to start a women's advisory committee within USA Hockey that would be committed to working on marketing and on expanding programming and opportunities for the women's program.

Before we broke and reconvened with USA Hockey in the main conference room, Meghan summarized our bottom line asks to make sure all the players in the room and on the phone were in agreement. She nailed it. She was on point and impressive—a perfect reflection of Meghan herself—and that grabbed John Langel's attention.

"All right, Meghan," he said. "You want to pitch this when we go back in there?" She was caught off guard; he wasn't exactly asking it as a question. "Just say exactly what you just said to the group," he said. "That's the way you're going to present it." The rest of us chimed in as if we were on the ice. "Yeah, Megs, you can do this. No problem. You got it."

John knew that the presentation would be much more powerful coming from Meghan, our team captain, than from a lawyer.

Meghan opened her pitch with an old Doc Hacker saying, "We did not come this far, to only come this far," she began. The folks on the other side of the table seemed to agree, and Reagan Carey, our general manager, who was across the table as well, put her head down and smiled. We all knew she was in our corner, despite being on the other side of the table. After some discussion, USA Hockey president Jim Smith said his next step was to present our offer to his board of directors. Despite some details and a contract still needing to be worked out, we felt pretty positive; we left the meeting thinking we had a handshake agreement. All the players scattered to our homes the following morning—most of us making final preparations to get to Michigan for the World Championships.

"The discussions were productive," we said in a release afterward, "and [they] will continue this week with the goal of reaching an agreement that will allow the players to get to camp in time to train for and compete in the World Championships."

MONIQUE

Three days later, on Thursday, March 23, we were shocked to hear that USA Hockey's executive committee had rejected our handshake. We had made significant compromises, as had USA Hockey, and thought we had come to a deal. USA Hockey did make a counterproposal, but it went backward in so many ways that we couldn't possibly accept it. By afternoon, we learned that USA Hockey was still attempting to field a replacement team for Worlds. In statements to the media and on Twitter, we reminded everyone that our issues went beyond the current national team players—and specifically beyond our compensation, which is how USA Hockey was trying to spin our dispute. We were advocating for larger, farther-reaching issues of more equitable treatment for female athletes now and in the future and not just in the United States, but around the world. Although our international counterparts steered clear of commenting on our negotiations publicly, we knew they understood what we were trying to do and wanted the "real" U.S. Women's National Team at that tournament.

The stress was hard to handle, and we all leaned on each other, some nights clinking wineglasses with each other through the phone but mostly offering each other pep talks and brief shouts of encouragement the way we did in the locker room and on the ice. When under extreme stress, I tend to lose my appetite. On the night Jocelyne, Kendall, and I were gathering information on D3 programs, I lost track of time and realized I hadn't really eaten all day. Since something is better than nothing, or so the saying goes, I took a trip to Qdoba for a queso burrito followed by a Dairy Queen Blizzard. I can say that I haven't had a queso burrito since that day, but I have enjoyed an occasional DQ Blizzard.

We drew energy from the fact that public opinion was so firmly on our side and gaining momentum. The constant support from what seemed like everyone reaffirmed no matter how this ended, we would end up on the right side of history. On Friday, all of the women on the team posted individual pictures on social media, holding a sign with a single word communicating our resolve. Powerful. Bold. Ambitious. Together. Historic. Brave. Fearless. Fierce. Strong. Family. Devoted. United.

The Players Associations of Major League Baseball, the National Hockey

League, the National Football League, the National Basketball Association, the Women's National Basketball Association, and the U.S. Women's National Soccer team all added their support across social media. Corporate sponsor Dunkin' Donuts chimed in with an official tweet saying it stood in solidarity with the women's national team.

On Monday, March 27, soccer star Abby Wambach added her voice to our cause, as did tennis legend and activist Billie Jean King and North Dakota's United States Senator Heidi Heitkamp. Nineteen additional US Senators, including Elizabeth Warren, Patty Murray, Diane Feinstein, Cory Booker, and Maizie K. Hirono, also signed a letter calling on USA Hockey to treat the women's national hockey team fairly. Twelve of those senators were women.

Amid that groundswell of support, USA Hockey's board of directors—more than ninety people, an overwhelming majority of them being men—had an emergency meeting via conference call to vote on our original proposal, the same one the executive committee had turned down earlier in the week. Everyone on the board was notified of the meeting, including Meghan Duggan, who served as the player representative on the board. Her presence on the call and her performance made her the hero of the day.

She listened to USA Hockey's description of the deal and surrounding conversations, and while what she heard wasn't untruthful, some of our positions were mischaracterized and exaggerated. Unable to break into the conversation, she punched at the button on her computer that indicated she wanted a turn to speak. I can only imagine her frustration. Finally, she was recognized and had the chance to articulately and powerfully set the record straight from the players' perspective. It was a revelatory, game-changing moment. As she did in our previous meeting, she went through our position point by point, calmly, clearly, logically, and pretty convincingly.

After she was finished, the board rejected the USA Hockey negotiating committee's offer to us and also our offer to the organization. At the same time, the board ordered USA Hockey's executives to meet with the players again and come to an agreement in the middle, and most importantly, to make a deal. And that's what happened. John and Dee had a contract already prepared and sent it to USA Hockey. They spent the rest of the day and night filling in the blanks.

JOCELYNE

On Tuesday morning, March 28, I was at our local indoor swimming pool, watching my sister-in-law's nephew and visiting with her parents. It was hot and humid, the air heavy with the smell of chlorine and the playful sounds of kids splashing in the water. I was doing things to distract me from thinking about the ticking clock. We were three days from Worlds, and if anything was going to happen, it had to happen now. Then I heard the ping of an email on my phone, indicating a new email. It was from John and Dee. After a deep breath, I opened it up and read, "Contract finalized, good to sign."

A second or two later, the text messages started pouring in. *Congratulations. We did it. Yes! Amazing.* They went on and on. And yes, we had done it. We had made change happen. We had banded together with a common goal and an unbeatable resolve, and the world for girls who wanted to play hockey had changed forever.

MONIQUE

When we got the final green light to sign our contracts I was in my basement. It was early afternoon, and we had all been told to wait until Ballard read through the final draft of the contract before signing. I was trying to kill time, but all it seemed like I was doing was checking my phone every other minute to get an update. When word finally came, I leaned back on the couch and took a deep, deep breath. I felt a sense of relief and pride that wouldn't quit. It was the first time I let myself take in the enormity of our battle, both the risk we took and the victory we won.

The mission we had been on had been singularly consuming, between managing the flow of information and calls, media requests, social media, internal communication, while also training as elite athletes, and still going to work every day. And also just putting everything on the line—the opportunity to represent our country at another World Championship, which might jeopardize our position on the Olympic team the next year and our twenty-year dream to win an Olympic gold medal. We had put it all on the line because we knew we were doing the right thing for the right reasons, and everyone saw that.

What they didn't see was the personal toll it took on all of us and our loved ones. As I sent in my signed contract, I knew of all the victories we had shared on the ice together, all the years spent working to achieve our dreams, this was the sweetest moment. And ahead of us was the good part, the fun part, the part all of us loved most of all—and we let the world know in a team video we all posted on social media. "To our dearest fans, together we dared to make history, and we couldn't have done it without you. See you at Worlds!"

The support we received from fans and followers throughout this time and especially after our deal was made public, was heartfelt—and heartwarming. The comments and messages meant so much to all of us. That night after we signed the deal, Jocelyne, Anthony, Brent, and I went out to dinner in Grand Forks, along with a few of our coworkers from the gym, and instead of giving us a check at the end of the meal, the waiter dropped off a piece of paper on which someone had written, "On behalf of little girls everywhere (including my daughters) THANK YOU! #BeBoldForChange."

And that was just the beginning.

There were the letters, notes, emails, texts, social media posts. Jocelyne and I personally received hundreds and hundreds of them. Some were from people we knew or had met. Most were from strangers. Some came drawn in crayon. All shared the same basic message, like the one we received from Avery Hakstol, the eleven-year-old daughter of Erin and Dave Hakstol from Grand Forks, the former head coach of the Philadelphia Flyers who had also coached at UND. We had babysat Avery a few times, so we knew she was a huge hockey fan and a pretty awesome young player herself. Her note said, "Hey, I think it's pretty cool you guys are standing up for girls' hockey; my mom showed me the article, and I wanted to say thank you!" (This was followed by two fist-pound emojis.)

Pretty cool, indeed. She was why we had put everything on the line

24

PERFECT TIMING

"The selflessness that had made us unbreakable now made us unbeatable."

JOCELYNE

Like everyone else, my bags had been packed for a few days, just to be ready to jump on a plane in a few hours if I had to—and I did. We all did. Monique and I arrived in Michigan for Worlds on March 29, a day and a half before our first game. As we rounded the corner in the airport baggage claim area, we saw half a dozen of our teammates with their hockey bags, waiting for the rest of us. Hilary Knight and Meghan Duggan from Boston, Maddie Rooney from Minnesota, and Kendall Coyne from Denver. I almost cried when I saw everyone. We always hug when we see each other, but this time every hug was held just a little longer and a little tighter.

We had time for only a couple of practices before our first game, while the rest of the world's elite teams had been practicing for weeks. Unlike the world's other elite players, our team had just gone to battle, and no amount of training or team-building could have created what the previous two weeks had done for us. The confidence and trust in the locker room was unlike any other group we had ever been a part of. Our bond was stronger than ever. We were Team USA!

But Monique and I were unable to fully revel in the joy. After landing in Detroit, we turned on our phones and found out the University of North Dakota's women's hockey program had been eliminated. Right on the eve of the World Championships. The men's and women's swimming and diving teams were also terminated. But losing the women's hockey program was like being told it was no longer going to get cold in North Dakota. It was impossible to fathom. Budget cuts were cited as the reason. The players had learned of the news at practice that morning through leaks on social media. Pictures and displays were removed shortly after the announcement. Staff members were left to look for new jobs.

We were stunned. Hockey was the state's religion. UND's hockey program was an integral part of our entire family. Our dad, two of our brothers, and my husband had all played for the program, as had we. From the time we began skating with the Fighting Sioux, the women's team had become a force in its conference and nationally. Last-place finishes were replaced by two NCAA tournament appearances and one WCHA title game. Our triple-overtime game against Minnesota was still talked about, part of UND lore. Eight UND alumni played in the 2014 Olympics.

We were especially disappointed to find all this out on social media. In response, we posted a picture with our graduating class of seniors and wrote that "how you handle the hardest and toughest decisions is a true indicator of character. The players and staff at UND deserve so much more than what they got today. A complete lack of respect for people's lives was on full display, and today I am not UND proud." United States Senator Heidi Heitkamp shared our sentiments. "It's an unfortunate step for all female athletes, and especially those from a program that has created some world-class players," she said in a statement.

Others spoke out, and some of them pushed to revive the program. Nearly a dozen former players attempted a discrimination lawsuit, which a judge dismissed. The university had made its decision; the program was dead and available only to those who wanted to search the internet to revisit a time when hockey at UND was played by both men and women.

MONIQUE

We got on the team bus and headed to the rink for practice. Finally, all we had to do was skate, which was such a relief. Even at practice, several dozen fans were in the stands as we got on the ice and held up handwritten signs that said "#BeBoldForChange." One young girl had a sign that said, "Thank you for being bold." The feeling of mutual respect ran both ways. Our stand may have been built around women's hockey and the long-term inequities faced by the women's national team, but it addressed much more, and we were gratified that so many saw and felt that. Their support was really appreciated, and we were thankful the time had come when we could get on the ice and show it.

Before we flew to Detroit, our team believed that if we were on the ice for the first game, we were going to win the tournament. Again, confidence, not arrogance. We'd told each other that if we could get through the USA Hockey negotiations, we could get through anything. We had survived the hardest thing we had ever been through as athletes and as young women. Now all we had to do was go out and do what we were born to do—play hockey. Fittingly, our opening matchup was against Canada, and we shut them out 2–0. It was one of the better games we had ever played against Canada. It was also obvious that the way we stuck together during the boycott was an asset at game time too. In the next round, we beat Russia 7–0, and then momentum carried us past Finland 5–3 to put us in the semifinals.

Having played in seven World Championships, sometimes you have a single line that is clicking and seems to have a finishing touch. In these games, though, we had contributions from everyone. No one line was being relied upon to get it all done. We needed everyone, and everyone was up to the task.

The selflessness that had made us unbreakable now made us unbeatable. In the semis, which followed two more days of practice, we overpowered Germany 11–0 to send us into the gold-medal game against none other than Canada. The pressure was on us to win.

USA Hockey didn't issue a memo, but we sensed an attitude that was like, "You guys got what you wanted. You better go out and win." We also put pressure on ourselves. We understood what was on the line other than a gold medal. We were playing for pride. We had made plenty of statements in the media. Now we wanted to make one on the ice.

Our parents and Anthony were in the stands (Brent couldn't make it because he was at a work event), along with our brother, Jacques, his first time watching us in person at Worlds. Having family present always brings an added element of pride and wanting to do it for them. Our Ballard Spahr attorney Dee Spagnuolo was also in the family section with her daughter, Marina.

Canada took a 1–0 lead right at the opening-minute mark. Getting a goal scored on you early can be a punch in the gut, but we didn't let it rattle us. We came back and took a 2–1 lead early in the third period, but to know the Canadians is to know that they never feel as if a game is out of reach. They will battle and claw with everything they have, and like so many times before, they tied it up to make it 2–2 and send us into overtime.

It was just one of those tight games where the margin separating the two teams was as thin as could be. Nicole Hensley, who was playing goalie in her first World Championship gold-medal game, performed like she had been there for years. Shannon Szabados of Team Canada, who faced off against us in net more times than we can count, continued to scramble and keep the puck out of the net whenever there was a little ounce of hope that it could go in. Both teams showed the USA-Canada rivalry was alive and well.

Nearly ten minutes into overtime, Hilary Knight scored off a three-on-one rush. She took a pass from Kendall, teed one up in Hilary fashion, and boom! The next thing I knew, I was part of a huge dog pile. It was a celebration of our negotiation with USA Hockey as much as it was our fourth straight World Championship and seventh in the last eight years. No amount of team-building activities could have forged the bond this group had after going through the biggest battle of our lives off the ice. Now we were congratulating each other on the ice for winning the World Championship.

JOCELYNE

I remember standing on the blue line with Monique, waving up to our parents and the rest of our family and seeing Dee standing on her seat, waving a flag back and forth. It was one of those moments when I thought of everything that had happened in the past three-and-a-half weeks. Then I saw not only those weeks, but also years of our life, play out in front of me—the years we'd spent walking up to our confrontation with USA Hockey, and long before that, our mom driving us to practices and our dad telling us that if we had an idea of how to improve our team, it was up to us to talk to the coach, to fight our own battles.

And so it was with our whole team. We had grown as players and people. We had changed in ways that paralleled the way we had changed the game. Going forward, our battles were no longer about us as much as they were about expanding and redefining the opportunities for the next generation of girls and those coming up after them. Our victories, starting with this World Championship, were so much bigger than the score of any game.

25

EVEN STRONGER

★

"We approached every day as if it was a make-or-break try-out. Our job was to go out and play."

MONIQUE

That summer, Meghan Duggan, Kacey Bellamy, Alex Rigsby, Brianna Decker, Jocelyne, and I agreed to pose in ESPN magazine's Annual Body issue, which meant taking off our clothes and stepping in front of the cameras wearing nothing but our skates. The magazine captured the fun and confidence we brought to the photo session. "Six members [of the U.S. Women's National Team] posing nude on the ice?" they wrote. "Not even their bravest move this year."

But it was the coldest. The photo shoot was an unexpected opportunity that grew out of our new stature as advocates for change and equity. When we got the offer, all of us wanted to take advantage of our notoriety to send out a much-needed body-positive message—that even though we were successful elite hockey players, we came in all shapes and sizes. One look at the six of us, and you could see that we certainly did. Tall, short, lean, muscular. The hardest part of the shoot was smiling through the chilly temperature and trying to synchronize our movements for the photographer. It was challenging to get six naked women on skates, holding nothing but a hockey stick, to pose in an action shot without showing anything.

We laughed our way through the six-hour shoot. But the subject matter was serious. None of us hesitated when asked what size pants we wore. Jocelyne and I were a six or an eight, depending on the fit, and we all dove right into the difficulty we had finding pants that fit properly as female athletes. There was no reason to ever pretend we were a two or a four because…well, we weren't.

We were equally honest about our weight. Health and fitness was more important than a number—something that can't be said enough. Being proud of our strength and owning it was something we wanted to display because so many girls are taught to take up less space, to be thinner, to look a certain way, to blend in, not to stand out, and to be good but not too good. We wanted to flip the script and show that you can be strong and beautiful; you can showcase your talent and still be humble; you can take up space in the conversation and still want more; and you can and should strive for your own standard of excellence and never settle for anything less.

JOCELYNE

In early 2017, Comcast SportsNet (now NBC SportsNet) produced a documentary called *Tomboy*, a discussion of gender in sports, including the continued inequitable treatment of girls post-Title IX. Hilary Knight and I were among the women athletes featured in the film, along with Billie Jean King, Lindsey Vonn, and many others. Dee Spagnuolo asked if I wanted to participate in a panel discussion that was happening in July at Comcast headquarters about the documentary. This was one in a series of events that Comcast SportsNet and Comcast were presenting around the country to help promote the film and the cause of gender equity in sports.

It turned out that a top Comcast executive, David Cohen, the company's senior executive vice president and chief diversity officer, was hosting this series of events. David was also the former chair of Ballard Spahr and a good friend of John Langel's. When Ballard Spahr heard about this project, John and Dee Spagnuolo reached out to David and offered me up for the panel discussion, which unbeknownst to me (or anyone else) turned out to be a tryout.

After the panel, David introduced himself more informally and complimented me, saying that I had a compelling, powerful, and authentic story that had really grabbed the audience, including himself. He offered to talk more—and to help in any way he could. I didn't even know how to react. Was this complete stranger and busy corporate executive just being polite? And how could he help? But John and Dee told Monique and me that we shouldn't take that offer from David lightly, that he was personally passionate about diversity and inclusion issues and in particular gender equity, that he loved taking the side of the underdog, and that we should not underestimate David's ability to "help" on any issue and in any space.

I emailed David shortly after the panel. By then, he had already talked to John and learned the details of our negotiations with USA Hockey—all of them. Sometimes we thought David knew more about the negotiations than we did! He told me how impressed he was with the risks we had taken as a team and the courage we had demonstrated, and then he simply asked what we needed help on. Who does that? I soon learned that David was one of those rare individuals who not only asks but also delivers.

I came up with two needs off the top of my head: 1) help in organizing the marketing committee that we had agreed to create with USA Hockey and 2) sponsorship support for us as players and for the team. I could feel his smile through the phone. Within days, he introduced us to the leader of the Comcast Olympics marketing team who helped us brainstorm marketing opportunities for women's hockey. Shortly thereafter, our agent received a call from the team putting together Comcast's set of sponsored athletes for the Pyeongchang Olympics. By November, Hilary Knight, Monique, and I would be named three of Comcast's thirteen 2018 Olympic athletes, our first major sponsorship. It was just the beginning of our relationship with Comcast and David, but it was a welcome boost given all that had happened in the tumultuous negotiations with USA Hockey.

MONIQUE

In May, we were among the twenty-three players selected for the women's national team, the group we assumed would be on the roster for the 2018 Winter Olympics in Pyeongchang. On the advice of the medical staff and with the coaching staff's blessing, I did not have to participate in tryouts due to a separated shoulder I suffered in my last shift in the gold-medal game at Worlds. I took that as an indication the coaching staff wanted to keep the players free of as much stress and pressure as possible as we started the season leading up to the Olympics.

Then we saw Kelli Stack didn't make the team. We were stunned when the two-time Olympian and scoring machine wasn't one of the twenty-three players on the roster. Kelli was one of the most skilled players we had ever played with, and she wasn't afraid to display her skill on the ice. She was an effortless skater who had deceptive speed. This decision sent a message to this very close-knit team—and it wasn't necessarily a good one.

From the outset, something was off. Kelli not making the team was just the beginning. The full import of our unease might not have been immediately apparent in August when we packed our bags, said goodbye to our husbands, and moved to Tampa, Florida, for our six-month residency leading up to Pyeongchang. Hurricane Irma passed through the area shortly after we arrived, and thankfully we were spared anything more than a scare, but its threatening nature was an omen. When USA Hockey's director of women's hockey Reagan Carey announced our roster to the press, she made two points: the first was that these twenty-three players were going to be the team going to the Olympics; the second was that it was a long time between now and January and anything could happen.

JOCELYNE

At the end of October, we had a poor showing in an exhibition game against Canada in Boston, losing 5–1. We had played really well in our previous game against Canada, but like any good team, the Canadians had adjusted, and they just beat us. There was no need to panic. We still had an entire season ahead of us, and six games against Canada before the Olympics.

In attendance at that game in Boston were ten young girls who were a part of the Snider Youth Hockey Program, based in Philadelphia. Snider Hockey is a nonprofit that uses hockey to teach kids from under-resourced communities the game of hockey and the game of life. In addition to running hockey clinics and leagues, Snider Hockey provides homework assistance, career counseling, and college scholarships. Monique and I had worked with Snider Hockey for a few years. So we decided, along with our teammates, to fund a trip for these girls to go on college visits and come watch our game. Although the outcome of the game wasn't what we wanted, the presence of those ten girls was a reminder that our impact would go well beyond games won and lost. It felt like our coaching staff did not feel the same sentiment.

A couple days later, the coaches added U18 team captain and Boston College defenseman Cayla Barnes to the roster. We adored Cayla, but her arrival put the team on notice that the roster, seemingly set, was now in flux, and nobody's job was secure.

The following week, several players spoke to us confidentially about feeling unsettled by weigh-ins our coaching staff had initiated, and follow-up discussions citing player weights as evidence that some players weren't in shape. We brought this up in a meeting between the leadership group and our general manager before the Four Nations Cup, which was being played in Florida where we were living.

I don't think the irony was lost on anyone that six of us had been featured in the ESPN body issue talking about health and fitness being more important than a number, which we not only believed but also was backed up by research. All the reports we had read on elite female athletes said there was no ideal weight or magic formula for body composition. Each woman's body was different and unique to her. The bottom line was that these new weigh-ins created unhealthy stress for some of our teammates.

We weren't trying to be critical. We wanted to raise awareness of an issue that was sensitive to some players. That was our job as team leaders.

The next day, Monique and I were called into separate meetings with the coaching staff. Our head coach asked if I remembered what happened to Kelli Stack. "She's not here," I said. "Exactly," the coach replied. I had no idea what that meant in terms of Kelli having been left off the roster, but I understood the inference as it related to me.

MONIQUE

In my meeting, I found out that we would not be dressing in the first game, and one of the coaches would let us know when we would be back in the lineup. As it turned out, no one ever got back to us. Jocelyne and I didn't play the entire tournament. Obviously, something had changed between the coaches and us; we just didn't know what or why. We weren't injured. We didn't receive any feedback that indicated we were playing poorly. No explanations were provided. We were simply scratched from the lineup for an entire tournament.

Before each game, we sat through the pregame meetings while the lineups were read. We dealt with all the raw, up and down, difficult emotions of not hearing our names even though we were healthy, prepared, and ready to play. Ordinarily, if you are a healthy player who doesn't dress, a coach runs you through an extra practice since you aren't playing in the game. But Jocelyne and I found ourselves asking for ice time and then skating on our own without a coach. I can only imagine how this looked to Team Canada, Sweden, and Finland.

Jocelyne and I leaned on each other more than ever. Calls home to our husbands were important. They were great listeners, but it was hard for them to imagine everything we talked about unless you were there and saw it with your own eyes. We were able to lie to our parents about why we didn't play in the first game by saying the staff was resting us. After the second game, we didn't say a whole lot and hoped we would dress for the third game. When that didn't happen, we had a tough conversation with our parents and filled them in on everything that was going on behind the scenes.

Our teammates, who were under their own stress from the coaching staff, but still winning games and advancing through the tournament, saw what was going on, and their private support helped us manage all the emotions we were feeling at the time. We hung out with "the three kids," Kelly Pannek, Nicole Hensley, and Maddie Rooney, who lived across the parking lot from us, and they shared smiles and laughter with us at a time when they were hard to come by. Hilary Knight checked in with us daily, and Hannah Brandt took us out for frozen yogurt. In reality, everyone was checking in with each other. But we knew our teammates were there for us, and that support kept us sane and strong as the adversity continued.

Despite all of this noise and stress, the team won the Four Nations Cup, beating Canada 5–1 in the final for our third straight Four Nations championship. Our involvement in the tournament was summarized by USA Hockey as, "On roster, did not play," and we were relegated to watching the action from the stands.

After the tournament, we returned to practice for a week-and-a-half of training before our Thanksgiving break. At our first practice, we were congratulated for winning another Four Nations tournament. Our immediate reward was a day of practice without pucks. It was more like a punishment, as we were pushed past the point of exhaustion. A couple of our coaches stood on the glass and laughed as we tried to catch our breath. The following two days were more of the same.

We were trying to figure out how we were going to get through another practice without pulling a groin or having some type of lower-body injury. Thankfully, we got news that we were going to get the day off and then head into Thanksgiving break. As everyone was packing up their stuff and getting ready to head home, I received a text message to go to the coach's office for a meeting. My heart dropped, as my immediate thought was they were going to cut me from the roster and send me home. What came next caught me off guard. It wasn't the greatest news, but it was also a bit of a relief considering the other options.

At the time, Meghan Duggan was our captain, and Kacey Bellamy and I were the two assistants. The coach now told me I would no longer be an assistant captain and explained this was for my own good, so I could focus on myself, or, as I recall them saying, "So you can worry about yourself." Casual conversation followed with them asking what my plans were for my day off, as if it mattered to them. I was actually so speechless that the only thing I said on my way out was, "Thank you."

Our Thanksgiving break couldn't arrive fast enough. But on our way to the airport, Jocelyne and I both got a text alerting us to a mandatory team call. We parked and dialed in. Moments later, Reagan Carey announced that two more players, Sidney Morin and Haley Skarupa, a forward and a defenseman, were being called up to the team. The two of us did some quick analysis. We had been scratched from the entire Four Nations tournament, and now with two months before the Olympics, the coaches had brought in a forward and two defensemen. The roster was clearly in flux; it did not take a genius to know that Jocelyne and I were on the chopping block.

JOCELYNE

At home over Thanksgiving, we talked through the drama and tension with our husbands and family. We were able to clear our minds at the gym. When we train, unlike a lot of people, we don't wear headphones and listen to music. We want to be involved in the workout, not a song. In this instance, we were also listening to our bodies and our thoughts and, of course, to each other. In the end, as always, it came down to the two of us agreeing to face the reality of this situation together. We had one month to make the team that would go to the Olympics in Pyeongchang, South Korea, and to compete for a gold medal.

We returned to Tampa, knowing the coaches were not our biggest fans. To this day, we have zero explanation as to why the way we were treated changed so drastically. We approached every single day like it was a make-or-break day at tryouts. We knew everything we did was being watched and judged, and that we had to be "on" at all times, which was something we had to accept and deal with, even if by some chance we were wrong and the coaches didn't have us under a microscope. Our job was to go out and play, be the best teammates with great attitudes, and make it impossible for them to cut either one of us.

We had four games against Canada scheduled in December. We figured that we would only play in two of them if we were lucky. Which gave us zero margin for error when we were on the ice. Given the new players that had been called up, we knew the line between making the team and going home was razor-thin. It was a stressful way to play, but all of the preparation we'd put in over the years gave us confidence in our ability to perform.

MONIQUE

We lost our first game against Canada 2–1 in St. Paul. Two days later, we played the Canadians again in Winnipeg. Before the game, I was informed that I was moving from defense to forward and playing on a line with Jocelyne and Annie Pankowski. "Okay, cool," I said, mustering a can-do enthusiasm even though I hadn't played forward for three-and-a-half years. We lost that game 2–0, and then we dropped the next two, making that four straight losses to the team we expected to play for gold in Pyeongchang in February. The four losses showed a team struggling to come together without apparent reason.

Jocelyne and I sat out only one of those four games, but at least we sat out together. "If they really wanted to torture us, they would have sat us separately," she said.

Halfway through our final game against Canada, I separated my shoulder again. I had it numbed for the third period and continued to play. After the game, our doctor wanted to put me in a sling. "Absolutely not," I said, knowing the coaches were making cuts over the next few days, and they would send me home if I was in a sling.

The next morning, I was in the trainer's room at 4:00 a.m. to get my shoulder numbed again before our flight home. At the airport, I wore my backpack as I always did, except it was empty. I had put everything into Jocelyne's backpack. Back in Tampa, I got my shoulder numbed again before each of the next two practices. Unable to shoot like I usually could, I got rid of the puck as quickly as possible when it was on my stick. I don't know if the coaches ever noticed. I was giving it my best and resigned to whatever fate brought. This was a long way from being allowed to sit out tryouts so I could get healthy.

I tried to make sense of it all one night as I sat with Jocelyne, talking about the politics and injuries, the pressure being put on us, and some of the point-less instructions we'd been forced to follow, and I remember saying something like, "You know what? They would've already cut us if they thought they could win without us."

But maybe I had spoken too soon. Jocelyne and I received a text message from one of the assistant coaches, summoning both of us to a meeting. There it was, we thought, the bad news we had anticipated and feared. We were only days away from the final roster getting announced, and this was the time when the staff would make their final cuts. We talked through every possible reason for this meeting and tried to lessen our anxieties by agreeing the message would have come from the head coach or the team's general manager if we were being cut. Something else was up, we decided—and we were right.

We were met by head coach Robb Stauber and his two assistants. We all sat at a large round table, with the two of us facing the coaches, waiting for one of them to start the conversation and reveal what was going on. It seemed like they might have planned this moment of uncertainty for its effect on us before one of the assistant coaches finally broke the silence and said, "*If* you make this team, you're going to be the best f#@*ing fourth line in the world."

All three coaches looked at us intently, studying our reactions. We instantly understood that he was giving us an order that was also sort of a threat. But not a problem. We nodded, trying to come across as compliant and apprecia-tive. As I did so, I realized this meant I was playing forward. It also meant Jocelyne and I were going to play together, which was one positive detail in the conversation. And I said to myself, "Call us whatever line you want, but if you put the two of us together, there's no f#@*ing way we're anybody's fourth line."

Then, as I was processing these thoughts—and I am sure Jocelyne was doing the same—the head coach spoke up. "*If* you make this team and we can't send you home because you aren't doing the things we ask of you, what leverage do I have over you?"

Suddenly, I got it and realized that they really wanted to send us home, but for some reason that we will never know, they weren't going to. "Ice time," I said. Jocelyne quickly agreed.

"Exactly," Coach Stauber said. "If you don't do the things we ask, you're going to be sitting on the other side of the glass."

This whole interaction was really bizarre, but later, Jocelyne and I tried to see both sides. The coaching staff was probably working through their own anxieties after we had dropped four straight games to the Canadians. They had unexpectedly released Annie Pankowski after our loss in Minnesota, and then just a few days before Christmas, they cut Megan Bozek and Alex

Carpenter, both of whom were impact players. That was a shock to everyone. In our view, neither of those two should have gone home.

Under almost any other circumstance, we would have spoken up and asked questions. But we couldn't say anything. The two of us weren't just on a short leash. We didn't have any leash left at all. This had been the toughest tryout of our lives. It felt like we had fought our way through every single day of this residency, and I suppose we had, right down to the end. It took a while for it to sink in that we had made the team. The Christmas break came at just the right time. We needed to be with our families, to relax and regroup, and to shift our thoughts from trying to make the roster to winning Olympic gold.

JOCELYNE

Coach Stafford had always talked about finding the very first layer of passion for the game in your heart. When things got bad on the ice, he said it was important to go back to the purest reasons you were there: You loved to play the game. It was fun. Find the fun again. Go back to the fun. I didn't have to look hard to find that place.

On the Wednesday after Christmas, my brother Pierre-Paul, his childhood friend Matt Marchelle, and Brent and I put on our skates, bundled up, grabbed a handful of pucks, and played two-on-two on the coulee across the street from our parents' house, like we had done countless times throughout our childhood. It was late afternoon, and the temperature was only about three degrees. With Monique watching from the sidelines due to her injured shoulder, the four of us skated, bumped into each other, and laughed.

"This is the most fun I've had playing hockey in months," I said to Monique before she went back inside to escape the bitter cold. Beneath my knit cap, all she could see was a big smile plastered across my face. I know because she looked exactly the same. There was no doubt about it. We were back in our happy place. *Family...home...the two of us...hockey outside on the pond...waiting for Mom to put dinner on the table...dreaming about winning a gold medal together in the Olympics...*

We were going to be okay, and although I know it sounds strange, I just knew we were going to do it. Somehow. Some way. We were going to do it. The next time we came home, we were going to have Olympic gold medals.

26

PYEONGCHANG

★

"The time to prepare is over when it's time to perform."

JOCELYNE

When we returned to Tampa after the holidays, it appeared the coaching staff was trying to move past the negativity of the last few months and focus on getting the job done in Pyeongchang. We were back to a more familiar and positive routine of arriving at the rink early, getting in extra reps, and putting in as much time on the ice as was available. Whether or not we played as much as we wanted in South Korea, we were going to be ready. We saw the same intensity in our teammates. The fire was back.

About ten months earlier, someone close to the team shared an observation with several of us. She said if our team won the gold medal, it was going to be in spite of the coaches. Although we know how it sounds, it's a statement that is more a testament to the types of players and leaders we had within the locker room than a criticism of our coaches.

And our closeness as a team paid off. We all returned from Christmas break with a shift in mindset—we all realized that we were part of something bigger than ourselves. There was a singular focus on winning gold in Pyeongchang no matter what challenges came our way, whether it was our coaches or something else. Every time we stepped onto the ice, we had a lightness about us that we hadn't had for a while. We skated faster—our passing was crisper. It seemed like we had been through it all as a group over the past two years, and we were still up for whatever challenges came our way.

Toward the end of January, we played a mock Olympic schedule, which left the team with a significant amount of downtime between games. Players used the time to get in extra skates and training sessions. Everyone took it upon themselves to do whatever they thought necessary to feel their fittest and most prepared physically and mentally. Routines didn't need to be talked about or shared; everyone just took care of business.

We needed to let go of everything that had happened in the past—in Vancouver, in Sochi, in Tampa—and get to South Korea. Once we got there and stepped on the ice as a team, we knew things would take care of themselves. We had the talent. Even though we were missing certain individuals who deserved to be there, we still had a great team, and we kept the others with us in spirit. We had the desire. We just had to play. Despite everything that had transpired, we knew that when we got on the ice, we would win.

MONIQUE

The trip to Seoul was seventeen hours. We flew to Atlanta, which was a short hop, and then changed planes for the long haul to South Korea. Jocelyne, Hilary, and I settled into a row together. As the pilot and copilots ran through their checklists in the cockpit, we went through ours. We had our headphones charged and our Netflix shows downloaded onto our computers, iPads, and phones. Check, check, check.

In Pyeongchang, we settled into the Olympic village surrounded by buildings and venues and signs that reminded us this was the biggest stage in all of sports. After getting photos and media out of the way, we concentrated on our practices. In between, Jocelyne and I zipped around the village on scooters we rented in order to limit our walking. We heard about all the great coffee shops, so we found one nearby where we went every day. The barista got to know us and had our drinks ready every morning. We ate lunch and dinner in a building the USOPC set up for Team USA. Like our teammates, we were confident, excited, and ready.

Before our last practice, Jocelyne and I left the locker room and headed to the bench early to sit and take it all in. After talking about the 2018 Olympics for the past four years, we took a moment to appreciate the opportunity of being there again, both the enormity of it and also the meaning it held for us personally. It had been a long road for us to get to this point. Through the tangle of emotions, the one that dominated was our sense of relief as we sat there and said, "We're here."

The next day, we opened play against Finland. As we knew from past experience, the Finns are a dangerous team that can beat any team on any given day. Finland scored first, and with the world's best goalie protecting the net, even one goal was a dangerous lead. But I tied the game midway through the second period. Jocelyne chased down a loose puck in the corner. One of Finland's players fell awkwardly on her as I poked the puck free. I took the puck to the net and, with limited space, was able to get a backhand shot off her pad and then slammed home the rebound.

Jocelyne was pumped for the goal, but something was wrong with her knee. She later found out she had a grade-two MCL sprain that she played on the rest of the tournament. (Those scooters really did come in handy.) Less than three minutes later, Kendall Coyne put us up 2–1 thanks to a pass from Hilary that Kendall one-timed just under the crossbar. Finally, in the last few seconds, Dani Cameranesi sealed the deal with an empty netter. It was a good game, a test that left us sharper and even more dialed-in.

JOCELYNE

Right after the game, we got to see our parents, Brent, and our aunt and uncle. They were a welcome sight, being so far from home. I hadn't seen my husband since Christmas. Monique's husband, Anthony, planned to join us by the semifinals. Our parents had been with us through this entire journey, and we couldn't imagine not sharing these moments with them. I saw our dad wanted to comment on the game, and sometimes, if a game went well, we threw him a bone and said, "Okay, Dad, give it to us." But this time, knowing what we had been through to get this far, we all sat back and enjoyed each other's company and a good opening game. No hockey talk.

Two days later, we enjoyed a 5–0 win against Russia. Kacey got us on the board midway through the first period, and then, in the second, I scored off a shot from Monique's rebound, and six seconds later, notched another goal off a broken play. Those two shots set an Olympic record for the fastest two goals ever scored by one player. The Russian defender mishandled the puck, and I was able to poke it past the Russian D, go in on a breakaway, fake the shot, and backhand it past the goalie. After the game, my dad said, "You sold the sizzle."

We had plenty of goals after Gigi Marvin and Hannah Brandt added to our lead. The win ensured us a place in the semifinals.

MONIQUE

We went up against Canada in the third game of the first round and lost 2–1. We outplayed them in stretches and had more in-zone time than Canada, but goalie Genevieve Lacasse played a very solid game, which included denying Jocelyne's penalty shot in the second period. Jocelyne also hit a post, and we had a few scrums in front of the net where we weren't able to finish. It was just that kind of game.

But we outshot Canada 45–23, which was a positive statistic to take with us, and we felt good about how we played as a team, especially considering we had lost the last four games to Canada leading into the Olympics. We didn't just lose those games—we didn't play well—and we weren't the better team. This time was different. Despite the loss, we left the rink feeling like we were the better team and confident about how we played.

With four days between games, we traveled to see the Olympic torch up in the mountains and enjoyed some time with our family. Anthony arrived two days before the next game. Our practices were short and intense. In a meeting with the team's sports psychologist, Dr. Colleen Hacker, we revisited different situations the team had been through and reviewed various tools she recommended to stay focused, confident, and relaxed. Her advice was simple: You're ready to win this thing. Be confident in the work you've done. The time to prepare is over when it's time to perform.

Anthony had a similar saying: The hay is in the barn. In other words, there was nothing we could do now that would change the way we were going to play. There was nothing to practice that was going to make us play better. We'd done the work. It was just a matter of staying in a routine that would keep us sharp.

For our semifinal match against Finland, the game plan was to score early and force the Finns to play catch-up. Once the game started, we got that early lead from Gigi Marvin and never gave Finland a chance to come up for air. Dani Cameranesi scored two goals, and Hilary Knight and Jocelyne each connected on one. Maddie Rooney was perfect, stopping all fourteen shots that came in her direction. It was a solid team win—exactly what we wanted and *needed* as we advanced into the finals against Canada.

Afterward, we went up to the family section to celebrate with our husbands and parents. "Just one more game," said our dad, whose emotions prevented him from saying anything more. Our folks were next to the Duggans, the Knights, the Steckleins, and the Bellamys—all parents like ours who had been with their daughters every step of the way—and all of them were like my dad, pumped up and ready to take on the Canadians. I was literally yanked away from my husband. I turned around, and it was Kacey Bellamy's mom, Maura, giving me a big hug. "One more f#%*ing game. You girls just need one more."

27

GOLD

⭐

"It was a lifelong dream..."

JOCELYNE

February 22, 2018—game day. Relying on routine and preparation, we treated it like any other game, except it was the biggest game of our hockey careers. With the action scheduled to start at 1:00 p.m., we got up early. Jim Radcliffe, our strength and conditioning coach, led a warm-up in the basement of our building to get us moving and to get our legs going for the day. There were two sessions, one early and one later. Monique and I were at the early one; Hannah Brandt and Kendall Coyne also showed up.

Then it was time for breakfast—pancakes that I made from scratch the night before. Really good pancakes, with chocolate chips, bananas, and berries. If we had a superstition before games, this was it. My pancakes, which the team dietician and training staff cooked up for us. We ate as a team in our unit, which saved us from having to go to the universal cafeteria, gave us some more time to hang out together, and treat this like any of the many other game days we had experienced away from home.

Except we were in South Korea, this was the Olympics, and the game was the women's hockey final between the two teams everyone predicted would be vying for the gold, the same two teams that had met in four of the five gold-medal games since the sport was added to the Olympics—the United States and Canada.

Monique and I took our time getting ready in our room that we shared in the village. We took turns brushing our teeth and making sure our hair was straight. We met in the living room and checked the bags we would be taking to the arena. The little things mattered. Finally, we put on our Team USA jackets and prepared to head down to the bus. We sat down on our beds for a minute and absorbed the calm and quiet. Right before it was time to go, we looked at each other the way others who aren't identical twins might look in the mirror. We didn't have to speak to know what each other was thinking or what we wanted to tell each other. We knew.

We didn't come this far to only come this far. We have worked too hard, gone through too much. We are going to be difference makers.

We stood up, got our stuff, and walked toward the door. Just before we walked out of the apartment, I broke the quiet. "You always score when it matters." Monique smiled without saying anything, but I still heard her.

MONIQUE

The bus ride to the Gangneung Hockey Centre took about fifteen minutes. One player sat in every two-seat bench. Jocelyne was on the right side in the row just behind me. Everyone listened to their own music on their headphones. No one said a word the entire way there. The mood was quiet, confident, and intense. We were one team, unbreakable, and we were ready to make history.

I hadn't been this nervous since the national championship game our freshman year of high school when we were fifteen. But it wasn't a bad nervous. It was good, powerful energy that was hard to contain. I was ready to be on the ice. We all were. This was our time.

JOCELYNE

As game time approached, we taped our sticks, warmed up, played soccer, listened to music, sat on the bench, put on our gear, sat in our stalls, and did all of the things that players do to prepare for a game. We eventually gathered together and went through the routine of handshakes before walking down the hall from the locker room and skating onto the ice. We all had routines for this too. Some players had special handshakes. Some had superstitions. In our case, Meghan Duggan and the two of us made sure we were always the last three players leaving the locker room after having our little "get-together."

Moments after we skated onto the ice as the visiting team, we were joined by our Canadian opponents. We were not strangers. Many of the members of the U.S. Women's National Team, including us, had played with and against many of the Canadians in college, in all of our seven World Championship finals, and in prior Olympics (ten members of our team had played in the heartbreaking loss to the Canadians in Sochi). While off the ice, we were cordial and respected each other, but I can't say we really liked each other. We were elite athletes, all wanting the same result, all fighting for the same-color medal. We were rivals in every sense of the word.

There are a lot of great sports rivalries. But the US vs. Canada rivalry in women's hockey stands up to any of them. No rivalry in sport "pays off in entertainment-cardiac distress more reliably than this one," said Canadian journalist Cathal Kelly of the *Globe and Mail*. It has to be the most intense sports rivalry that most Americans have never focused on. But our team—and the Canadian team—were certainly focused on it, as were the 4,500 hockey fans filling every seat in the Gangneung Hockey Centre. The atmosphere was electric.

We looked toward the section reserved for family and found our parents and our husbands. It was a huge lift to see them in the stands. In that split second, we were incredibly grateful for their unquestioned support and for everything they had done to prepare us for a game like this. We were also deeply appreciative of the constant support from our friends, neighbors, and people we had never met back home who'd helped raise money so we could look up in the stands and see our family. The generous support we received was a reminder of the connections we'd made over a lifetime, and it reflected the pride a small city and state took in being represented in the Olympics.

For instance, one night, as we signed T-shirts at a UND men's hockey game, a woman asked Jocelyne if she remembered her son. "You played him in Pee-Wees," she said. "You checked him, and he broke his collarbone." Jocelyne didn't know whether to smile or apologize, but she remembered. "That was my son!" the woman beamed. "He's fine. He's grown up and married."

After the Olympics, we had a chance to meet and talk with Carson Wentz, the Philadelphia Eagles' star quarterback who was from North Dakota and played at North Dakota State. After we said hello to him, he smiled and said, "I know you. You used to kick my older brother's ass all over the ice."

This is one of the reasons athletes tear up during medal ceremonies. You don't just play for yourself. You play for your country, your state, your city, your neighborhood, and for all the people who were on teams with you in Bantams, PeeWees, and Termites and, although grown-up, still point at the TV and say, "I know them. I was on their team," or, in some cases, "She broke my son's collarbone."

It was cool how the many different strands of effort and history all came together at this special point in time. As an Olympic athlete, what you realize is that you're all still on the same team. You never leave. The team just gets bigger.

Finally, warm-ups ended, and before the opening faceoff, we had one last routine that we carried out with our line-mate Kelly Pannek. Kelly would sit between the two of us, we would give each other one pound on the knee and say, "Let's go, Millie; let's go, Diesel; let's go, Leo." Making us all smile as we thought a moment about our dogs back home.

It was game time.

At 1:10 p.m.—or 10:10 p.m. the previous day in Grand Forks—the puck was dropped. The biggest game of our lives, and a game that some predicted might be the biggest game in the history of women's hockey, began. Too often, big games don't live up to their advance billing, but from the start, this game more than delivered. Those of us playing could sense that.

During the first five or ten minutes, our two teams felt each other out. Canada had three penalties in the first period, and we capitalized when Hilary Knight scored on the power play from a deflection off a shot from Syd Morin—with twenty-six seconds left, giving us the lead and an important psychological boost.

Canada carried the play during much of the second period. Haley Irwin scored to tie the game from an impossible angle, leaving me wondering how she was able to put the puck in the net. Five minutes later, Canada went up 2–1 on a goal by our nemesis from two previous Olympic finals, Marie-Philip Poulin. "Not again," I said to myself on the bench when I saw her shot get past Maddie. I couldn't believe she was working her same heartbreaking voodoo again.

But toward the end of the second period, the flow of the game seemed to shift in our favor. Monique and I had a couple of shifts with some good in-zone time; as a team, we were outshooting our rivals; and the period ended with momentum favoring us.

We didn't score, but neither did Canada, and as was the case the entire game, whichever team had the lead—in this case, the Canadians—was never up by more than one goal. Nothing was safe. Anything could happen.

MONIQUE

Although down 2–1, we had been in this position with Canada in the past. There wasn't any panic. No one was saying, "Oh shit, we're down a goal." We shared a singular belief that we were going to find a way to win this game. Come hell or high water, someone was going to tie it up, and we were going to put gold around our necks. We just had to keep doing what we were doing, and one of our efforts was going to pay off.

A few minutes before we went back out, Haley Skarupa put her usual songs on before we hit the ice. It was just like any other game. We had work to do.

JOCELYNE

We continued to feed off the energy as we opened play in the third period. But we didn't capitalize right away, which created a test of will and concentration. Despite the frustration, you can't let up. We had a quiet confidence that someone, somehow, was going to score the tying goal. And that someone turned out to be Monique.

With about six minutes left in the period, we got beat on a faceoff in Canada's end and gave up a two-on-one rush. Monique was behind the goal line, the last player back. The Canadians' shot hit the knob of Maddie's stick. It was like time froze for the briefest moment, and when it started up again, Monique saw the puck coming around the corner.

MONIQUE

I was at the far blue line assessing how the play was going to develop. One of Canada's players went off for a change just as the puck came back up the ice. Jocelyne had picked off the defenseman, allowing the puck to continue up the boards where Kelly retrieved it. As soon as I saw Kelly was about to get the puck, I came off the wall and started yelling for it. If she managed to get it to me, I was going to be on a breakaway.

Kelly saw me and made an unbelievable pass. The puck traveled between the Canadian defender's stick and skates. With everyone in motion, there was one small opening to create the opportunity I had seen, and Kelly found it at the exact right instant. I caught the puck on my backhand with no one around me, a rarity that is nothing less than a gift from Coach Stafford's hockey gods, especially in a critical moment like that one.

I remembered getting a semibreakaway in the first game against Canada, the one we lost, when I tried to go to my backhand and lost the puck. I heard the echo of wise and true words from our old coach Peter Elander, who said when you have an opportunity to shoot, you should always shoot it. So this time, I wasn't thinking about anything but taking the shot. After I got the puck, I stick-handled it once and then shot the puck on Canadian goalie Shannon Szabados. The puck found the space just under her glove and went in.

I can't remember ever being more excited after scoring a goal. No sooner did I raise my hands in celebration than Gigi Marvin barreled into me. Emily Pfalzer came in next, a five-foot-two cannonball, and then Lee Stecklein crashed into me against the boards. It is a moment I can recall—and physically feel—to this day.

The score was tied 2–2—and regulation play ended with it that way. Up to that point, the game, as the *New York Times* reported, "had it all—lead changes, slick passing, game-saving goaltending, and a healthy dose of contact" with the Canadians "using their skill and physicality to bully the Americans around the ice," and the US countering with "puck possession, creativity and slashing attacks through the seams in the [Canadians'] defense."

Overtime delivered even more—more excitement and more momentum changes. We took nine shots in overtime, forty-one in total for the game, thirty-nine of which were turned away, leaving one social media commenter to ask whether we had considered that Canadian goalie Shannon Szabados was not human. With less than two minutes left, we were hit with a penalty and had to kill off a four-on-three power play. With less than thirty seconds to go, Canada's Rebecca Johnston got the puck in a similar spot where Poulin had it four years earlier, maybe a little lower. This was not going to happen again, I thought. I put my head down. I thought she was going to score, and I didn't want to see it.

But Maddie Rooney, our fantastic twenty-year-old goalie and an Olympic rookie—who was maybe too young to even understand the pressure—made a miraculous, desperation save. We survived—and the game and the gold medal came down to a shootout.

This was new territory, where none of us had been before in an Olympic final.

Per international rules, in a shootout, each team chooses five shooters, each of whom takes one shot, the shots alternating between teams. If the score is still tied after five shots, the two teams proceed to a sudden-death shootout, and the coach can pick any player to shoot, including players who have already shot.

JOCELYNE

Normally, the players have an idea of who will go if the game goes into a shootout. But I don't think anyone knew who the coach was going to pick before he announced the choices for our initial five shots: Gigi Marvin, Hannah Brandt, Emily Pfalzer, Amanda Kessel, and of course, Hilary Knight. We were going up against Canada's two-time gold medalist Shannon Szabados, arguably the best goaltender in the world, while the Canadians were taking aim at our amazing young goalie, Maddie Rooney.

Canada went first and didn't score. Then Gigi Marvin was first for us, and although she mishandled the puck, she got her stick on it and scored. Everyone on the bench let out a sigh of relief and went nuts at the same time! Then Canada's Meghan Agosta tied the score, sniping the puck blocker side past Maddie into the net. After another back-and-forth without a goal, Melodie Daoust zigzagged her way toward the net and put Canada ahead 2–1 with her own highlight-reel goal. I can't say how those watching the game felt, but from the bench, I know it was impossible to take a breath.

Amanda Kessel was the fourth person to shoot for us, and she tied it up, 2–2. She skated down the middle of the ice and kept the puck in a shooting position the entire time. When she hit the hash marks, she hesitated and dropped her shoulder slightly, just enough to freeze Szabados for a split second. She then shot it right over her glove. Amanda probably had the most pressure-packed shot of the entire shootout because if she didn't score and Canada did, it was game over. Her goal was huge. Right before Amanda went, I was told that I was going to be the sixth shooter if it was still tied up. I gave the coach a quick, crisp nod, took a breath, and refocused my attention.

But first things first. Canada's next shooter was up. And when we looked down at Maddie, she was cool as a cucumber. She had a slight smile on her face, and it looked like our twenty-year-old goalie, in her first Olympics, was having a ball out there. Why not? She stopped Canada's shot, which sent Hilary Knight up for us.

I was standing by the door as she got ready, and I was 100 percent convinced that she was going to score. We all were. The score was tied. She was the fifth shooter in the shootout. The Olympic gold medal was on the line. Hilary Knight was born for this exact kind of moment, and she stepped into it like she was putting on her favorite jacket that fit perfectly. Only Szabados made an extraordinary glove save, clearly defying the hockey gods and rewriting history as it was supposed to have happened.

With the score still tied 2–2, my turn arrived. The sixth shooter. True sudden death. I always wanted the puck when the game was on the line. And this was the sixth shot in a shootout for the Olympic gold medal. Like most athletes, I liked stepping into the drama of a high-pressure situation and, of course, was eager and even a bit impatient, if that makes sense, for the opportunity to help my team win. I had been doing well in shootouts in practice leading into this game. Time to do it for real.

I was standing beside Brianna Decker. Nicole Hensley opened the door for me, and I skated slowly towards Maddie to give her a pound, clearing my mind, shutting out the noise, and entering the moment. Then I slowly circled back, keeping my eyes on the puck at center ice, focused on the one task I had been asked to accomplish.

MONIQUE

I saw the look in Jocelyne's eyes, the expression on her face, her whole demeanor, and I knew what was going to happen. It was the most pressure-packed situation you could ever be in as an athlete. You are in the gold-medal game. It has gone into and through overtime. It has gone through the first five shots of the shootout. And the game is still tied. Now you are the sudden-death shooter in the shootout. You are playing for your country. Every person on your own team wants you to score. Your parents are in the stands. Your husband is in the stands. Everyone you have ever known is watching on television or streaming. Millions of people around the world are tuned in. The pressure doesn't get any greater. But I saw Jocelyne turn the corner and take a deep breath as she started to come down the ice, and I thought, "She's got this."

JOCELYNE

I was in the zone. I had already done my homework. I had watched video of NHL players Patrick Kane and T.J. Oshie in shootouts. I had listened to an NHL goalie talk about how players who slow up their pace and change their angles on approach throw off the goalie's timing. I had worked on a lot of different moves in practice, not because I was preparing for a shootout—let alone a shootout for Olympic gold—but because if you want to score on your own goalies, you can't keep doing the same thing over and over.

But I knew exactly what I was going to do on this attempt. I had practiced it going back to the days Peter Elander drilled us time and again at UND. It was a fake shot—fake backhand and drag to the forehand—with a good amount of head-and-shoulder movement thrown in, like Britney Spears on the dance floor. Hence the move's name, "Oops, I Did It Again."

Coach Elander, in his thick Swedish accent, had critiqued every rep we did. "Number three, you didn't push out wide enough." "On number one, that was good." "Number two, you got to get on your edge more." It was feedback overload. We performed those moves hundreds if not thousands of times with him critiquing each one, breaking them down and repeating them until they were second nature to us.

This was my go-to move—that is, when I could pull it off. Because I had messed it up hundreds of times, maybe more, trying to incorporate Peter's feedback. But that's what practice is for, to make the difficult stuff seem easy, automatic. This was a brand-new reality, though. In this situation, at this moment in time, nothing that had come before mattered, not the misses or the successes. All that mattered was this one shot. This was for the Olympic gold medal. It was me, the puck, and the goalie. A test of will, talent, and fate. "I'm going to end this thing right now," I said to myself.

I had paid attention to the way those before me had attempted their shots. Everyone had come down the middle at pretty much the same pace without changing up the angle of their approach. I recalled the importance of alternating styles, speeds, and rhythms to throw off the goalie's timing and ability to anticipate. I heard the ref blow the whistle, which meant I could go when I was ready. I picked up the puck and went wide to the left and really slow, changing it up from everybody else's approach. I took an inside edge back out wide to the right before I took my final strides toward the net down the middle. I tried to gauge how far out from the net Szabados was as I came down. I kept my eyes up and the puck in a shooting position in case the goalie's angle was terribly off and there was a big hole to shoot at, which was very unlikely.

Once I hit the bottom hash mark, I started the sequence that has turned into the most important play of my hockey career. I opened my blade, faked a shot with my weight on my right leg, and let my left leg kick back, getting the goalie to flinch at the movement. I slid the puck to my backhand and transferred all my weight to my left leg, getting Szabados to drop to her knees and lean all the way to her right. Finally, I brought the puck back to my forehand and had a foot and a half to slide the puck into an open net. I could hear Peter yelling down the ice, "Great fake, perfect weight transfer."

"Oh my gosh, that's electrifying, that's as good as you're going to see anywhere," NBC Sports announcer Pierre McGuire said on TV. (I saw it on the news later and was electrified myself as I watched.) "Great move. Great hands. Great deception," added his broadcast partner AJ Mleczko, herself a gold medalist on the 1998 US team.

The drama of actually taking that shot boiled down to maybe ten seconds, with the shot itself—later called the greatest shot in the history of women's hockey by the *Washington Post*—taking a fraction of that, probably less than two seconds.

But what often goes unappreciated in such moments, when everything literally comes down to a second or two, is the lifetime of work, preparation, sacrifice, and learning that came before it. In our case, it was two lifetimes of getting up at 4:30 a.m. for work, then training, then going to the rink for skates, and eventually making our way back to work. It had been years of that, and before that, it was working out at the gym and going to school. And before that, it was being driven around by our parents to hockey practices and games. And all along the way, we received support from family, friends, and our community who believed in us as much as we did ourselves, sometimes even more. All for such a moment.

But here's the thing.

We were in front, 3–2.

But we hadn't won yet.

Canada still had a chance to tie and keep the shootout going.

I skated back around and gave Maddie another pound. The fierce look in our eyes mirrored each other. I said, "Game over," and then went back to the door and threw my stick behind the bench, where Brianna Decker and Amanda Kessel each gave me a pound as I took my place next to them. Then we held our breath as we watched Meghan Agosta come in with her shot. I already had a leg over the door and was ready to jump on the ice. "This game's over," I said out loud to no one in particular. "Maddie's going to stop this. Come on, Maddie. Come on, Maddie…"

Then Maddie made the biggest stop of all of our lives. Agosta, who had already scored earlier in the shootout, got in close, and Maddie didn't give up an inch of room. Her right leg halted all forward progress of the speeding puck with a thud that filled the Gangneung Ice Arena. The puck drizzled to the left before Maddie flipped it away with her glove and raised her arms in triumph.

I was ready to launch myself out the door as Maddie was making the final save. Then it was chaos in the arena and on the ice. We were throwing our gloves, jumping up and down, and diving into a huge dog pile on top of each other. I was at the bottom next to Maddie. Our heads stuck out; we looked at each other with expressions of unrestrained excitement. The hugs were amazing. I embraced Gigi, Lee, Meghan, and everybody else close enough to grab. It is impossible to put the absolute joy into words. "We did it!" I said over and over again.

We had won! We had won the gold medal.

We were Olympic champions.

Monique was still somewhere in the frenzy of the celebration when I skated over to the bench to grab my American flag. The flag, which had flown over the US Capitol, had been given to me in 2010 after the Vancouver Olympics by North Dakota Senator and former governor Kent Conrad. We didn't win four years later in Sochi, so I put it away. Before we left for Florida, though, I got it out, folded it properly, and put it in my hockey bag. I carried it with me everywhere we went the rest of the year leading up to the Olympics. Before the gold-medal final, I gave it to our trainer, Sherri Walters, and asked her to keep it on the bench for me after we won—because we just knew that we were going to win.

I draped it around me. With the stars in my right hand and stripes in my left, I skated back into the frenzy, where I finally spotted Monique coming toward me. As close as we are, we don't hug very often. But we had just realized our childhood dream and won Olympic gold. That merited a hug. A long, tight one. The American flag draped around our shoulders as we shared a moment with just the two of us. We had done it together. But in that hug was also a sigh of relief. We had sacrificed so much to accomplish something that was never guaranteed. We skated together toward our teammates and around the rink, taking it all in together, enjoying this very intimate, private moment in front of millions of people, our smiles as bright and wide as the stars and stripes themselves.

MONIQUE

I was the first player to shake hands with our coaches and give them hugs. After hugging all other staff members, I looked up in the stands for our family. I spotted our husbands and our dad at the top of the family section, waiting for the crowd to disperse before trying to get all the way down to where they could congratulate us. Our dad was standing on top of the railing with his hands in the air like Leonardo DiCaprio on the *Titanic*. He had the biggest smile on his face I had ever seen. I saw Meghan Duggan nearby, climbing into the stands to get to her mother. Then I looked to my left. And I saw our mom, her cheeks streaked with tears. Somehow, she'd managed to get all the way to the railing by our bench.

"We did it! We did it!" I said. Anthony was right behind her. He took my face in his hands and said, "*You* did it," but I shook my head and corrected him. "No, *we* did it." Our families were the team behind the team. The win belonged to them too.

The actual medal ceremony was almost dreamlike. We had been through it in two previous Olympics but had never experienced the gold-medal celebration. I can report that the view from the top was as breathtaking as we had always imagined, and we were filled with joyous anticipation as we watched Finland receive their bronze medals and the Canadians their silver. Finally, it was our turn. Angela Ruggiero, our former teammate and mentor who was an athlete representative on the IOC and also a member of the gold medal–winning 1998 women's team, presented us with our medals.

We had shared this journey with her just as she'd shared hers with us, and for Ang to be part of our gold-medal experience in such a special way was pretty awesome. For many of us, it was a poignant and profound illustration of the way women of one generation were there for those in the next and the responsibility we all have to keep that going and to be there for each other.

Part 4

BIGGER THAN US

★ ★ ★

28

ALMOST FAMOUS

★

"It felt like we high-fived with half of America."

JOCELYNE

Somehow, we were still on our feet—but just barely. The game was over, and the medal ceremony was long past. We finally made it through the media mix zone following over an hour of interviews. Around 7:00 p.m., showered and changed, we met up with all our families at a restaurant near the village. We only had about an hour with them before starting up more rounds of interviews. But it was enough time to exhale and take in the celebration with our families. Dad was quiet and patient as we enjoyed some wine and laughter. He bided his time, waiting for his turn; we knew he had something to say about the game since he always did.

Finally, it was time to let him speak. "Okay, Dad, what'd you think?" I said. Smiling, he recalled the shot I had missed in the second period and said, "You should've had two." Everyone cracked up. We had won the Olympic gold medal, and in fact, were wearing them around our necks, and our dad still found something we could do better as he always had done our entire lives. Enjoying our victories, and simultaneously pointing out areas for improvement.

The *Today Show* was next. Backstage, all of us were starving. They rustled us up some McDonald's, the only thing available on short notice and in large quantities. We all ate pretty healthily, but you would have never known it from the way we inhaled our Big Macs, quarter-pounders, and fries. Monique was vegan and hadn't eaten meat in eight months, but she scarfed down a burger and then promptly stepped outside and threw up. The glamor of winning a gold medal only went so far.

Then, at 7:00 a.m. ET, all twenty-three of us led off the morning broadcast of the *Today Show*. We had to pinch ourselves. A bunch of women hockey players appearing at the top of the *Today Show*, as the opening story. Really? We were a bit starstruck by Savannah Guthrie and Hoda Kotb. But it turned out that they were a little starstruck by us too.

MONIQUE

Of course, they wanted to hear about the game, including my tying goal and Jocelyne's winning goal. They also brought up our negotiations with USA Hockey the year before. When you thought about it, we had gone through some remarkable experiences over the course of our hockey careers, especially in the past year. In one year, we had moved from watching a clock tick in a conference room as we approached the negotiating deadline for us to make the World Championships to watching the scoreboard clock tick down in an arena in which the gold medal in the Olympics was at stake.

While we weren't in any rush to stop talking about and savoring our gold medals, Jocelyne and I were already pivoting to the future—What did it all mean? What had we learned? What were we going to do with that knowledge? Not that we knew or had thought through all the next steps. But we knew that our battle with USA Hockey and our gold medals were not the end of the story. They were important chapters that we were continuing to write.

So we started to think and talk about not just the thrill of winning the gold medal, but also about the awesome power and platform that medal gave us to continue to fight for gender equity in hockey and in the larger world. Although we didn't use these exact words, we were beginning to consider our agenda to cheer for the one behind and to make a difference in a world broader than hockey and sports.

The week and a half after the Olympics was a whirlwind of travel and media appearances across the country, a blur of questions, airports, flight schedules, security lines, hotel check-ins and check-outs, fast food, healthy food, and calls home to let our husbands know where we were even if we had to check our itineraries because we didn't always remember. In LA, we guested on *Ellen*, met *This Is Us* star Justin Hartley, and tried to sweet-talk *Bachelor* host Chris Harrison into telling us who Arie Luyendyk wound up with at the end of season twenty-two. Even as gold medalists, we had to wait for the season finale to find out.

Before leaving LA, we made one of several appearances at NHL arenas, this one at the Staples Center. The NHL players, coaches, referees, and fans gave us a tremendous reception. On our way out, we were intercepted by a mother who asked if she could take a picture with her two young daughters. "My girls are twins, and they are big hockey fans," she said. "They'd love to have their picture taken with the two most famous twins in hockey!"

Although we were being told to keep moving, we still stopped. How could we say no?

The funny thing is that when we saw the picture, both girls were ignoring the camera and our gold medals. Instead, they were looking up at the two of us, as if seeing an older version of themselves.

JOCELYNE

After LA, Monique and I took a detour to New Jersey, where we were on air with the NHL Network for its first all-female broadcast. We were in New Jersey for less than twenty-four hours before we were back on the ground in Tampa for one last team signing of all types of apparel. That night, the team was off to Washington, DC, where we were introduced during the intermission of the NHL Stadium Series game at the Naval Academy.

Next was the Big Apple, New York City. New York was jam-packed with heady appearances. We were on the *Tonight Show* with Jimmy Fallon. Hilary guested on *Saturday Night Live*. We visited Times Square—posed on top of taxi cabs. The following morning we were asked to ring the bell to open the stock market at the New York Stock Exchange. We really were on a roll. After four dismal sessions in a row, the Dow Jones surged up 1.4 percent on the day we rang the bell!

That night, we made an appearance during a Rangers game at Madison Square Garden, one of the iconic sports arenas in the country, where we received another standing ovation from that city's rabid hockey fans. The best were the people we met in airports, restaurants, and on the sidewalk. It seemed like we high-fived half of America. As much as we were ready to go home, the warm receptions we got did not get old.

Just before we were scheduled to leave, I received an email from David Cohen. He was hosting a post-Olympics event in Washington for leaders and influencers in the Asian American community, and he wanted to know if we would be interested in being the special guests at this event to give it some splash. This event was not tops on our list of things to do—we were pretty tired—and eager to get back to Grand Forks. But Comcast had been very good to us—and I liked David and appreciated all his support throughout the past year—so we said yes and delayed our return home for an extra day.

When David found out we had not yet made it home after the Olympics—and that we were delaying our return home to do this event—he emailed me and told us we should go home, that this event wasn't sufficiently important. He apologized for even asking and for not realizing that we hadn't been home yet. We talked and decided we wanted to honor our commitment and do the event. It was a life-changing decision.

The three of us talked late into the night. And while David had his usual insane schedule the next day, he made time for another few hours to talk at lunch—and more time after the event. Monique had not even met David before this trip, and beyond a few phone calls and emails, I had only met him once in person. The fact that he was willing to spend so much time with us was a testament to his commitment to equity—his belief in us—and to his wanting to fight for the underdog and try to right what he perceived to be wrongs.

David had a lot of questions for us. What were our goals? What did we want to accomplish? Did we have any concrete plans? Did we want to compete in the 2022 Olympics? Did we have any sponsorship irons in the fire? We told him right then that we planned to train and compete for a place on the 2022 Olympic team, but our more immediate goal was to start families of our own.

This appeared to please him more than anything. As we got to know David better, we saw why. Family was at the core of everything he believed in. He really respected that our winning a gold medal had not turned our heads and that our basic value structure remained in place. As we talked about developing our brand and post-Olympics career, David helped us organize our thinking and even helped us draft a comprehensive written plan. Whether it was building a social media presence, making ourselves go-to sources for reporters writing about gender-equity issues, finding appearances that promoted social causes that were important to us, writing a book, or even considering the development of our own personal foundation to support causes that interested us, he always brought us back to basic questions: Who were we as people? What did we believe? What did we want to accomplish?

It's hard to express how much David challenged us. He took our dreams and our thoughts, gave them structure, and then dared us to think much bigger than we had ever imagined. We might have known hockey, but David knew business, brand development, and communications, and he believed in us—maybe even more than we believed in ourselves. He urged us to dream as big in our post-Olympic life as we had dreamed about winning an Olympic gold medal.

Interestingly, almost every discussion we had on these topics brought us back to the way we had been raised and the core values instilled in us by our parents. Everything boiled down to family and trying to share with others the sense of love, strength, and support we got from our parents and brothers. With time to reflect, we knew this was core to us too. And David kept encouraging us never to forget or walk away from those values.

Our almost two-week national victory tour was pretty special. But as Dorothy so poignantly noted in the *Wizard of Oz*, there's no place like home. And our return home was a vivid reminder of the importance of a lifetime of North Dakota values that had influenced our lives. It was March 8 when we finally arrived in Grand Forks, but it was like the Fourth of July in our neighborhood. My garage was wrapped with a welcome-home message and picture, and Olympic rings were painted in the snow.

By six that night, we were at the Ralph Engelstad Arena, where we had played so many games and practiced so many times, for a welcome-home celebration. The Ralph wasn't Madison Square Garden or the Staples Center, but we weren't prepared for the emotional punch of this congratulatory event.

As we arrived, the main entrance windows were filled with signs kids from local schools had made. Little girls and boys wore their youth-hockey jerseys. Kids were hanging their arms over railings from an upper-level balcony because that was the only place they could find to stand. Old teachers, coaches, friends, and strangers filled the arena, and in the front row were our husbands, parents, grandma, and extended family.

Our eyes filled with tears of joy as we waved and smiled at the crowd. The warmth and enthusiasm of the reception was almost indescribable. Forget about the glitz of LA and New York, this not-so-intimate Grand Forks welcome from our friends and neighbors—people who had supported us for our entire lives—hit us in the gut with much more power and emotion. We really were home, the place where this all started.

29

PLAYING FOR TWO

★

"Being moms is the most important job we'll ever have."

MONIQUE

Before I left for the team's six-month residency in Tampa leading up to Pyeongchang, Anthony and I made a plan to start a family after the Olympics. Since Jocelyne and I tended to do everything together, motherhood was also a priority for her, and on the same timetable as me. In Pyeongchang, it was a running joke on the team: who was going to get pregnant first?

As it turned out, I had to give up wine before Jocelyne. We were having dinner with Julie Foudy and her parents the day before an event in California when I had my last glass of wine. Jocelyne and I were on our way to Chicago for an event when I found out I was pregnant. Being that I am not a great keeper of secrets, I, of course, told Jocelyne right away and then waited until we got home to tell Anthony.

I gave Anthony a card that read, "Get ready, you're going to be a dad." He was overjoyed and so excited. Within two weeks of finding out I was pregnant, I started throwing up every day, multiple times a day. This became my new normal throughout pregnancy. I gave up my very part-time gig as an in-studio analyst for the NHL Network. I just didn't feel comfortable going on the air for an hour doing live shows and potentially having to step off set to throw up.

I surrendered to the reality that every day was going to be different, but working out was usually the one part of the day when I felt "normal" or like myself. As an elite athlete, I'm used to being in control of my body and having it feel a certain way, but I had to embrace the fact that my body was going through some amazing changes.

JOCELYNE

In March, I was traveling home from Philadelphia (Monique, who had started to tell family and close friends that she was pregnant, had returned before me). My dinner that evening did not agree with my stomach, and I just felt off.

As soon as I arrived home, I took a pregnancy test, and it was positive. I wanted to tell Brent, but he wasn't getting home from work for a couple of hours. I found it impossible to sit by myself with such happy news without telling someone. So I called Monique. "I knew it," she said. Apparently, she really did know. She had told Anthony she thought I was pregnant while I was in Philadelphia. Both of us burst out laughing, excited for each other. As always, we were going to go through this experience together.

During our pregnancies, Anthony, who'd now trained us for the past four years and knew our bodies and workout capabilities better than we did, monitored us closely and created modifications for our second and third trimesters. We wanted to stay fit and feeling strong, but to be smart about it. Every day was different. Listening to our bodies took on a whole new meaning.

We also maintained a full work schedule, attending over fifty events around the country, mostly for Comcast. The company worked around our training schedule and gave us plenty of time to rest. Everyone was particularly solicitous of Monique because of her morning sickness. No one was more focused on our prenatal health than David Cohen, who was often the one telling us to take it easy. The company wasn't just amazing – everyone was enlightened. And this enlightenment and respect for us as mothers continued after our babies were born.

MONIQUE

I checked into the hospital on the night of December 10, expecting to be induced in the morning, as planned. But my water broke, and I went into labor. As labor progressed, Anthony asked the doctor what he could do to help, and she started telling him how to deliver a baby. "You're going to let him do *that?*" I asked in a panicked voice, looking over at Jocelyne, who was standing next to me. But things went fine, and at 9:48 p.m. on December 11, 2018, Mickey Salvatore Morando was born, weighing in at seven pounds, fourteen ounces, and our worlds have never been the same since. Two days later, Anthony and I took Mickey home and introduced him to our other family member, our basset hound, Millie.

I was tired but blissful. My nausea disappeared. My heartburn went away. It was almost magic. And in their place, I had the greatest gift anyone could imagine, a beautiful little boy.

JOCELYNE

My last workout was on Friday, January 18. Three days later, I checked into the hospital and started the most physically uncomfortable thirty-six hours of my life as this little person inside me debated when he wanted to make his first appearance in this world. After two nights of contractions, Monique arrived with breakfast for Brent. Later that morning, as I gritted my teeth through contractions, I snapped at Brent to stop pacing beside the bed. "Pick a spot and stand there."

"Be nice," Monique said. "He's nervous."

Later that morning, at 7:28 a.m., the doctor turned to Brent and said, "Congratulations, you have a little boy." He was eight pounds, eight ounces—a big boy like his dad. We named him Nelson Maurice, after Brent's and my grandfathers. After a few days in the hospital, we took Nelson home and started our lives as parents and falling in love with our little guy all over again every day.

Soon, Monique and I were back in the gym training together. Fortunately, we had my mother to fill in and babysit the boys while we worked out and got our feet underneath us. Seeing how hard this was, I wondered how she had managed to do this with six kids under the age of five—plus training for twenty-five marathons? Her ability to tune out the crying and manage the chaos with ultimate patience was a great lesson.

MONIQUE

I stepped back on the ice for the first time at the end of February, almost exactly one year from the date of our gold-medal win in Pyeongchang. Jocelyne started to skate again seven weeks after Nelson was born. At first, skating was just to shake the rust off and get back into the groove—simply getting a feel for being back on the ice. We worked on our hands, our shooting, and our skating. We did the same drills we did as kids. Getting back into hockey shape was going to take time. It was going to be a process.

As parenthood would be, too. That much was immediately obvious to both of us. Watching our parents and grandparents hold our babies opened our eyes and infused our hearts with the big picture of parenthood. There was so much joy. Parenthood also came with responsibilities: some big picture, like working to create a better future for our children and those who might come after them, and some more immediate. We felt right away the motherly instincts to protect, nourish, and care for our babies. We also recognized that our workout schedules took a back seat to feedings and naps. We weren't ever going to come first again, and we knew that was as it should be as parents.

We kept up with news about other female athletes having babies and returning to their sports, such as track great Allyson Felix, tennis legend

Serena Williams, and WNBA All-Star Skylar Diggins-Smith. We also had many friends outside of athletics who'd had babies and were in the same situation as us. Motherhood was the greatest job we would ever have, but what about the careers we had before having children and the goals we still wanted to achieve? Our sights were set on continuing to build out our gold-medal platform and pursuing our ongoing fight for gender equity and making a difference in the lives of underrepresented populations. Further in the distance was potentially playing in our fourth Olympics in 2022 and winning another gold medal. But first, we had to make the team. And before that, we had to get back into shape.

It was, as we told ourselves, a process that started with questions all too familiar to women in our same position. Did we have to choose between our careers and being mothers? Could we still achieve at the same high level and be excellent moms to our children? Were there any reasons we couldn't do both? Would we receive a fair evaluation from the coaching staff? Those were important questions, but we had more. And for us, it was even more complicated. Because we had already had a taste of our ability to make a difference in other people's lives. Could we also continue our fight to level the playing field for girls and ensure they had all the same chances to succeed in sports, school, work, and life in general? Could we continue to battle for gender equity and diversity and inclusion throughout the country? Could we make a difference in our own North Dakota community?

What became apparent was that these weren't new questions. They were simply new ways of looking at old challenges. We had time to figure things out. That's what life is all about, figuring things out. We knew a day would come when we'd step away from the game, hoping we'd left it in a better place than when we entered it. But we weren't done with the sport—and we certainly weren't done with fighting to change it for the better.

We still had the passion, drive, and motivation to compete. Although we were just getting back on the ice, we still had fun. We were going to bring a different perspective to working out, making the team, wanting to win another gold medal, and fighting for a more equitable playing field. And we planned to do it all while changing diapers, juggling day-care schedules, and applying to preschool. Striking this balance would be the hardest thing we had ever done. But we had amazing husbands to share the responsibilities. We also had the maternity benefits that we were able to negotiate with USA Hockey in 2017. We were proud of the way USA Hockey had emerged as a leader among the governing bodies of Olympic sports because of its strong maternity-leave policies and benefits. Without them, we wouldn't have been able even to think about coming back as quickly as we planned, if at all.

Mickey and Nelson ensured that our transition into this new stage of our lives and careers would be realistic. We weren't playing for ourselves any-more. Not that we ever had. Not when team always came first. Not when we were expected to make a difference. Not when we were taught to cheer for the one behind. But now we were playing for our boys—and they would have a lot to say about our path going forward, even before they could talk.

30

CHEER FOR THE ONE BEHIND

★

"Making Mom and Dad proud never gets old."

JOCELYNE

I n July 2018, during the middle of our pregnancies, we announced a unique multiyear partnership with Comcast that expanded our existing relationship. This partnership was not about selling cable services. Instead, we were being asked to help amplify Comcast's community values initiatives tied to promoting a more level playing field, more equitable treatment of underrepresented populations, advocacy for those in our country who were being left behind, and making a difference in the community.

This felt very comfortable. We'd built a platform as athletes. Comcast was giving us a new platform as human beings. The partnership was a remarkable alignment between what the company stood for and what we believed.

At least in the immediate aftermath of the Olympics, it was easy to revel as the toast of every town we visited. Invitations were plentiful. But we tried to be volitional about the process of building appearances and opportunities to advocate for gender equity and, ultimately, a broader equity agenda—our core beliefs.

One of our appearances for Comcast was with a class of kindergarteners in Boston. As I spoke to the kids, Monique noticed one little boy had separated himself from the rest of the class and hid under a table on the other side of the classroom. She crawled under the table with him and showed him her medal. "Do you want to see this really big coin?"

Soon he had the medal around his neck and was back among his classmates. We hoped it was the beginning of another dream, his dream. I think we are quick to recognize people who don't fit in and help them feel included. During a Q&A in that classroom, kids asked where we kept our medals, if we had to shine them, if we wore them, and were they heavy. Then one little boy who'd been scrutinizing our medals raised his hand. "So what do you do with them?" he asked.

This was the question we had asked ourselves even before the Olympics. It was the question we had been discussing with David Cohen and that he had challenged us to answer. What do you want to do with your medals? Part of that answer was our decision to become brand ambassadors for Comcast's corporate values initiatives, including especially Comcast's renowned internet-adoption program for low-income Americans, Internet Essentials. Tony Dungy and Jackie Joyner-Kersee had each served as national spokespeople for Internet Essentials before us, and the company was looking for a new spokesperson. As soon as we heard Jackie Joyner-Kersee, we were ready to sign up and get to work.

MONIQUE

It was tempting to allow large audience-speaking opportunities and big events to dominate our schedule. They were easy—and good for your ego.

But we didn't want to let these large-scale opportunities replace our ability to interact with individuals. We had discovered that the magic happens when you actually sit down with people, look into their eyes, listen to their stories, and try to figure out a way to help.

We found a way to do this by getting involved in trying to help close the digital divide. As much as everyone we know relies on the internet, it's hard to believe that almost 30 percent of Americans don't have an internet connection at home. It's hard to believe until you see it and hear the stories. And those households on the wrong side of the digital divide are disproportionately poor and disproportionately people of color. And they are being left behind. This was exactly the type of big—really big—equity issue we were passionate about tackling. Hard to do on our own, but the partnership with Comcast helped both of us amplify our impact.

So we jumped in. The Internet Essentials program provides a low-cost, high-speed data connection, a heavily discounted laptop computer, and massive amounts of digital literacy training to drive internet adoption. Comcast has connected millions of households to the internet through this program.

We saw the impact of this program firsthand. We traveled across the country to more than seventeen cities—one hundred-plus events—talking about the importance of closing the digital divide—and giving away thousands of free laptops in classrooms, recreation centers, senior centers, public housing developments, veteran centers, YMCAs, Urban Leagues, libraries. We met mayors and governors and attorneys general, senators and members of

Congress, and hundreds and hundreds of children, parents, teachers, seniors, veterans, and people with disabilities.

Each Internet Essentials event is emotional. Whether the laptop giveaway is to kids, adults, seniors, or veterans, there is always a short, stunned silence followed by unbelievable joy as what is happening sinks in. One senior citizen at an Urban League office stood up and started singing her thanks to God. At the Minnesota State Fair, we got hugs from veterans with tears in their eyes. One little boy told his teacher that this was the best day of his life. We got a thank you note from a girl who said, "PS, this is being typed on my new laptop." We could sense her pride. Her dreams were unlocked.

In a Seattle classroom, one little girl went straight to the back of the room and cried. "Are you okay?" we asked. She nodded. "My parents have been saving up for two years to get me a computer," she said, looking up at us with her big, tear-filled eyes. "They still don't have enough money. But now I have one." This was real life, cheering for the one behind.

The importance of closing the digital divide was driven home with the coronavirus pandemic in 2020, with widespread school closures and reliance on remote learning. Unfortunately, a large segment of students, particularly in urban America, didn't have an internet connection at home or a laptop. We were so proud to support, through our social media channels, Comcast's extension of the Internet Essentials program to offer sixty days of free Internet service to any qualifying low-income family living in the Comcast footprint. That is really leveling the playing field.

On a trip to Washington, DC, in 2018, we helped announce the expansion of the Internet Essentials program to cover low-income veterans. Jackie Joyner-Kersee joined us for many of the Washington events, as did our mother, who brought along her old copy of Jackie's autobiography (which Jackie autographed for her). Having a chance to meet Jackie and talk with her up close and in person was a highlight for all three of us. We also enjoyed talking with Jackie about her foundation and the impact she is having in her East St. Louis community. That doubled our resolve to start our own foundation.

Our Washington visit closed with a gathering in the famous Kennedy Caucus Room, which has served as the venue for many historic hearings such as those investigating the Vietnam War, the sinking of the *Titanic*, and Watergate. We were joined by several hundred guests, with almost one hundred senators and members of Congress, including former Senator Elizabeth Dole and our home state senator, Heidi Heitkamp, stopping in to say hello and congratulations. There were a lot of VIPs there—plenty of people our mom and we recognized from television. But only three Olympic medalists.

At the reception, David surprised both of us with a framed copy of the letter a group of senators, including twelve women, had drafted in support of

our battle with USA Hockey back in 2017. Except this version was individually signed by all twenty senators who had lent their name to it.

JOCELYNE

We also had numerous opportunities to participate in events that helped us
to continue our fight for equity.

We became contributors to Mika Brzezinski's Know Your Value platform
that the MSNBC *Morning Joe* cohost started to advocate for a broad variety
of gender-equity issues. We've blogged on the Know Your Value site and been
interviewed by Mika.

We delivered a talk at the TEDx program in Fargo. TEDx talks are noto-
riously difficult—and even harder with two speakers. We prepped for the
strict twelve-minute limit and no-notes rule by working with renowned
speech coach Michael Sheehan, whose résumé includes coaching Bill Clinton,
Barack and Michelle Obama, Joe Biden—and us. We studied hard in school,
but we never worked as hard as we did on our TED Talk. We revised the
speech ten or fifteen times—and practiced it dozens of times. And then, when
we thought we had it down, we practiced some more.

At the conference, we were introduced by ten girls who played hockey in
North Dakota, including some who had attended our hockey camp. We told
the story of our fight for gender equity with USA Hockey. We obviously
talked about winning a gold medal in Pyeongchang. We talked about the
outpouring of reactions we had received from young girls all around the
country, including Avery Hakstol, who was present at the talk. And we closed
by asking the two thousand people in the audience to join us in our fight to
make sure there was a level playing field for the next generation of girls with
dreams of excelling in sports, education, and their careers. The crowd
applauded enthusiastically.

Then, something unexpected happened. Their applause turned into cheers.
And a standing ovation. Clearly, our talk had hit a nerve. Many of them were
parents of little girls with big dreams of their own, and they knew the importance of continuing this battle for gender equity. No one's dreams should be
hindered by gender, ethnicity, skin color, income, or any of the other unnecessary barriers many people have to face. Avery Hakstol was on her feet, standing
next to her grandfather. Off to the side, we saw our parents beaming.

In October 2018, we spoke at the Global Citizen annual festival in Central
Park in New York. There were about sixty thousand people in front of the
main stage, and more than a million all around the world watching on
MSNBC and over the internet. Two girls from a small town in North Dakota
were announcing a new set of goals for Global Citizen related to gender
equity around the world.

We tried our best to keep our work personal. Six months later, we offered a progress report as featured speakers at an event on the UND campus.

The speech was well-received, but the real "wow" moment came afterward when an older woman came up and introduced herself as Justin's grandmother. "Do you remember him?" she asked. Justin was the boy with Down syndrome in Monique's sixth-grade class who we invited to start having lunch with us because he sat by himself, which he did until he became the most popular boy in the lunchroom, with everyone wanting him to sit at their tables! "Of course, we remember him," we said. We shared that moment with her and appreciated the memories we had of making a difference in someone's life. "Tell him hi." His grandmother smiled. "He still says that you're his girlfriends."

MONIQUE

As we were exposed to more people and communities with less, we didn't just want to show up and leave the work to others. We wanted to make our own personal financial contribution to address certain issues. We wanted to be thought leaders and philanthropic leaders. We felt particularly strongly about this in our home state of North Dakota, where 30 percent of children live in low-income families, and nearly one-third of the state's students are eligible for participation in the National School Lunch Program. North Dakota is also ranked thirty-sixth among all states for children living away from their parents in foster care.

In July 2019, we created our own foundation to put us in a position to put our personal dollars where our hearts and brains were already and to give us a mechanism to help lead on initiatives to level the playing field. We weren't very creative with the name—we called it the Monique and Jocelyne Lamoureux Foundation. We wanted it to benefit underserved children and communities, as well as other causes that aligned with our values, primarily in the state of North Dakota. Our goal was to work with local organizations that supported disadvantaged children through education and extracurricular activities. We wanted to have reach beyond hockey and sports.

To fund the foundation, Jocelyne and I decided to dedicate the net proceeds from our annual summer hockey camp to the foundation as an ongoing source of revenue. From the outset of our planning, David Cohen said he wanted to host a fundraiser for the foundation to help jump-start its work. Sure enough, David and his wife hosted a fundraiser for the foundation in Philadelphia. We didn't fully understand what that meant until we arrived and saw David's version of this fundraiser wasn't some stuffy event in a hotel ballroom—it was actually a major carnival for kids with tons of games (hockey, basketball, soccer, football and baseball toss, and badminton) and prizes, including Lamoureux Foundation T-shirts and backpacks and Olympic medals specially branded with the Lamoureux Foundation logo for everyone. More than two hundred people showed up, including one hundred kids from Snider Hockey.

There were also some surprise guests, including Herb Douglas. The bronze-medal winner in the long jump in the 1948 Olympics, Herb, at ninety-seven, was the oldest-living African American Olympic medalist, who had won his medal almost seventy years before we won Olympic gold. Talking with him about his experience, including the obstacles he faced as an African American athlete and his relationship with Jesse Owens, was inspiring—and a big reminder that the Olympics have been an important vehicle to help the world embrace and appreciate all of our differences.

David didn't want to charge admission, so he did all the fundraising in advance—except for one contributor. It was Dee Spagnola's ten-year-old son, Beau, who came up to us at the event and explained he had emptied his piggy bank to make a contribution to our foundation. We may have embarrassed him by how tightly we hugged him as we said thank you. But his desire to help really tugged at our heartstrings because not only were we trying to make a difference by providing financial support to causes important to us, but we were also trying to inspire others to do the same.

We spent some time researching where and to whom we should make our first foundation grant. As in many cities, we learned that Grand Forks had a multitiered school lunch program. There was a free school lunch program for the very poorest of kids. There was also a reduced school lunch program where kids who were still really poor had to pay something toward their school lunches. If they couldn't pay, they received a different school lunch—usually a cold sandwich instead of a hot meal. But more importantly, it singled those kids out. This was not just a Grand Forks problem. This happened all across the country.

So we worked with the Grand Forks Foundation for Education and arranged for our foundation to cover the costs so that every child in Grand Forks would receive a hot school lunch for the 2019–2020 school year. For us, school was always the place where everything important to us came together—sports, academics, friendship, learning, and a sense of what can be possible in the future. If a kid is hungry or singled out, how can he or she be expected to learn? To play? To dream? To be a normal kid? The many positive and heartfelt social media messages we received from the Grand Forks community confirmed that we had hit the mark.

We felt good about this grant as the kickoff for our foundation and hoped it would inspire other people to get involved and cheer for the one behind. The spillover impact of our grant was beyond anything that we could have imagined. First, in 2019, we heard from Fargo business owners and philanthropists who wanted to discuss our grant in Grand Forks and whether we could work with them to solve the same problem in Fargo. Then, in the midst of the coronavirus pandemic in 2020, some in the Grand Forks community realized that, with our schools closed, we were creating a big food insecurity problem since kids were not getting their free or reduced school meals. So we joined again with the Grand Forks Foundation for Education, local retailer Kittsona, and other businesses to make another foundation grant to help fund meals and delivery of them to over three hundred and fifty families a day, plus to provide supplemental weekend meals to families in need. We're learning that when you make a gift, not only do you make a difference in someone's life, but you also provide thought leadership and help leverage support from others in addressing important problems. It's a team effort where everyone wins.

Our partnership with Comcast, our appearances, and our work with our own foundation has driven home the opportunities and obligations we have as a result of our gold medals to reflect and comment on some of the critical issues that confront us in America. To be silent is to be complicit. As we have traveled the country, we've learned about the unfair impacts of poverty and discrimination in our country. This exposure led us to post the following statements on social media in the wake of the overwhelming outcry in the country following the murder of George Floyd by Minneapolis police officers:

> It's no secret that North Dakota is one of the least diverse states in the country, but I will not let that be a reason to be silent and be a bystander. We should all be treated as equals, we should all respect each other, love each other, and support each other. I will never pretend to know what it's like to be judged by the color of my skin, but I do know that all human life should be valued as equal. [Monique]

> We all have to be a voice for change, and we all have to know when to LISTEN. We can all stand up for what is right. I want my children to grow up in a world where people don't see color and make judgments based on race but make judgments based on their character. [Jocelyne]

To us, George Floyd represents an important challenge to fight for the ones behind—people of color who have suffered from the ravages of more than four centuries of discrimination and racism. It's an important challenge for us to join with others to make a difference.

In June 2020, we received a surprise telephone call from the governor of North Dakota, Doug Burgum. The governor told us that he was presenting us with the North Dakota Theodore Roosevelt Rough Rider Award, which is the highest commendation that a citizen of North Dakota can receive. Joce-lyne and I would be the second and third youngest recipients of the recogni-tion—Roger Maris edged us out by one year.

This North Dakota recognition meant a lot to us. And while the gover-nor's statement announcing the award obviously referenced our Olympic gold medals and the fact that we were the first North Dakota athletes to bring home Olympic gold, the governor also called out our "dedication [off the ice] to promoting equity, diversity and inclusion and improving access for disad-vantaged youth" and our foundation.

31

BIGGER THAN US

"Don't be like us. Be better."

JOCELYNE

September 2019. We made the team.

About a week after our first camp since our gold-medal win in South Korea, we were at home when we received word that both of us had made the roster for the 2019 Four Nations Cup. In many ways, we were as excited as we were when we made our very first national team as high school juniors in 2006. Although we hadn't played in a game for more than eighteen months, we had showed up at camp close enough to Olympic form and demonstrated that we still had the right moves, muscle, and motivation to compete at an elite level. We had proved that we could be mothers and still make an elite U.S. Women's National Team. Mission accomplished, and point made.

We took pride in being the first two women hockey players to benefit from the maternity benefits we had negotiated in our 2017 pact with USA Hockey. While the statistics are a bit all over the place, numerous sources report that fewer than 15 percent of working women in the US receive some sort of paid maternity benefits. It's past time for the United States to join the vast majority of countries around the world—178 of them—including all the so-called developed countries—and provide paid maternity leave as a matter of law. We were proud that USA Hockey was setting a positive example.

Then, we ran into an ironic roadblock when the Swedish Ice Hockey Federation canceled the Four Nations Cup tournament because its team's players were boycotting the event. Sweden's players wanted more compensation and better working conditions that considered the women's personal and family obligations. It sounded familiar. They had our full support, along with that of the Professional Women's Hockey Player Association (the PWHPA), a union created in 2019 to launch a new professional hockey league that would provide the pay, stability, and professionalism we felt our sport deserved.

The existing professional options were not real. The Canadian attempt at a professional women's hockey league went out of business in 2018. And the US effort was a professional league in name only—disorganized, inadequately financed, insufficient compensation, no health or disability insurance, and little to no promotion or sponsorship support.

The PWHPA was the next important step in our battle for gender equity in hockey. Reminiscent of our 2017 negotiations with USA Hockey, one hundred and seventy of the best players in the world banded together and formed the PWHPA. We immediately pledged that none of us would play in an existing professional hockey league in the 2019–20 season as we worked toward the creation of a bona fide professional league, which we believe needs to be under the auspices of the National Hockey League.

For women's hockey to reach its full potential, we need the same continuum of opportunities in hockey that the men have—from youth hockey to high school and college hockey to the national team and the Olympics, and ultimately professional hockey to provide opportunities to play in between Olympic cycles and for the dozens of elite women players who will not make the national team. We have had some productive discussions with the NHL, which seems interested in helping to make a professional women's hockey league a reality, under the right circumstances. Demonstrating its interest, the League has invited female participation in two successive NHL All-Star weekends in 2019 and 2020, which have proven to be fan favorites.

In 2020, with the help of Billie Jean King and Illana Kloss, the PWHPA organized and executed an amazing exhibition tour, which we dubbed the Dream Gap Tour. The tour brought the best players in the world to six cities in Canada and the United States, which hosted a total of twenty-four games as well as a series of hockey clinics and other appearances. The players were able to attract enough sponsorship dollars to make the Dream Gap Tour a breakeven proposition.

During the course of the tour, we saw hundreds of young girls showing up and waving signs of support and thanking us for our leadership. Girls lined up for autograph sessions and hockey tips. The warm and enthusiastic embrace was just like the aftermath of our negotiations with USA Hockey and winning Olympic gold. We believe we are demonstrating again the appeal of women's hockey.

Ours had become a real family sport. Meghan Duggan, taking time off to have a baby, consulted with Anthony about a workout program. After giving birth to her son, George, on February 29, 2020, she joined an Olympic moms support group that we started with track and field gold medalist Allyson Felix and Olympic bobsled gold medalist Elana Myers-Taylor, who also had her first baby in early 2020. (It may not be a coincidence that Allyson, Elana, Monique, and I were all Comcast-sponsored Olympic athletes.) Besides knowing the unique demands each of us had as elite athletes and moms, we wanted to set an example for the younger women in each of our sports and others coming up behind them.

At thirty years old, age was on our minds. Not that we were old—or felt it. But every athlete has a finite competitive lifespan, and the national team roster was filled with players at least five to ten years younger than us. Like Monique and me a decade ago, they were climbing the ladder up the ranks, looking to carve out a place for themselves, and ultimately play in the 2022 Olympics in Beijing. Many of them had grown up watching us play. We relished the opportunity to serve as examples the way players like Angela Ruggerio had done for us—and also as links between generations who fought on the ice and battled just as hard off it for the betterment of our sport.

If the time ever came when they had to face the same challenges that confronted us, we wanted them to feel a connection to the past and use it to find the courage to do the right thing for themselves, for the team, and for future generations of female hockey players.

MONIQUE

Even without a Four Nations Tournament, we continued to train full time—five days a week at the gym, skating at the Ralph in the early mornings. We attended three more USA Hockey camps. And we reveled in the continued growth of Mickey and Nelson. They seemed to get bigger every day—and were developing real personalities. Watching them grow up filled our hearts with love—and grounded us as to what was really important in our lives.

In January 2020, we participated in three of the five games in the US-Canada Rivalry Series, created by USA Hockey and Hockey Canada to provide more highly competitive games in between the Olympics and World Championships. The games were hard-fought and fun. The US won the first two, although we were not on the roster for those games. We had been sent home after a five-day camp, along with twenty other players. This was the first major roadblock we had faced in a while as hockey players, and contributed to our developing thought process as to our priorities going forward.

We were back for the final three games of the series. True to form in any US-Canada series, Canada stormed back to win Game 3 in overtime by a score of 3–2 in Victoria, British Columbia, and then we won the fourth game of the series in Vancouver by a score of 3–1. The final game of the Rivalry Series was in Anaheim, California, where we played in front of the largest crowd ever to see a women's hockey game in the US. I scored the tying goal to send us into overtime, and we eventually pulled out a 4–3 victory to take the series.

But the real win for those of us who had been around a while was looking up into the stands and seeing young girls, their moms, and even some of their dads wearing USA jerseys and holding up signs that said, "We love you," "You're our heroes," and "Thank you, USA." At intermission, the ice filled with little girls ten and under who came out in their hockey gear and played shortened games. The cool part was that only a few years earlier, our teammate Annie Pankowski had been one of them. The sport was growing for a reason.

The game in Anaheim came at the end of a really tough couple of weeks. This was the longest we had been away from the boys since their birth. We thought we had done a good job balancing our roles as mothers and as elite hockey players, but those twelve days were really tough on us. In fact, if there is anything beyond "really tough," that's what it was like. Bottom line: we were pretty miserable.

We also had to interrupt camp to fly to Edmonton for our grandmother's funeral. She had passed on the day we left for camp. It really wasn't a close call—and the coaches said they understood. It wasn't ideal to leave, but we had our priorities, and family was always top of mind. Our grandmother had always prioritized us—we needed to be at her funeral with the rest of our family. So after our game in Vancouver, we flew out Thursday morning to be with family in Edmonton. The funeral was on Friday, and we woke up at 5 a.m. on Saturday to go to the airport and made it to Anaheim in time for the pregame meal and to play in the final game at 7 p.m.

The challenges of this camp caused us to accelerate a tough, critical look at what we were doing, which had been percolating for several weeks. People always ask us how we think we did in camp, and this time, answering honestly, we couldn't say that we crushed it. We were proud of how far we had come—proud that we had battled back to elite physical shape after giving birth—proud that we were competitive with the best women's hockey players in the world, even if we weren't totally back in Olympic shape. We felt like we still had a lot of hockey left in us. But were our hearts and minds as committed? As our dad had taught us so long ago, we needed to carefully assess our priorities.

As we did that, we looked at our new coaches and wondered how committed they were to us. It was pretty clear that they were making at least tentative decisions—and that those decisions were not putting us in a position to be fully competitive. The coaches weren't very familiar with us as players or as people, and based on our limited playing time, we could see they were more interested in giving quality minutes to new, younger players, who reminded us of ourselves when we were first trying to compete for a national team slot. Based on the vacillation of the coaches as to whether I should play defense or forward—almost leaving it up to me where I wanted to play—we sensed some disinterest in us as members of the team. While there was a part of us that wondered whether we were being given a true, fair shot to come back after our maternity leave, that might have been unfair. But in any event, as our dad had drilled into us long ago, you can't take on your coaches. There is no upside to that. You can only do the things that you have control over.

JOCELYNE

Following this twelve-day camp, we received the disappointing, but not very surprising, news that we had not made the cut for the national team for the 2020 World Championships. (As it turns out, the 2020 World Championships were canceled because of the coronavirus pandemic.) We had missed national teams before, but that was when we were eighteen, with a huge future and coaches asking us to be patient. This was different. Our coaches told us that we would be invited to attend the next USA Hockey camp, in August, but they also warned us that there was a group of younger players that they wanted to look at and that making the team would be an uphill climb.

For the first time, we thought about whether we wanted to control our own exit strategy—and not leave it up to a group of coaches who really didn't know us that well on and off the ice. We still loved hockey—and we thought we could compete on an international elite level if we were given a full and fair opportunity. And there was a big part of us that believed that if we put our hearts fully into it, we could overcome the coaches' skepticism and make the next team. We had turned around coaches' skepticism before, including our coaches for the 2018 Winter Olympics, where we won gold.

But we also loved the rest of our lives, which were richer with opportunities than we ever imagined would be the case. First and foremost, we had our boys, and we now knew that nothing in our lives would ever be more important than Mickey and Nelson—until we had other children, which was also something that was increasingly on our radar screen. We knew that the tough twelve-day trip was the first of many tough twelve-day hockey trips to come, and it was hard to process that.

Our ongoing work with our teammates for the future of the sport was also really important to us. So was our work with the Players Association to pursue a real professional hockey league for women in North America. And we were looking at upcoming negotiations with USA Hockey to make sure that we held onto our hard-fought gains from 2017—and maybe expand on them.

We thought back to our musings as young hockey players in our teens and twenties that being Olympians, winning an Olympic medal, and winning an Olympic gold medal were important not just for the hardware, but for the platform that being Olympians would give us to advocate for causes that we cared about. Through our appearances and partnership with Comcast, we had gained much more insight into how to use our visibility as Olympic gold medalists to be difference makers for the future.

We were also passionate about activating our foundation and seeing how much change and impact we could create in North Dakota. And we knew we wanted to continue to advocate for gender equity, closing the digital divide, racial justice, and other issues that could help level the playing field for under-represented populations around the country.

As we began to reflect on our future, we realized that, over our careers, we have achieved all of our hockey dreams. Winning three national champion-ships at Shattuck. Check. Helping to turn around the women's hockey pro-gram at our hometown university, the University of North Dakota. Check. Making countless national teams—and winning twenty international medals between us. Check. Playing in three Olympics—together. Check. And winning two silver medals and one gold medal in those three Olympics. Check. Prov-ing we could work ourselves back into Olympic shape and make a national team after giving birth. Check.

As our dad told us back in high school, sometimes you have to make choices in your life. When we were in college, we chose hockey and academ-ics over our social lives. We are blessed today to have at least three fantastic choices—our young sons and families, our community engagement, and hockey. In the end, ordering our priorities is actually pretty easy. We choose Nelson, Mickey, and our families, and our community commitments, includ-ing our work to fight for gender equity, to advance the sport of women's hockey, and the work of our own foundation.

MONIQUE AND JOCELYNE

While none of these types of life choices is easy, we are comfortable with and proud of our legacy. The individual games will likely fade from memories (maybe except the gold-medal game in Pyeongchang). Our medals will be mentioned (we will always be Olympic gold medalists). But the changes we have brought to women's hockey and the opportunities we have created for girls to dream big, just as we did, will have a lasting impact. They will go down in history. And we will be remembered for the difference we made in our sport—and for changes we have helped bring to underserved communities around the country—and the difference we will continue to fight for in the years ahead.

We have been and will continue to be part of a movement. In January 2020, the WNBA and its players' union signed a new agreement that provided a signif-icant increase in caps on top salaries, a potential revenue share of television and media rights, and more benefits, including a dedicated space at arenas for nursing mothers. Commissioner Cathy Engelbert called it "a big bet on women." A few weeks later, Jocelyne participated in a women's three-on-three game during the NHL All-Star weekend, televised live on the national NBC Sports Network. And I provided national television commentary at the event from down on the ice while Kendall Coyne helped with the broadcast by being mic'd up on the ice.

Many of the columnists writing about the weekend said our three-on-three game was the most exciting part of the entire NHL weekend.

Something is happening. As we have traveled the country, we have sensed an awareness in the public of the challenges women and girls face in pursuing their interests and careers and a desire to change the culture to ensure more equitable opportunities in sports, education, and the workplace. This movement is about power, freedom, courage, and an insistence on not just breaking but ignoring barriers. Katie Sowers was the first female to coach in the Super Bowl for the San Francisco 49ers. Laura Yeager became the first woman to lead a US Army infantry division. NASA astronaut Christina Koch set a new record for the longest space flight by a woman. More women ran for president of the United States in 2020 than ever before, daring to make history of their own. One day a woman will win and make history.

Maybe you are a little girl reading this who will grow up to be that first woman president. Or you will be something else. As we know from firsthand experience, change doesn't happen overnight. But it does happen. We have always bet on women, including ourselves, and we always will.

It might seem far-fetched to think that two small-town girls who first put on ice skates at age three and a few years later began to dream of competing in the Olympics would one day bring a gold medal back home. But we never doubted our ability to turn dreams into destiny. Neither should you. We hope our story inspires you to dream like we did. Only bigger. In the same way that we have followed hockey into areas bigger than sports and battles that are more important than wins and losses.

Our struggle for fairness and equity for women and girls—in hockey and in life—and for anyone or any group that is being left behind—has not ended. It goes on. We're not skating off into the sunset until we know that the many girls we hear from through social media, email, in arenas where we play hockey, and old-fashioned letters get equal treatment with their male friends. We're not unlacing our skates until we know that maternity-leave policies in the United States match those available essentially everywhere else in the world. We're not taking off our gloves until pay equity for women and people of color is a reality in this country instead of an embarrassment. And we're not laying down our sticks until the digital divide is closed in this country.

Join us! Even if you can't skate, we want you on our team. Despite all of the challenges, or perhaps because of them, life can be truly amazing. You have to set goals, work hard, embrace the adversity that will undoubtedly come your way, be a great teammate, know that the hockey gods are watching, and dare yourself to make history.

That's what we did.

LETTERS OF CHANGE

★

"Dear Jocelyne and Monique..."

2017
Mae_k13

This is awesome! Passion isn't defined by gender. Hockey is for everyone, male or female. You guys deserve better. This is setting a great example for other women's sports leagues and for girls all over the world! You have my support. It takes a lot of guts to do what you guys did. You have my support!

March 2017
Alex Hunter

Good to see that you are being an inspiration for the next generation of young hockey players.

March 2017
Just Me

As a former junior hockey player and father of two daughters, good for all of you for standing up for what is right.

April 2018
Connie Zhary

On behalf of my children, I want to say thank you for bringing the world champion Lamoureux twins to Laura Sims to meet the children, coach them, play with them, and send them the generous gifts of laptops and winter Olympics glove and hat sets.

My children have been very excited about the event and couldn't help sharing the news (bragging) with their friends. And we've got a plan to use the laptop to learn foreign languages this summer.

April 2018
Danni Declerico

It was awesome to meet you and spend some time on and off the ice. Being on the ice with you was great and something I will never forget. It was super cool to see and touch the Olympic gold medal. This is something I will cherish forever.

I am currently a fifth-grade student at Mastery Charter Thomas Elementary School in Philadelphia with first honors. I am in my fifth year playing for the Ed Snider Youth Hockey Program. I am also a three-time academic all-star. During the off-season, I also enjoy playing soccer.

I would not be playing hockey if it was not for women like you. You both are heroes that we look up to and idolize every day. If not for women like you, there would not be us. You pave the way for females in hockey and make it possible for us to dream. I hope one day I get the opportunity to play at your level, to win a gold medal. If dreams like this come true, there is no one to thank but you!
Good luck in the future.

June 2018
Ericka Schott-Juelson

Facebook Post

Very exciting to watch the clips of the Olympics when the women won the gold, but to think they risked it all! You ladies are trailblazers, earthshakers, mountain movers, and game-changers (quite literally)! Two of the hardest-working and bravest women I have ever met! Monique and Jocelyne, hometown heroes, national sweethearts, world icons!

March 2020
Avery Hakstol

Dear Jocelyne and Monique,

You've always been role models to me in so many ways. Of course, I've always loved watching you play the game, but you've also shown me friendship, hard work, and shared your knowledge of the game, how to be a good person, and now, how to be a high-level athlete while being a mom.

I feel so lucky to train at the same facility, so I get to see firsthand what it has taken you to get to the Olympic level. When I was younger, I thought it was so cool that you were always willing to give myself or other girls tips on our game—whether it was a quick tip about puck skills or an hour at the shooting station behind the lake house. When you let me come on the ice after practice with the Olympic team, I was starstruck. But now that I'm old enough to reflect on that, I realize how lucky I've been to count you as friends, coaches, and mentors.

But the biggest lesson I've learned from you comes off the ice and out of the gym. You've taught me that I can do anything I really put my mind to and to stand firm in my beliefs—know who I am and be proud of that. I watched as you went through the fight for equal rights and pay for women's hockey. I saw that it wasn't easy or popular in some cases. I knew how hard you had trained to be on your third Olympic team and that your goal was a gold medal. As an eleven-year-old, I knew you and your teammates put your dreams of that third Olympics on the line for equality and what was right, and I knew that was in jeopardy. I thought you were so brave. And when you won equal rights, I was ecstatic.

I'll never forget when you won Olympic gold. My mom and I sat on the couch in the middle of the night in New Jersey. I don't even know how to put into words how excited I was—but it didn't surprise me that it was you. I've seen you two be clutch so many times before. And when Joc scored the shootout goal, I woke up the rest of the house with my yelling. I texted you right away. I couldn't believe you texted me back…from the ice…as I watched you celebrate a gold medal with your teammates. It's hard to properly put into words how awesome it was watching you win gold, but I was celebrating with you that day.

Thanks for being my role models on and off the ice. I'll forever be trying to score shootout goals with the "Oops, I Did It Again" shot.

March 2020
Jasmine Martinez

Dear Monique and Jocelyne,

Thank you for being amazing inspirations. You have not only inspired me, but also many other young female athletes to strive and fight to achieve their dreams. I used to think that I would never be good enough to make any women's hockey team after college, but once I met you both, you inspired me to keep believing in myself no matter what anyone said. You taught me to never take to insult when someone says, "you play like a girl" because it is not an insult, but a compliment. The way you led Team USA to threaten a boycott of the 2017 International Ice Hockey Federation world championship took a lot of bravery and courage. It's amazing how you were and are willing to risk so much to break barriers to fight for the equality of female athletes everywhere.

The first time that I met the both of you was back in 2017 at Scanlon Ice Rink in Philadelphia, Pennsylvania. I was a little nervous at first because you are both amazing women and great hockey players. I loved how interactive you were with everyone, including my 6 year old sister and me, and how you both made each and every one of us feel special. It was hard to believe that we were in the presence of Olympic gold medalists. When I held your medals that day, it made me think of how if I work hard enough and dream big, I could potentially earn a gold medal of my own. When I think of how inspirational you both are, a quote that comes to mind is "cheer for the one behind". No matter how hard someone strives for their goal, there is always a little motivation needed to get there. I will always remember to support my friends and family with whatever it may be that they are working toward and show them that I will always be there for support no matter what.

One of my favorite memories was when I was given the opportunity to interview both of you while I interned for David Cohen at Comcast. I was honored to be the one to interview you both about gender equity in the work force and sports and also ask a few questions about how you both felt about becoming mothers together. It is amazing how you both were able to fight for not only more equity in sports, but also more equity in the workforce as well.

Thank you for being the two women athletes that I look up to the most. Without you, I may not have had the courage to go and try out for Team USA's ball hockey team. Thanks to both of you, I am now representing the United States of America playing for the Women's U20 USA Ball Hockey team and traveling the world playing the sport I love. My future goal is to one day play for USA Hockey's Olympic Ice Hockey team just like both of you. I can't wait to see what other memories I will make when I meet you both again.

With much gratitude,
From one of your biggest fans,
Jasmine Martinez

ACKNOWLEDGMENTS

O n and off the ice, we have always valued being called team players and team leaders. We have learned that our life experiences can be defined as embracing all of us being part of the same team, which means that we have to play, behave, and live as if we are working toward one common goal. That means playing hard and fair and lending a helping hand to teammates when they need it.

We would not have enjoyed the success and blessings in our lives without learning these fundamental lessons as children from the two most important examples in our lives, our parents, Linda and Pierre Lamoureux. As we look back through the pages of this book, the examples you set and the lessons you taught us are evident from the first page to the last and will be recorded in chapters of our lives yet to be written. So thank you, Mom and Dad. We love you.

We were also blessed with exceptional teachers and teammates, starting with our four older brothers: Jean-Philippe, Jacques, Pierre-Paul, and Mario. Thank you for setting the bar high and never taking it easy on us.

Every day, we treasure the support that always came from our crowded family section, something we carry with us every day.

Grandma Edith: "To whom much is given, much is expected." We have always recognized the privilege and opportunities we have been given and the responsibility that flows from them. The way you lead your life is the greatest lesson you have taught us.

Grandma and Grandpa Lamoureux: Although you have recently passed, we know that your candles are lit in heaven for our biggest days ahead. Thank you for showering us with your love our entire lives and showing us the importance of family.

And Jerry Reske: We know that you are up in Heaven taking care of Grandma and Grandpa. Thank you for always supporting us and being a part of the family. We couldn't have asked for a better godfather. We miss you!

Outside of immediate family, we have been helped and influenced by many extraordinary teachers, coaches, and mentors who have shared their best and challenged us in order for us to reach our potential. The lessons we have learned on and off the ice have helped us to see the bigger picture and inspired us to help the next generation be even better. Those standing front and center include:

David Cohen: There are very few people in life who "really really" take the time to get to know you. You have challenged us to do more than we thought possible, encouraged us to see an even bigger picture, and pushed us to reach beyond our comfort zone to make a bigger difference. We would not have written this book without your encouragement and guidance. You are a mentor, teacher, coach, friend, and guiding light all in one. Without you, our gold medals would not shine as brightly. And we can't forget about Rhonda. You have quietly been an example that we have looked up to through your own accomplishments in your career and as a mother.

Coach Stafford: Thank you for always understanding our drive and passion and for taking a risk on two girls from North Dakota who you had never even seen play. It has always come back to that first layer of the heart, and you have been a reminder of that throughout our careers. Your influence and mentorship has guided us since our time at Shattuck St. Mary's and will continue in the years ahead.

John Langel: Thank you for taking our first call and being an ally and advocate for us. You have amplified our voices and showed us what it means to give selflessly to those who have been unheard. You and Jackie have become extended family to us, and we are forever grateful for your friendship.

Diane Spagnuolo: Like John, you have been an advocate and have given us a microphone to use our voices. You have also become a friend through this process, and you and Sasha have become role models for us as working moms. You amaze us! And Beau. Everyone has the capacity to make a difference, and you represent that. You emptied your piggy bank at our foundation launch and told us you wanted to cheer for the one behind. We will never forget this and never stop sharing your story!

Everyone at Ballard Spahr LLP: Thanks to Mary Kate Gordon, Ashley Wilson, and Kimberly Magrini for being a part of our journey to fight for more, to fight for what Team USA deserved and earned. And thanks to Mark Stewart and the rest of the firm for believing in our fight and continuing to work for the women of Team USA. We would not be where we are without your work.

Mrs. Carney: We have come a long way since seventh-grade English class. Thank you for teaching us that good work is not always your best work. You have been encouraging us to write a book since we graduated high school. Well, here it is!

Speaking of this book, we spent many hours alone in front of our computers, just as we have done in the gym, but actually writing and publishing a book requires a big team. We benefitted from, and we enjoyed the experience and efforts of an especially talented group of people: our agent, Dan Strone, the CEO of Trident Media Group, and Trident's head of business affairs, Sara Pearl; Scott Waxman and Mark Fretz at Radius Book Group, our publisher; and our editor Susan Canavan, whose children made her very familiar with life at the rink. Thank you all for helping us tell our story.

This book would not have been possible without many others, starting with all of those women who came before us. There are too many to name individually, but we honor all those women on and off the ice and in and out of sports who created openings for us and on whose shoulders we stand.

Julie Foudy: Thank you for your mentorship since 2015. You were instrumental in helping us navigate through our negotiations and have been a role model for us and our teammates since you and the rest of the 99ers blazed new paths for female athletes around the world.

Angela Ruggerio (Sissy): Thank you for taking us under your wing when we were seventeen years old and teaching us that what you can do with your platform is limitless.

To all of our hockey teammates over the years, and especially our Team USA family: Thank you for pushing us to be our best, challenging us to be better leaders and people, and sticking together to leave the jersey in a better place than when we started wearing it.

Margot, Max, and Kathleen: No matter where we have been, you guys have always helped ground us in our lives—and we have shared some pretty good laughs along the way. Thank you for your friendship since we entered through the arch at Shattuck.

Alyssa and Lindsay: Our bond formed because you befriended the seventh graders playing high school soccer. We can go months without seeing or talking to each other, but our friendship has never wavered over the past seventeen years.

Peter Elander: You sat us down when we were twenty years old and asked us what you could do to make us two of the best players in the world. You have never stopped helping us over the last ten years. You're the unsung mastermind of moves like "Highway Patrol" and "Oops, I Did It Again." But what stands out is the way you always said, "It's nice to be important, but it's more important to be nice." Thank you for demanding execution and being the encouraging voice when our confidence was shaken.

Greg, Heather, and the Lotysz Family: You let us into your home and let us become a part of your family over the years. We have shown up unannounced more times than we can count, and you welcome us with open arms no matter what. Greg, you have always been honest with us, even when we didn't want to hear it, and it has pushed us to always strive for success and be better. We have always been treated as people first in your home, and athletes second, and we appreciate that.

O'Keefe/Hakstol family: Our families have crossed paths through a couple of generations and in so many different ways over the years. Your friendship, guidance, mentorship, babysitting services, and everything in between has had a ripple effect throughout our lives.

Youth coaches: Tony Bina, Mike McNamara, Brandon Lunak, and Kelly Kilgore. Thank you for always treating us like hockey players and not making us feel less-than when we were the only girls on the team. You always made us feel like we belonged and respected us and what we brought to the team.

UND coaches and staff: Playing for the Fighting Sioux was a dream come true, and helping to turn the program around is one of our proudest accomplishments.

Team USA medical staff: Katie, Sherri, Doc Jamie, Doc Howe, Carrie, J. Chee, Katie, and Shelly: If it wasn't for you, who knows how 2018 would have turned out. We shared laughs and smiles when they were hard to come by some days. We will always be grateful for everything you have done to help our team succeed! And when you need some doughnut holes, you let us know!

Strength Coaches Jim Radcliffe, Mike Boyle, Sarah Cahill, Anthony Donskov, and Kevin Neeld: Your passion for helping athletes reach their potential is contagious. Thank you for all of the time you spent with the team and us as individuals and answering the many questions we always had for you.

Doc Hacker: You have been that sound advisor when we needed it most. You have provided encouragement and reality checks through the toughest moments of our national team careers.

Danielle: Over the last five years, you have been there for us as athletes and people. Between figuring out meal plans, cheering us on with your pom-poms as we conditioned, and making gender-reveal cakes, you have seen it all with us. Thank you for sharing your kindness and friendship with us since day one.

Jody Hodgson: Thank you for approving endless ice times and giving us a facility to call home while we trained and skated over the years. You didn't owe us anything, and you never said no to the two of us chasing our dream. You also helped make it possible for our family to come to Pyeongchang and be there by our side. Thank you!

Jason Carlson: Thank you for helping design shirts and promote a fundraiser to help our family get to Pyeongchang.

Karen Schuler: The endless emails back and forth to schedule our ice times at all hours of the morning will never be forgotten. You were always so kind and flexible with us.

Our neighbors, friends, and community who have supported us from the beginning: We have always felt the support of our community, and we are proud to be from North Dakota and especially Grand Forks. Thank you for making this a place we are proud to call home.

The Comcast team: Corporate Communications (Jenn Khoury, Steve Restivo, Matt Dickman, Charlie Douglass, Jane Maybury, Carla Grzywacz); Internet Essentials (Karima Zedan, Trinity Thorpe-Lubneuski, Christina Wiskowski, Carly Morris); Community Impact (Dalila Wilson Scott); and Jennifer Paternostro. We don't think any of us knew what we were embarking on the first time we sat down together, but you have all helped us accomplish so much since 2018. We appreciate all of your hard work and willingness to help us.

And to our husbands and children, thank you for being our guiding light, our reason why, and everything in between. Brent and Anthony, you two probably had no idea what our lives would turn into over the past few years, but you have kept us grounded through it all. You have supported us in every challenge we have faced and every opportunity that has come our way. Our success on and off the ice would not be possible without you, and we can't wait for what the future holds.

Finally, we want to thank YOU. Thank you for cheering for us. Thank you for reading this book. And if you are someone with the dream and determination to make your own history and cheer for the one behind, let us know so we can cheer for you.